WHEN THE WAR CAM

WHEN THE WAR CAME TO AUSTRALIA

Memories of the Second World War

Joanna Penglase and David Horner

ALLEN & UNWIN

Note

All photographs are from the personal collections of people interviewed. The photograph on page 239 is from a newspaper but was unable to be traced. The photograph on page 42 is reproduced with kind permission of *The Sun* (Melbourne). The line from 'In My Arms' by F. Loesser and T. Grouya © 1943 Frank Music Corp. For Australasia: Allans Music Australia PO Box C156, Cremorne Junction NSW 2090

First published in 1992
Allen & Unwin Pty Ltd
9 Atchison Street, St Leonards, NSW 2065 Australia

National Library of Australia
Cataloguing-in-Publication entry:

When the war came to Australia: memories of the Second World War.

ISBN 1 86373 320 5

1. World War, 1939–1945– Personal narratives,
Australian. 2. World War, 1939–1945– Australia.
I. Penglase, Joanna. II. Horner, D.M. (David
Murray), 1948–

940.548194

Set in Times and Garamond by DOCUPRO, Sydney

Printed by Southwood Press, Marrickville, NSW

Contents

Preface

In February 1992 the ABC premiered a four-part television documentary series called *When the War Came to Australia*. This was the culmination of ten years' research and development by the producers, Will Davies and Bee Reynolds of Look Television Productions Pty Limited, and of two years' intensive interviewing and production by the authors of this book, along with many others.

The series was made possible by the support and encouragement of the NSW Film and Television Office and the Australian Broadcasting Corporation, and was made with the participation of the Australian Film Finance Corporation Pty Limited.

There will never be another war like the Second World War. Although more Australians were killed in the First World War than in the Second, the latter war touched the lives of a larger number of Australians and helped shape the nation as it is today. The outstanding episodes of the war—Tobruk and Alamein, Greece and Crete, Singapore and Kokoda, the bombing of Germany, the sinking of HMAS *Sydney* and *Canberra*, and many others— have been told in numerous books. The great debates about policy and strategy have been described, as have the lives of the prominent leaders. However, the effect of the war was also the sum of the experiences of millions of Australians who did not serve overseas, but contributed in their own ways to the war effort.

The aim of the series, therefore, was to record the memories and retell the experiences of the people who lived through the Second World War in Australia, and in doing so pay tribute to the homefront which played a vital but less acknowledged role in the war. Over the two-year period, the production team advertised widely throughout Australia, asking that people write in their reminiscences. Letters were received by the hundreds, and every writer was contacted so that eventually we had a nucleus of people who could be interviewed for a cross-section of opinions, responses and experiences. This formed the basis for months of interviewing throughout the country, in cities and in towns.

Special thanks are due to the senior researcher for the series, June Henman, who was indefatigable in setting up and pursuing this original research and whose efforts were so vital to the ultimate success of the project.

The source of this book, then, is the many Australians who contributed their stories to the series. Dr David Horner, historical adviser to the series, has written the introduction to each chapter. The series' writer, Joanna

Penglase, who along with the director, Peter Butt, conducted the majority of the interviews for the television series, has edited and organised the interviews for the book. The choice of material for the book was often a difficult one because of the richness and variety of people's recollections and the wide range of topics covered; but all the interviews in their complete form are lodged with the Australian War Memorial, as an important repository of the social history of the period.

Many people made a significant contribution to the making of the series, out of which the book has arisen, and the authors would like to acknowledge the work of the series' director and editor, Peter Butt; camera, Gordon Dein; sound, Ken Fryer; archive editor, Annie Marles; researcher, Peter Rees; production assistant, Michael Neil-Smith; and transcript typist, Susie Gibson. Thanks are also due to Rhonda Grande, Barry Videon, Helen McAnulty, Margaret Southcott and Vicky Miller, who gave so readily of their time and expertise. As producers, Bee Reynolds and Will Davies were unfailing in their inspiration and support.

The authors would like to thank above all everyone who gave so generously of their time, memories and photographs, without whom this book could not have been written. Their names are listed at the end of the book.

Abbreviations

AAMWS	Australian Army Medical Women's Service
ABC	Australian Broadcasting Commission
AGH	Australian General Hospital
AIF	Australian Imperial Force
AMP	Australian Mutual Provident Society
ARP	Air Raid Precautions
AWA	Amalgamated Wireless of Australasia
AWAS	Australian Women's Army Service
AWL	Absent Without Leave
BHP	Broken Hill Proprietary Company
CMF	Citizens' Military Forces
CO	Commanding Officer
CWA	Country Women's Association
GHQ	General Headquarters (South-West Pacific Area)
PMG	Post-Master General's Department
POW	Prisoner of War
PX	Post Exchange
QC	Queen's Counsel
R & R	Rest and Recreation
RAAF	Royal Australian Air Force
RAN	Royal Australian Navy
RANVR	Royal Australian Navy Volunteer Reserve
RSL	Returned Servicemen's League
TPI	Totally and Permanently Incapacitated
US	United States (of America)
VADs	Voluntary Aid Detachments
VD	Venereal Disease
VDC	Volunteer Defence Corps
WAAAF	Women's Auxiliary Australian Air Force
WANS	Women's Australian National Service
WOI	War Organisation of Industry (Department of)
WRANS	Women's Royal Australian Naval Service

1

Our Melancholy Duty

Fellow Australians, it is my melancholy duty to inform you officially that, in consequence of the persistence by Germany in her invasion of Poland, Great Britain has declared war upon her, and that, as a result, Australia is also at war . . .

No harder task can fall to the lot of a democratic leader than to make such an announcement. Great Britain and France, with the co-operation of the British Dominions, have struggled to avoid this tragedy . . . But, in the result, their efforts have failed, and we are therefore, as a great family of nations, involved in a struggle which we must at all costs win, and which we believe in our hearts we will win.

The Prime Minister, R. G. Menzies, broadcasting on the radio at 9 p.m. on Sunday, 3 September 1939.

The first seven months of the Second World War was a period of confused emotions for most Australians. It was a little over twenty years since the end of the First World War, and they fully appreciated the tragedy of war. They had no desire to take part in another. But there was general acceptance that Hitler's Germany had to be opposed, and in the main Australians saw themselves as loyal members of the British Empire. The question was—how could Australia contribute?

The resolution of this question was not helped by the lack of military activity during the so-called phoney war. After overrunning Poland in September 1939, Germany began moving forces towards its western frontier, but throughout the northern winter of 1939–40 it conducted no further offensive operations. In Australia the government, led by Robert Menzies, was faced with conflicting pressures. It wanted to aid Britain, but needed to prepare against a possible attack from Japan, which had been pursuing an aggressive expansionist policy throughout the 1930s. Australia was largely defenceless. While there was a small permanent Navy with relatively modern ships, the Army was based on an under-trained and poorly equipped part-time militia. The Air Force was tiny and equipped with obsolete planes, and it seemed doubtful whether Australian industry had the capacity to build modern planes.

On 15 September 1939, Menzies announced that Australia would raise a force of one division for service at home or abroad, but it was not until November, after assurances from Britain concerning Japan, that the government decided that the division, known as the 6th Division, Second Australian Imperial Force (AIF), would be sent to the Middle East. In the meantime, the government had also committed Australia to participation in the Empire

1

Air Training Scheme, by which Australian air crew would be trained for service overseas.

Not every eligible male rushed to enlist in the AIF. For some, the Air Force seemed more attractive and they put their names down for the RAAF. Others hesitated to join a force that might not see action overseas. The adventurous and those with a high sense of duty enlisted, and so too did those who were out of work or, in the aftermath of the Depression, did not have a secure job. The number who were actually unemployed was much lower than some have suggested. Many who listed their occupation as unemployed did so to escape the regulation that prevented the enlistment of men in Reserved Occupations—those civilian occupations considered vital to the war effort. Some, though actually unemployed at the time, stated their usual occupation. According to the Australian official war history, of 14 953 men chosen at random from those who enlisted in 1939, 200 stated they were unemployed. Initially the Second AIF numbered 20 000 men.

The first brigade of the 6th Division sailed for the Middle East on 10 January 1940 and the remainder left in April and May. Meanwhile, from 1 January 1940 compulsory training for a month at a time was introduced to maintain the militia at a strength of 75 000. Then, in February, the government decided to form another AIF division, the 7th, plus corps troops, to enable the formation of an Australian Corps. Enlistments in January and February were slow, picked up in March and April, but were still not sufficient to fill the 7th Division.

Germany's attack on Denmark and Norway in April, followed by its blitzkrieg against France and the Low Countries on 10 May, ended the phoney war and changed Australians' perceptions overnight. Whereas previously the government had rather unfortunately spoken of 'business as usual', it now called for an 'all-in' war effort. A new Director-General of Munitions was to be appointed and parliament was asked to introduce a bill enabling the government to requisition property, to direct businesses to carry out war work, and to call up and train the nation's manpower.

Both the AIF and the Home Army, comprising a small permanent component and garrison and militia units, were to be expanded, additional naval ships were to be manned, a graving dock was to be constructed in Sydney, and the Empire Air Training Scheme was to be pushed ahead. Men crowded into the recruiting offices and quickly brought the 7th Division to its full complement. In addition, it was possible to raise not only the 8th Division, which the government had announced was to be formed, but also to form another division, the 9th. Of course, there were insufficient weapons for these forces.

The German army advanced rapidly through France and by early June the British army was being evacuated from Dunkirk. On 10 June, Italy declared war on France and on 17 June France asked for an armistice, leaving Britain and the Dominions alone fighting against Germany and Italy. The increased danger caused by the fall of France changed the Australian government's attitude to internal security. The Australian Communist Party claimed a membership of some 5000 in 1940 and actively opposed the war effort, but on 15 June, under National Security Regulations, it was declared an illegal organisation. In the federal election of September 1940 the Communist Party, while banned, attacked both Menzies and the Leader of the Opposition, John Curtin, as 'Fascist monsters' and supporters of 'monopolists, bankers and profiteering warmongers'.

National Security Regulations were also used to intern enemy aliens. Initially some Germans had been interned, and with the entry of Italy into the war Italians were included. By October 1940 the internees totalled 2376, of whom a quarter were Germans and three-quarters Italians. While undoubtedly there were some injustices, there were nearly 20 000 recent arrivals from Germany and Italy, and about 45 000 persons of German or Italian birth in Australia, so the proportion interned was relatively small. Nevertheless, it was bitterly resented by naturalised Australians and native-born Australians of foreign origin who were interned.

In the latter half of 1940 the war came closer to Australia when several German armed merchantmen operated in Australian waters, but few Australians were in combat with the enemy. Australian ships operated in the Mediterranean, and in July the cruiser *Sydney* sank the Italian cruiser *Bartolomeo Colleoni*. Only a small number of Australian airmen were serving in Britain, although a Sunderland flying-boat squadron, manned by regular airmen, was in Britain at the beginning of the war and served there throughout 1940. Australians were keenly aware of the Battle of Britain, which began in July 1940 and extended into 1941 with bombing attacks on British cities.

The defeat of France and the Netherlands had repercussions in the Far East, where Japan, already at war in China, took the opportunity of moving into the northern part of the French colony of Indochina. After some consideration the government decided to continue the build-up of the AIF in the Middle East, where by December 1940 the 6th, 7th and 9th Divisions were training, but for the time being the 8th Division was retained in Australia. Defence problems in the Far East were discussed at a conference in Singapore in October, and when it was revealed that the British were extremely under strength in Malaya, the Australian government offered to send a brigade there. The British government accepted the offer, and in February 1941 the headquarters of the 8th Division and one brigade set sail. Meanwhile the Prime Minister, Menzies, who had been re-elected with a reduced majority in the September elections, decided to visit Britain to ask for further reinforcements for Malaya.

Thus by the end of 1940, few Australians had been in action and the Australian homeland had not been touched directly by the war in any substantial way. The economy and society were still gearing up for total war. In the Middle East, however, the AIF divisions were preparing for action, the first graduates from the Empire Air Training Scheme were about to arrive in Britain, and the chances of war in the Far East were growing. Australia's relative insulation from the full impact of war would not last long into 1941.

1 Not Another War!

I don't remember very much myself but I can remember my parents,

and they were both in tears—that's what impressed me more than anything because they were so upset about it. But I was nine when the war started.
Margaret Maxwell, schoolgirl, Swan Hill, Victoria

We'd been fearing it for a long time and I remember the scene in our own drawing room at the time, in fact my cousin burst into tears. We listened to the smug voice of Robert Menzies saying that Britain was at war and therefore Australia was at war. And my father jumped up like a firecracker and said, 'That's constitutionally wrong!'. And of course he was proved right; that was one of the stupidest things that Menzies ever said. But it added to the tension in the room at the time. It was the end of possibly two or three years of fearing that there would be war, so when it came there was a certain amount of relief.
Niall Brennan, university student, Melbourne

We were coming back from the evening service at St Mary's in Leederville, in Perth. And people were rushing out of the doors, saying war has been declared and Mum got very upset. I was twelve, and my brother was fourteen. And Dad kept saying, 'It's all right Kate, it'll be over long before the boys are of military age'.
Maurie Jones, schoolboy, Perth

I just felt absolutely terrible. I felt the whole world was going to drop into pieces, my whole life seemed to me to be going down the drain. I felt terribly depressed and terribly worried.
Margaret Holmes, pacifist, Sydney

We heard it at the Congregational Church and I remember how it seemed to be almost despairing. We walked round, my friends and I, for hours and hours discussing the whole position. We thought it seemed to be like the end of the world—it would be from the air, there would be poison gas and all this would be pouring down on Europe—it was as though the world had gone mad.
Ted Hartley, pacifist, Sydney

I guess my reaction was pretty typical of people my age. It was exciting to a point, and it was a little bit mysterious because of the things that we'd read and heard since the First World War about the invincibility of the British—we thought Germany was going to be a pretty easy snack I think.
Bill Graham, wheat farmer, Gulgong, New South Wales

It was terrible. We had friends in, and we heard it in our library and we were appalled. We talked about what would happen 'til very late and then they left. And when they arrived home there was somebody to intern them already, quick like that—all our friends were interned practically immediately.
Irmhild Beinssen, German-born resident, Sydney

I was a roustabout in a shearing shed at that time and I was sharing a shearer's hut with one of the farmer's sons. And I'd gone to bed at about 9.30 and he came down and he shook me and he said, 'They declared the bloody war'. And I just couldn't believe it—that Hitler would be such a maniac as to launch the world into war. But he did it just like that, thought nothing of it.
Bob Bahnsen, farm labourer, New South Wales

That night I'd gone with a friend over to the paper shop and on the way back we stopped, and this old fella was telling me how we had to keep the flag flying—he was drunk obviously—and that frightened me because I understood there'd be enemy troops coming down the hill, I didn't know if I'd get home in one piece.
Kevin Shepherd, schoolboy, Adelaide

I was visiting a friend at Watson's Bay and the news came over that we were at war. Not long afterwards I took my departure because it was getting late and I had to get a bus and I remember walking down the street from her home past various houses and one house had a light on and the blind was a little bit up and whoever was in that house was on her knees saying a prayer at her bedside. And that is when I realised to a greater extent what the war meant—it had gone already into people's homes.
Nell Stronach, welfare worker, Sydney

I was at a friend's place at the time and that night when I heard it over the air, within twenty minutes, I'd run all the way back up to the barracks to join up, to be there, and when I got there every one of my friends that was on leave was there also, waiting to join up.
Sandy Rayward, sergeant, Permanent Army, Sydney

2 God Save the King

That night my father had nightmares, having been in the First World War. He was up and walking about through the night and then next morning out at our farm there was a congregation of his brother and cousin and two or three ex-servicemen of World War I and oh! what they wouldn't have done to those Germans! They talked and told yarns about the First World War; I suppose they would have been there two or three hours, and I remember how one of them finally said, 'We better go home else we won't be able to wait for the call-up'—they were all in the Army reserve.
Charles Janeway, schoolboy, Mt Gambier, South Australia

Oh, we were all for Britain and King and Empire and the whole bit, it wasn't unfashionable to be patriotic in those days.
Margaret Maxwell

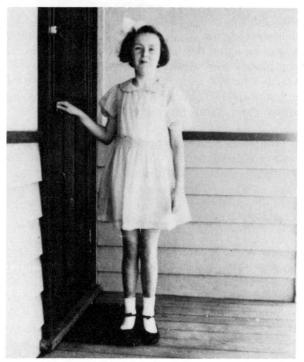

'It wasn't unfashionable to be patriotic in those days': Margaret (Pickett) Maxwell, Swan Hill, Victoria, was 9 when the war began.

It was automatic that we went to war. It wasn't questioned, except by supposed traitors. And certainly our culture was a very British one.
Maurie Jones

At that stage, we were nearly all of direct British descent. The Royal Family still meant a great deal to everybody in Australia, and nobody thought of anything else other than being British; and there was no question in those days that 95 per cent of the people were intensely patriotic. World War I really was no direct concern of Australia's, but we were one of the first countries into it, and the same applied in World War II. We weren't under threat, but everybody felt—Britain's in it and so we're in it as a matter of course.
Ralph Doig, Premier's Department, Perth

We always alluded to Britain as our mother country. And we paid our tribute—when we were going to school, we were all lined up in front of the flagpole every Monday morning: 'We honour our God, we salute our flag, we honour the King', or words to that effect. So to my generation it was truly the mother country. They had developed Australia, they had helped to populate Australia, and so we were just one of the family of the British Empire.
Bill Graham

Looking after mother, that's the way I read it to be—looking after mother, we were all as one in those days.
Charles Janeway

And so it was always that you went to their side. I can remember Mr Menzies announcing this and the way he announced that Australia was going in—he didn't ask or anything, he just said 'The lion has roared, the cubs are with you'—meaning Canada, New Zealand, South Africa and Australia. And this great cartoon came out the next day with the lion roaring and the little cubs at the feet of Mother England.
Patricia Penrose, dress designer, Melbourne

3 First of the Second AIF

I think there was an immediate response from a large number of people. The first was the intensely loyal section, who wanted to be in right from the beginning, and who were military-minded; and there was quite a lot of unemployment in Western Australia still, following on the Depression, and a lot of people enlisted early who really had no regular jobs, in any case, to go to. So from those two avenues there was a large enlistment.
Ralph Doig

Thousands and thousands of characters on the dole and the breadline knew they'd get a job in the Army and this is what did happen. When you joined the Army you met them all, and they were all in there for the three square meals a day and 5 bob a day—big money.
Merv Lilley, rural worker, Queensland

It think it was high adventure: going to places we'd never seen before, the thought of the First World War and the high hopes and the great actions that were instilled in us in history, Gallipoli and the whole of France; and we couldn't get away quick enough actually. It was just to get over there and let 'em know how good we were, because we were all terribly sports minded and everybody knew how good we were at sports so we thought well, we can do just as well over there and have a lot of fun as well.
Sandy Rayward

In those days leading up to the Second World War we were still living on the tradition of Anzac and it was a very important part of Australian folklore, the invincibility of the Australian soldier was something that we really thought, and relied upon.
Bill Graham

It is on record that about 95 per cent of the first AIF volunteers were unemployed. We were still in the wash of the Depression.
Niall Brennan

Left *'Within twenty minutes I'd run all the way up to the barracks to join up': Sandy Rayward, Sydney.* Right *'I joined the Army because the King was in danger and the Empire was in danger and the Nazis were unspeakably wicked': Russell Braddon, Brisbane, soon after joining up.*

From the very poor area I lived in where there was just no work for any of the boys, they were jumping the rattler—including my brother-in-law—and getting under the tarpaulins, getting down to Melbourne to enlist. We'd wave the fellows off to the war, not too many tears then, and of course the fellows were shouting and yelling and chiacking everyone—young men don't join up thinking they're going to get killed, they join up for something else, the excitement was in all their eyes.
Patsy Adam-Smith, Warragul, Victoria

I joined the Army because the King was in danger and the Empire was in danger and the Nazis were unspeakably wicked and I wanted to go and kill Germans—it's as simple as that. Very schoolboyish and the first time I went they wouldn't take me—they said I was too young and that I must get my BA [Bachelor of Arts] first and at that stage the university wouldn't fail you if they knew you wanted to join up so that's how I got my BA and I rushed down and joined up and there you are.
Russell Braddon, university student, Sydney

I'd been brought up on duty from my father and also my schooling: that it's part of your duty to go away and protect your own and your mother and your sister.
   My mother had gone through the First World War with two young children while my father was away, for four years, and he'd been

Alan Low marching with the 6th Division in Sydney on 4 January 1940.

hospitalised and wounded and she had a vivid memory of this because it was only twenty years previous, and she wasn't happy at all about me going in. But Dad, I feel that he was very proud that I would take that attitude.

So I went along up to Vic Barracks and they took my name and address and of course I hadn't even started to shave then, and I could see them looking with a jaundiced eye about my age but I said to the fellow, 'what's the score?' and he said, 'well you've got to get your parents' permission' and that was that. So I came back with all the papers and I took them in, but my mother never signed them, my Dad did.

Alan Low, 6th Division

The first recruits—there were razor gangs, there were the push mobs, there were some very very tough blokes, blokes out of the boob [prison]; and also at the same time complete surf clubs joined up, cricket clubs, University of Sydney, and all types—a great diversity of chaps. And I remember my initiation was to watch a chap that they caught stealing—we were actually quartered in the pig pens at the time—and they caught him stealing and marched him up the clock tower at the Showground and tossed him off the top and we could hear him squealing for miles but it stopped the stealing. But that's the sort of boys they were, they didn't muck around.

Sandy Rayward

There were a lot of fellows discharged dishonourably in the first few months because they weren't checking up on people, they wanted the numbers. They came from a very great cross-section, and I would say

the greater majority were from the bush, and a lot of farmers. We didn't talk too much about whether we had a job or not, and I feel also that the fellows that were on the dole at that time didn't want to own up to it.
Alan Low

My husband was a miner at the time, I didn't know him then, and he wanted to go to war, he had that adventurous spirit, and he went through the line and they said, 'What do you do?' And he said, 'Coalminer'. So they said, 'No, you're restricted, you're not to come through.' So he went back and got in another line and when he went through it he said, 'unemployed' and was straight in.
Sally Bowen, hotel cook, Wollongong, New South Wales

It was in a bad way when we joined—they said we had to bring our own cutlery and a plate and a cut lunch and everything when we came on the day.
Alan Low

We had nothing, absolutely nothing. We had just a few little guns from the First World War, 18 pounders and 4.5 Howitzers. And very very rugged uniforms. I think they must have been making them flat out. Half of them didn't fit, we used to have to swap amongst ourselves and try and do a bit of tailoring ourselves to make them fit, they were very rough.

How they got the stuff to us I'll never know, even to start us off with—the Lithgow Small Arms [munitions factory, NSW] making the rifles and ammunition for all these sudden thousands of troops that had to be moved, all in a big big hurry—like from September, and we left January 10th so they did a mighty job to give us what we had.
Sandy Rayward

At Holsworthy [NSW] where we trained there weren't any guns but we pretended there were guns and the officers used to get frightfully excited about it if we didn't squat the right way even though there was nothing to sit on. 'Sit at attention!' they would scream so we would all sit bolt upright on nothing at all and then we would be ordered to de-bus out of our non-existent lorries and set up the non-existent guns and load the non-existent barrels and slam the non-existent breach and fire—so we were very proficient gunners by the time we left Holsworthy.
Russell Braddon

I was matron of a country hospital and a telegram came to say, 'report to Victoria Barracks at such and such a time on such and such a day' and that was two days hence, so I rang up to find out what it was all about to find I'd been appointed matron of the first hospital to go overseas, and that was the first I knew.
Connie Fall, matron, 2/1 AGH, 6th Division

Nurses of the 2/1st AGH on board The Empress of Japan *en route to the Middle East. (Photo: Connie Fall)*

We marched on the 4th of January and the people were cheering, girls were running out and kissing us as we went past and shaking our hands and patting us and all this sort of thing and it was a great feeling. It made you straighten your shoulders a bit more and feel like you were doing something for your country and you wanted to get out there and really get into it and get away and show them that we were as good as what had gone before us.
Alan Low

We were about ten abreast with our rifles and everything and you've never seen a mob like it, cheering and everything right through Sydney, and ticker streamers. You felt pretty proud and we were all pretty fit by then, we'd learned to march properly and I had an old girl come out of the crowd, she's hanging on my arm, I'm trying to swing it, she's got a bottle of wine in one hand, and she's trying to give me a swig.
Sandy Rayward

They sailed on the 10th of January but I was called up two days after we'd marched to the CO's office and told that I was being held back, and they weren't going to tell me the reason. You can't get anything out of the Army, they just do these things. So it was you'll hand your uniform in and get back into your fatigues suit. I was most unhappy about it and I really put on a turn but it didn't do any good. And I didn't find out until well after the war—at my father's funeral, my mother admitted then that she'd gone up to Victoria Barracks with my birth certificate and showed them my real age.
Alan Low

There were thousands of people on the railway station at Sydney,

Constance Fall, matron of the first overseas hospital, on the beach at Gaza with colleagues, soon after arrival in the Middle East.

giving us flowers and God knows what, we were all laden down, and we went to Melbourne to board the ship. And at the railway station, the Matron-in-Chief met us and we were going towards the ship and she said to me, 'Of course you've got your white gloves?'.

And I looked at her, staggered, and I said, 'White gloves—what on earth for?'.

'If you meet the Queen, you've got to wear them, go down the street and buy them!'.

Down the street I went for a pair of white gloves. I was thinking about the war, I wasn't thinking about meeting the Queen or anybody else. But I took the white kid gloves. And I never wore them.
Connie Fall

Quite a number of people saw us off, mostly officials and Army people and streamers were thrown to us and I remember I caught one streamer and I hung on to that streamer for dear life because it was attached to a gentleman I didn't know on the quay and it just felt that so long as I had hold of that, I was holding onto Australia and something I knew. When that went I was going into something I didn't know, the unknown, and that was rather apprehensive, a bit frightening.
Betty Oldham, Army nurse, 2/1 AGH, 6th Division

4 No Medals

It was to my amazement and to my mother's *utter* amazement that they could go so quickly. Go so quickly to something that had been so horrific in World War I—we couldn't believe it, we thought they were mad.

My mother was a very socially aware person with a strong sense of justice, and she felt that because of the Depression, which she

considered the British financiers had had a lot to do with bringing on
in Australia, she didn't feel that Australia should be fighting for Britain.
Bob Bahnsen

We were brought up on stories of World War I and the incredible
hysteria that accompanied the volunteer system during the First World
War, so in a sense by 1939 we were psyched into a readiness for it.
But it never happened. Of course our generation had been brought up
differently. The First World War had exploded onto a generation that
had no experience or knowledge of war at all except maybe the Boer
War and that was a small time affair, but by the time it got to 1939,
we'd read *All Quiet on the Western Front,* we were familiar with the
pacifist movements, the League Against War and Fascism, and the war
hysteria just never came about.
Niall Brennan

The community at that point certainly wasn't united behind Britain.
People of British descent were, for the most part. But there were other
groups who certainly weren't—those of Irish descent, who are never
pro-British; those of German descent, a lot of whom were very fearful
of what would happen to them, because they were persecuted in
World War I and they were fearful it would happen again.

The Irish hated Britain. I can remember an old Irish farmer who
buttonholed me one day in this little town, and he was gloating, this
old boy. And he said in his very Irish accent, 'I say God speed
Hatler'—he used to call him 'Hatler'. And by that time I'd begun to
appreciate the consequences of a German victory and I was a bit
stunned. And I think he saw on my face that I didn't quite go along
with what he was saying, so he repeated it—'That's what I say: God
speed Hatler.'
Bob Bahnsen

The student population was divided along much the same lines as the
rest of the population. There were a lot of loyal Imperialist students,
and there were a few brawls as a result, and some of us were
regarded as disloyal ratbags, and there was a certain amount of
violence. The year that I was editor of *Farrago*, the student
newspaper, I in fact had a bodyguard, a couple of hulking mates who
steered me out of the university when *Farrago* came out, usually
because of some anti-Imperialistic stuff we'd published, and we didn't
want to be thrown in the lake like some of our predecessors had been.

We had an attitude of pretty blasé indifference to the war, as a
result of which we were censored and silenced and I was carpeted
personally by the Chancellor who called me a foolish anti-British
young pup who didn't know there was a war on. Of course we knew
there was a war on, but we saw no reason to get hysterical about it.
Niall Brennan

I don't think there was any great division about the war being

Laurie Aarons addressing the crowd in Sydney's Domain on behalf of the Communist Party, urging listeners not to support the war.

necessary and so there wasn't the anti-war demonstrations that you see today. We were prepared to leave it to politicians and we believed that if they had to make those decisions, well there was no question. My generation thought of pacifists as disloyal people; as a matter of fact to my way of thinking they were sabotaging the effort of the majority of Australia.
Bill Graham

To me, it was this ideal of the brotherhood of man, and the thought that wars would cease if people said no and refused to fight.
Ted Hartley

I just felt that we shouldn't be in the war. I had these pacifist convictions that you shouldn't overcome evil with worse evil—that the thing to do was to treat it in some other way. I felt Hitler should have been resisted by some form of passive, non-violent resistance. People die in a war anyway, and fewer people would have died if they had non-violently resisted. I don't mean to say you should let dictators do what they want but there are other ways of dealing with them.

But there wasn't any protest movement that I know of. None at all. The small pacifist groups here were putting out little statements saying that they thought this wasn't the right way to deal with Hitler but there was no peace movement at all really, although of course until Russia came into the war the extreme left-wing people were against the war too.
Margaret Holmes

I've always hated war from the time when I was a child—I can remember helping to form a branch of the League of Nations in the school because that was the great hope of the world at the time. So war to me was about the dirtiest word that could be.
Joyce Batterham, Communist Party worker, Newcastle

When the three months conscription came in, it seemed to be just the thin end of the wedge and it was very very simple, you go forward and you just refuse to take the oath. They tried to bluster you into it and so on, but that was that. So that was the first stage, but they left you alone and it went on for years, not hearing. Though you were told what to expect—six months' imprisonment, repeated by another six months and so on. It was a terrible strain in that sense.
Ted Hartley, conscientious objector, Sydney

I would never have enlisted for active service. I wanted to be a conscientious objector at one stage but there were family problems about that and I backed off. And I spent most of the war looking remarkably like a young man evading military service. Well, I've learnt to live with that—it hasn't won me any medals.
Niall Brennan

5 On Guard!

Most people I don't think knew nearly as much about Germany as they should have. I don't think any of us knew much, except perhaps some intellectuals—who were pretty thin on the ground in those days.
Bob Bahnsen

I think that we tend to feel that people were suspicious and hated Hitler long before the war and indeed there was a lot of suspicion and ill-feeling, but we didn't in those days know anything about the concentration camps, or very little. There were reports—they were doubted. And I remember on the day that war was declared we listened to the radio and heard Chamberlain [the British Prime Minister] telling us that we were in a state of war, and then the BBC announcer came back and his whole tone had changed, and he said something very sarcastic about Mr Hitler. It was something we'd never heard before and I remember there was a sense of release, as though we'd been very careful about this guy.
John Hinde, ABC journalist, Sydney

We tried to make them understand it. We certainly talked quite a lot about it. I can't tell you how much the average citizen understood it or was even interested in it. I think we were a strange new group, we behaved differently, we dressed differently, we talked differently.
Doris Liffman, Austrian refugee, Melbourne

Anything that happened outside Britain didn't really matter very much. It was mainly things in England that were reported on, and the rest of the world were unfortunate not to be British or Australian-born. Even if you'd been in Australia for four or five generation, if you went to England you went home—which astonished me.
Alfred Ruskin, German refugee, Melbourne

Doris (Oppenheim) Liffman, Melbourne, Austrian refugee; a photo taken in 1937 before she came to Australia.

As soon as war was declared they put a guard on the Swan Hill bridge and my father was one of them. I thought at the time it was hilarious, there was Dad and somebody else with a gun marching up and down on the bridge and the other side, in NSW, was just the Hay Plains and there was nothing at all. I don't know what they were expected to guard—if anyone was going to come and blow the bridge up I suppose, but of course they didn't and it didn't last very long.
Margaret Maxwell

They felt very keenly that there might be an invasion at that stage; it was only Germany of course, and yet they had that feeling. They even put a guard on the Millicent powerhouse—which was two diesel engines with about 60 horsepower. But they put a guard on to make sure that in case any Germans landed that they could repel them from taking control of the powerhouse.
Ren deGaris, schoolboy, Millicent, South Australia

The first thing they did with us at Victoria Barracks was to ship seven or eight heroic youngsters like myself off to a racecourse with instructions we were to guard it against Nazi parachutists who were due to land imminently, and to resist them, they gave us an enamel mug, a knife and a fork, an enamel plate and food for one day. Fortunately, the racecourse was covered in mushrooms, and full of patriotic zeal we ate mushrooms for about ten days and then they ran out—we'd eaten all of them. We had no money or anything but we had enough to ring Victoria Barracks, so I rang an uncle of mine who was a major there and a few minutes after that a lorry arrived and we were shipped off to Holsworthy to begin training as gunners.
Russell Braddon

I had an uncle, he was German-born Australian, and I used to think that he was a spy. We'd go to his house and he'd have radio sets—I mean to a young child, you've got a relative with the name of Otto and you know he's German and he's got a radio set under his bed—he just *has* to be a spy!

I kept that to myself—I was very influenced by movies and in the movies it was always the Gestapo who took you away and tortured you and I thought I've got to keep quiet about this otherwise that's going to happen to me.

Lillian Harding, schoolgirl, Adelaide

We had spies in our area and one of them was found by my auntie who was delivering milk. There'd been a German came out in about 1938 and there were Germans that had been sent out by Hitler around other areas, and he'd set a radio station in an old biscuit factory down the road from us and for some strange reason kids always know what goes on and we knew all about this, and we knew that he'd been captured.

Margaret Burton, schoolgirl, Adelaide

A German mine was seen out to sea, off Beachport, and a local fisherman towed it in to the jetty and they pulled it up onto the beach about two kilometres from the town, and the Army were notified and they sent down personnel to delouse this mine. Then they went behind the sand dunes to wait for it to go off and after the time had elapsed it didn't happen and two men were sent over to check it and of course it blew up and killed them. And it was a German mine, so they were really all around this country, they mined the whole place, Spencer Gulf.

There were tracks seen on the sand dunes along the Coorong [SE coast of South Australia] and it's believed that they were from bicycles and that these people had come ashore in a submarine and had put together these bikes and ridden across the sandhills and made their way to Melbourne where they were going to infiltrate or to spy. And that's what the local VDC [Volunteer Defence Corps] were to watch out for—this sort of thing happening.

Rosemary McCourt, schoolgirl, Millicent, South Australia

There were Germans in the area. Most of them were in the Barossa Valley and of course they were terribly loyal to Australia and this was the sad thing. The ones that I believe weren't loyal were ones that had families who'd recently emigrated in the late 1930s. But most of the Germans came out in the 1860s, 1850s and they were third or fourth generation Australian and had no connection at all with Germany. I think they were too hard on them really but they didn't know who were spies and who weren't.

Margaret Burton

We didn't have a boat but a young policeman came one day, one of the many people who came in and looked through the house, and he

Alfred Ruskin, German refugee, Melbourne. His medical studies interrupted by the Nazis, Ruskin eventually put his knowledge to good use when he joined the medical corps of the Australian Army.

said he had had a complaint from neighbours, and I said, 'Well what is it about?'

'Oh that you are running out to provision German U-boats.'

And one time they came from the 'Intelligence' (we used inverted commas always)—and they went to one bookshelf that was in the drawing room and opened every book and shook it, and then wanted to go into the next room and that was the library and that was crammed with books and they said, 'Who reads all these books?'—they were so disgusted. Some of the books I never got back and I'm sorry about that.

But my husband wasn't interned then—probably because he was born here. He wasn't interned until Russia came into the war, that was on his birthday. It was not unexpected because all the other men had been interned, no women at that time had been interned except a very few which had a reputation of being Nazis and they were in a place on the Hawkesbury River. But you expect things like that in a foreign country and after all I had not been in Australia very long and so much of it seemed absurd, but not unexpected.
Irmhild Beinssen

We suddenly became friendly enemy aliens—*friendly* enemy aliens. In Melbourne that meant that if I lived in South Yarra and wanted to go over to Windsor, which is directly opposite, I would have to get a permit to do that.
Alfred Ruskin

Thelma (Coyne) Long, extreme left, in Hamburg, Germany, in August 1938 after playing the final of the women's doubles in the German tennis championships. You can just see the swastikas on the ribbons hanging from the bouquets. Thelma's promising career in tennis was interrupted by the war and she later became one of the earliest volunteers for the Australian Women's Army Service.

We were Germans, we had a German passport, so on the official level we were enemy aliens. This was something which for us was a very very difficult name to accept. After all, we were the ones who only saved our lives by coming to Australia. My parents, who did not come with us, had been sent to Theresienstadt, and we heard nothing from them. We were Hitler's victims, we were his real enemies, so for us to be enemy aliens was a grotesque and very difficult concept but we were tainted as such from the point of view that we had to report every week to the police in the suburb in which we lived and we were not allowed to leave the suburb without the permit. Now the permit that was given to us was a worker's permit, so for instance I was not allowed to go in the evening to the pictures, and not allowed to go out on Sunday, and if you had friends who lived in another district, you were not allowed to go.
Doris Liffman

Any noted person or any noted family of Sydney, the Sirs and everybody, always pulled up outside the door with their chauffeurs and were served at de Luca's, it was the going thing of the day. My father had the pleasure of serving Dame Nellie Melba, big cattleman Kidman, also Heinz, Bushells and lots of other people, Arnotts, so we were the spot of Sydney in those days as far as fruit was concerned.

But on 11th June 1940 when Italy declared war, it made a big

Bob Donato snr. and sons Marino (left), *and Bob jnr.* (centre), *who were all interned, and John* (right), *who joined the army.*

difference to us. We were ostracised by our clientele, my father was interned on the 11th, the first day, and my uncle and my brother and myself were left to run the business.

They just picked him up, that's all. My father came out here in 1898, he became a British subject in 1908. But no explanations given, the same as when I was picked up, no explanations given. As a matter of fact, the day that I was picked up was 3rd August 1940, I was to go round to Martin Place to enlist that day. Instead of enlisting they took me out to Long Bay [Prison in Sydney] for a holiday.

All the naturalised were allowed to go to a tribunal which my brother, my father and myself attended, and what sort of a tribunal it was I can't say even to this day. You had to prove your innocence of nothing. Whether this tribunal agreed with you or not, it was up to them. They asked me questions about my family, and the QC that was against us—his family were customers also at the shop—his summing up was, 'I demand that these men be retained in a camp mainly for the position that they have—their shop is in the centre of the city which could be detrimental to the nation and to the war effort'. Mind you, I used to write to Mussolini every week.
Bob Donato, fruiterer, Sydney

They came to search the house and then they had to go and search the little café we had. Then he didn't come back so Mum said to me, 'Go and see where your father is'. So I raced up the street and raced round to the police station and they had locked my father up. And that was the first I knew that he had been interned, that he was going to be taken away from us. Then I had to go back and tell my mother

'The policeman said 'the
naturalisation paper, dear girl,
is not worth the paper it's
written on': Francesca Merenda,
a schoolgirl in Tully,
Queensland in 1940 when her
Italian-born father was interned.

and it was devastating. The feeling of being unprotected, of Mum and I just being there on our own in the house, not knowing what to do, not having Dad there; because Dad was a strong personality and he always made us feel nothing could happen, it would be all right. So those months that Dad was away were really very bad for my mother and myself.

I could not accept the fact that my father was an Australian and that he'd been interned, and when I said this to the arresting police officer, he said, 'The naturalisation paper, dear girl, is not worth the paper it's written on'. And that really hurt, very very much.
Francesca Merenda, schoolgirl, Tully, Queensland

Down at Burwood Road there was a beautiful fruit shop we used to go to and it was Italian and we were down there this day and all of a sudden, I've never seen so many police. And they came in, took these two men, just walked them out of the shop, pulled the shutters down and that was the end of it. That's all the warning they had. They were taken away because they weren't Australians.
Anne Pellew, staff canteen worker, Sydney

I was very young and didn't realise what it was all about but at nine o'clock in the morning the doorbell rang and there were two detectives with my father. They had come to take him away. My mother could not speak English very well and the first thing she said was, 'What has he done that they're taking him away?'. And he said, 'He is going to the Fremantle gaol, and I suggest you get some clothes for him together'.

She said again, 'For how long?' and he said, 'I don't know.' And my father was interned for three-and-a-half years. It was a very frightening time, we were alone at home, my mother couldn't speak English and we didn't know who our friends were—every time we put our heads outside the front door we were dagos and you should be in gaol with your father, and we were very afraid.

I was nearly fourteen when he went away and seventeen when he came home.

Amelia Donato, schoolgirl, Perth

We knew the Communist Party was going to be banned and we had all sorts of preparations for it, cover addresses, and the cloak-and-dagger stuff we went in for, and when it was finally banned there was a great scurry—people moved, and the place where I was living got raided by the police, but I was one jump ahead.

Joyce Batterham

It all happened on a Saturday night, Saturday 15th June 1940. All over Australia, the security police, the secret political police of that time, and the State police in each State, raided the homes of most members of the Communist Party, and there were all sorts of humorous stories from that. Like the police impounding copies of Shakespeare and the Bible and various innocuous and inoffensive and non-Communist things. But they raided hundreds of places across Australia.

Laurie Aarons, factory worker and Communist Party member, Sydney

I was living with the miners at Whitebridge at that period and I was there one night and I was sitting typing a bulletin when a little boy came running over from a neighbouring miner's cottage across the paddocks, saying, 'The cops are at our place and Daddy said I'd better run over and tell you because they'll be here next'. So Jimmy, who was the miner, he said, 'OK, out!'. And he threw the typewriter, and me after the typewriter, into the blackberry bushes outside the window. And the last thing I heard as I landed in the blackberries was his wife Doris saying to him, 'Jimmy, I've been telling you for weeks to clear out those bloody blackberry bushes!'.

So there I sat in the blackberry bushes while the police came and made a very ineffective search of the house and of course they found nothing and off they went again.

Joyce Batterham

I was one of the Post Office's first human shredders. I often wonder how important those documents really were. But of course in those days everywhere around us there were posters—'Walls Have Ears'—Hitler with his ear stuck out. They were all over the place, so we were very much aware of the need for tight security, and not to say anything.

Bob Taylor, Post Office worker, Adelaide

Almost as soon as the war started, that Australian propensity for censorship turned up and there were censors in every newspaper office, as far as I know.
John Hinde

We had to submit every newsreel to the censor in the city who sometimes said, 'Take that out,' or whatever. It was a time of censorship and some very incompetent people were in the jobs, like they do with government appointments, they get some duds, not just some, they get a lot of duds. I used to argue the point with them but it didn't get you far because they just said, 'No, that's out in the national interest'. The censorship was necessary of course because people were constantly being reminded, 'Don't talk'"because there's submarines off the coast, or whatever. It was not a real worry, we more or less censored ourselves.
Ken G. Hall, managing editor, *Cinesound Review*, Sydney

6 Business as Usual

In the first days of excitement I think everybody felt that they should join up, that it was more or less going to be an adventure, that was the sort of feeling that was about. But of course it went on for so long as a Cold War, nothing happening very much, and being remote from Australia, that those sorts of feelings dampened down after the first few months.
Bill Graham

We were put on radio to lift morale by saying, 'Business as usual, we'll carry on', so I went in and did my bit and so did many many other people. The war was on us and we weren't all that concerned because it was a hell of a long way away.
Ken G. Hall

People didn't really know what to make of it, they were just waiting and wondering what was going to happen. But I think a lot of people were something like myself—they had other commitments, they had families, and they felt they would like to wait a while and see what the requirement was and what the demand was before they made up their mind to enlist.
Ralph Doig

When war was declared I was not quite 21 and sufficiently involved with a girlfriend and my life working in the bank that I simply felt apprehension—what is going to happen? And that we can't do much about it, so carry on and go to work Monday as usual. I didn't feel any wish to be involved immediately.

Towards the end of 1939, the government announced that apart from recruiting for a second AIF there would be a call-up of young

men who attained the age of 21 years between 1 July 1939 and 30
June 1940 and I turned 21 in the October so I was in that first call-up.
George Telfer, bank clerk, Adelaide

The English called it the phoney war until Dunkirk, and here it was
even quieter, because we weren't at that stage at any rate in any
danger of invasion or being bombed. And for a lot of people I think
the war passed without great incident to them. If they had nobody of
military age in the family, life just went on as before.
Maurie Jones

I don't think anybody believed that the war was going to drag on
very long. You looked at the map and there was one-third of the
surface covered with the British Empire. Germany had already been
defeated only twenty years before and we didn't realise that they had
developed so much—their army and their navy and their air force. We
were living in the First World War euphoria, I think.
Bill Graham

Now that changed about the middle of the year, after Hitler's
blitzkrieg. After that things took a more serious turn, particularly after
the fall of France of course—this was obviously pretty serious.
Niall Brennan

When France capitulated, it was dreadful. We were just sitting around
the radio crying, because we realised the whole of France was then
exposed for Hitler to move troops and aeroplanes, whatever he
wanted, just over the channel from England. That was a dreadful final
feeling, and we just didn't know what lay ahead for England.
Patricia Penrose

With the overrunning of France and the evacuation of the remnants of
the British army, that was the first time I think, really, that the vast
majority of people took Hitler as seriously as they had to. I think they
all got a little bit carried away by some of the British propaganda at
the time which indicated that things were going to be all right, that
the war was going to be over before very long.
Ralph Doig

There was a wave of patriotism. I remember at our annual school
concert in the Town Hall, we had a very patriotic tableau and I was
dressed up as Lord Nelson and I held up my telescope and said,
'England expects this day that every man will do his duty,' and then
the girls burst into *There'll Always Be An England*, and the school
pianist was pounding away and I think the audience got up and sang
as·well—it was a sort of a real national fervour that we were British.
Ken Muggleston, schoolboy, Katoomba, New South Wales

My father enlisted after they started bombing Liverpool because his

'England expects this day that every man will do his duty': Ken Muggleston aged ten (right) as Lord Nelson, hero of Trafalgar, in a patriotic tableau in the Katoomba Town Hall (NSW) at the end of 1940. He is wearing white satin breeches with royal blue sash and jacket and frilled cravat, made by his mother from a picture of Nelson in a school history book.

family came from Liverpool and he started getting very concerned about the possibility of the Germans in fact taking over. And he wanted to go back and help, and see his family—he had his mother and his brother and sister still over there, and lots of cousins.

The day he went he didn't want us to come down to the station and I think that was one of the saddest days. He wanted us just to come to the gate. And we all stood at the gate and waved and kissed him goodbye and I can remember crying and saying, 'Dad I don't want you to go'. That was the first time I'd shown any emotion but I realised then—I was probably nine or ten at the time—I realised I might never see him again.

Margaret Burton

The real populariser, if I can use the word, was the Dunkirk retreat, which had romance and a plot and the whole thing. It was a terrific story. And then the popular songs began to do it—'There'll Be Blue Birds Over The White Cliffs Of Dover'—as the airmen began to get busy.

John Hinde

I began to notice my husband being moody and pensive and one day he said, 'You know I'm going to have to be in this, this is getting serious'. The Maginot Line was down and the Germans were marching right through to Dunkirk. He said, 'I want our daughter to be brought

'My father wanted to go back and help': Margaret Burton, Adelaide, aged nine (right) *with her parents, Jack and Ella Hayden, sister Jen, 18 months, and brothers John, 8, and Phillip, 6. This photo was taken in 1940 just prior to her father's embarkation.*

up in a free country'. I didn't say anything and he came home shortly after that and he said, 'I enlisted today in the Air Force'. I said, 'Why the Air Force?' and he said, 'Well it will be quick and clean'.

So he arrived in England and shortly after that I received a letter from him, he said, 'I've been posted to what they call the Suicide Squadron'. He said, 'I'm in coastal command, we have to bomb our targets anything from 50 to 100 feet'. And he said, 'We're in Beaufort Bombers, the bloody things are so obsolete they're only held together with bobby pins'. But he said, 'I'm proud to be here, when I see what the English have gone through, the craters, the destroyed buildings'.

Anyway, then he only lasted six months.

Lillian Malcolm, housewife and mother, Sydney

7 Their Faces Were Bright ...

At that time, I was going to high school and of course everybody's mind was filled with the resistance the British were putting up to the German bomber onslaught on England and I really became impressed with the idea of being a pilot. So I applied to the Air Force to join up and to go on the air crew.

I was seventeen and my mother was more concerned with me going away, being so young; she accepted the fact that my father went away and then my elder brother. But I pleaded with her to sign the forms

'All me mates were going, I thought no good me being like the bird on the outside of the biscuit tin, I might as well go and be with 'em too': Hilary Hughes, Gulgong, New South Wales.

to give permission for me to join up and she relented, and eventually I went into the Empire Air Training Scheme.
Gerry Judd, schoolboy, Newcastle, New South Wales

It was in the papers every night of course and on the radio and friends would be talking about it. Everywhere you went, people would be talking about the war, and more people were joining up, more of your friends leaving. I think a lot of people were joining up for the excitement. They didn't know what was ahead of them, nobody expected to be killed or shot or anything like that, or have to shoot anyone else, but they wanted to get it over and done with quickly. And of course you were meeting different troops in Australia and it was really livening up and people—like my mother—were going to different classes; I was going to first aid classes, everyone was joining in and helping as much as they could.
Phyl Proctor, technical college student, Sydney

More than half of the population from Gulgong went away in the Army or the Air Force or Navy or something, all the younger population, 'cause they had all these big call-ups.
Hilary Hughes, plant operator, Sydney

I would watch them going, marching off, bright-eyed and full of hope. Their faces were bright with the thought that they were doing something for their country, and yet I couldn't help thinking, 'what lies ahead for these boys?'. You just never know. And I kept thinking of the wives, the sweethearts, and the mums and dads who would be watching them go. It must have been tearful for them, and heart-rending.
Kathleen Loneregan, store proprietor, Gulgong, New South Wales

Left *Lillian Malcolm, whose husband Reg White joined up when France fell, and* (right) *at a dance with Reg, before the war; she knew him from the age of 16.*

When the boys were called up in groups, they would march from Loneregan's corner [the local store] right down to the railway. The townspeople would all go down to see them off and the town band used to play quite a lot of the old tunes while they were waiting for the train. Then when they got on the train they played them out until we couldn't see the train anymore. So it was very effective really, very sad but effective.

Mary Comer, soldier's wife, Gulgong, New South Wales

I was still going to school when the war broke out and when the 18-year-old boys were drafted, the troop train came through and they picked up all the way down the line until they came to Gulgong. My brother was in the draft, and my girlfriend June and I went down to see him off and I was wearing my flag dress—it was miniature flags of red white and blue and I had sent away to Melbourne for it. My parents didn't come down but there were a lot of people there to see the boys off and my future husband, Ossie Wallis, was on the train too although I didn't know him at the time and I can remember one of the women saying, 'Look at that poor Wallis boy, he's far too young to be going off to war'.

It was the mothers who suffered and the women who had husbands at war. The teenagers had a different attitude because it generated a lot of excitement, the men in uniforms.

Roma Wallis, store assistant, Gulgong, New South Wales

When the first contingent of men went from Swan Hill, all the

Roy Hall, barely 20 years old, who went to train in Portsmouth, UK, as a seaman with the Admiralty Yachtsman Scheme.

children from the school were taken down to say goodbye and we were all so upset. I know I was in tears, and they didn't do it again, I think it must have been too harrowing. And those poor lads must have been so embarrassed because they'd have been about eighteen and there were all these silly little kids down there waving them goodbye.
Margaret Maxwell

I wanted to join the Army very badly. I wanted to do something about the war, in fact most of the so-called refugees who came to Australia certainly wanted to join the Army and do something in the war effort. They were put in the employment company and used mainly for things like at Albury, to tranship goods from the Victorian to the New South Wales railway gauge. Then about a year into the war they were allowed to join other units. I ended up in the Army, in the medical corps.
Alfred Ruskin

I recall very clearly my brother coming home on what they called final leave before being transferred and then perhaps shipped overseas and my mother really fell apart and I remember her very clearly saying, 'Look, you can fight for Australia but you can stay in this country and do it here. I've got one son overseas and you are not going overseas, I'll turn every stone that I possibly can to prevent this from happening'.

And my mother went out one day and wherever she went I don't know. The Aboriginal Welfare Board had a lot of say in our lives at that time, and I think that's one of the places she went to, to have my brother stopped from going overseas. She didn't object to him being

in the Army, but she wanted him to remain here. She was successful—he remained in Australia.
Pansy Hickey, textile worker, Sydney

My boyfriend Ted went off and I just felt so proud that he was going. I didn't have any fears. I remember the day—I was a bit sad that he was going away and I wouldn't be seeing him but his mother was heartbroken. I realise now the difference between a young teenager who was only thinking of the glory of a solder going to the war, and a mother who thought, 'He might never come back'.
Nola Bridger, schoolgirl, Sydney

My brother joined up, I think probably because some of his mates were joining up, and he was in the Eighth Division. I didn't join up. I went to Sydney and got a job in a factory that made small tools—drills and milling gear and that sort of thing. No one said to me, 'You ought to be in the Army'. I don't think anyone said that to anyone, it was something that you chose to do or chose not to do and they were very tolerant of them. I don't think there was any unofficial recruiting such as went on in World War I, I believe. Australia had already become a more tolerant society than it had been 25 years earlier.
Bob Bahnsen

I didn't think much of it for a while but then things started to change and we could hear what Hitler was doing to other countries and you started to get that feeling then that you should try and do something. So I left the job I was doing and went and joined the bloody Army!—that's what I did.

Actually when I joined up, I didn't tell anyone. I told the boss where I was working that I was finished, and went down to Merrylands [a Sydney suburb] Drill Hall and joined up. And then I wrote home and told Mum that I'd joined the Army. I didn't do it for patriotism for England at all, but for Australia more or less, and 'cause all me mates was going I suppose. I thought no good me being like the bird on the outside of the tin, I might as well go and be with 'em too—which I did.
Hilary Hughes

I didn't know me husband had joined up and he came home this day and knocked at the door and of course he had all his uniform on. For a minute I didn't recognise him and then I looked at him, I said, 'What are you doing?'.

'Well, he said, 'Couldn't get a job, I got a job now'.

And I said, 'You're not going away are you?'—I thought he was in the home guard.

He said, 'No, no home guard'. 'Cause he went in the First War as well.
Queenie Shepherd, housewife and mother, Adelaide

Four of these little boys grew up to become soldiers in World War II: Auntie Dot Kent, of Millicent, South Australia, with husband Victor and six of their eight children, in a formal studio portrait taken in the 1920s. Reginald and Mick, extreme left, Jack (the toddler on the table) and Leonard, (standing extreme right) all volunteered.

Dad asked me to look after Mum and the boys and the rest of it and I was only ten or eleven years old myself but still, I saw that as just quite natural. I guess being the eldest I was always sort of responsible.
Kevin Shepherd

When the war started up I thought well, that's the worst part of it. Any rate, they enlisted of their own accord, they weren't called up. Leonard joined first, then Reg got itchy feet, then of course when Mick joined up Jack wouldn't give us any peace at all. But he was too young, he should never have gone. You can imagine how terrible it was, first one, then the other going, it was a terrible experience. But I was a mother, I just had to take it.
Auntie Dot Kent, farmer and mother, Millicent, South Australia

When I first applied to join the Army they knocked me back and I applied again, only because my mates had gone, that's the only reason I joined up, it wasn't for love of country or patriotism, nothing like that, and I think most Aborigines did join of their own free will, I never heard of an Aborigine being conscripted. I wanted to be in there not because I was potential hero stuff, but because my mates had gone, my yahoo mates—and that's what we were in civvy street, at seventeen, eighteen.

'I wanted to be in there not because I was potential hero stuff, but because my mates had gone': Harold Stewart, Sydney.

In those days I never heard anything complimentary about Aborigines and they said that all Aborigines were either drunk or leaning up against the pub post. Well I wasn't accepting that as an Aboriginal image and for that reason was embarrassed about being classed as an Aborigine in my own land. In my own mind, I never accepted that but I wasn't vocal enough to speak out in those days.

Before we were in the real thing it was always made clear to me that I was Aborigine, they didn't say that I was inferior but that was what they meant, I was a good mind reader in those days. But I found when we did get into the real thing, they treated me differently. We were real buddies and as close as the skin of one another, it was very noticeable, and they are some of the good memories I have. I found the closer we were to danger, closer we were to one another. The fellows put away all their prejudices and we were one, really one.
Harold Stewart, artilleryman, 2nd AIF

I joined up because these four mates of mine joined up so I thought I might as well be in it too, to defend the country. Major Andrew came up from Brisbane and asked for volunteers, so ten of us joined, four dark and six white. When I got to Redbank army camp and as we were going through, got our numbers, we went up before the recruiting officer and he said, 'What subject are you?'. I said, 'I'm British'—being a Queenslander. So he said, 'All right, you're in'.

When I left Thursday I thought, 'I'll never see Thursday Island again,' and then the same thing happened in Sydney leaving Australia, because you know what you're going to come up against and you said to yourself, 'I wonder if I come back again'—that was my feeling.

My mother was very very upset and while I was in the Middle East,

she passed away. She was very very brokenhearted. Well you know, I was the one at school.
Charles Mene, 6th Division

Saying goodbye to one's family wasn't easy because we were so terribly British in those days and Edwardian and no one must cry, so we barely touched and Mum said, 'Take care of yourself'. And when I got to the bottom of the road to catch the tram into town, then I had a blub and I've no doubt she went inside and she had a blub, but at the time nothing at all, and that was how we went to war.

We got onto ships down in Sydney Harbour, deadly secret, no one must know, only one's family even knew that we were leaving but no one else in Australia knew. With the result that Sydney Harbour was packed with vessels of every conceivable kind saying, 'Goodbye 8th Division and Good Luck,' and everybody was waving and as the ship pulled out away from the docks, there were streamers of course and everybody sang 'Now Is The Hour'—the Maoris' farewell, which is a very Australian song. It was sung on the occasion of every ship leaving for Europe for a long long time before we went to war and it was sung to every vessel that left in convoy to fight the war.
Russell Braddon

2

An Unlimited War Effort

It is my purpose to tell you in the plainest and most direct
fashion what is, as I see it, the prospectus of an unlimited war
effort by our country . . . Seven million Australians can do a
mighty and triumphant work in this war. But half a million
Australians in the armed forces and munitions factories cannot do
that mighty work unless the remaining six and a half million
devote themselves body and soul to their support . . . It is clear
that our national organisation must become one primarily for war.

**The Prime Minister, R. G. Menzies, broadcasting on the
radio during the evening of Tuesday, 17 June 1941.**

By contrast with the previous year, 1941 began with Australian forces
involved in combat, and operations continued in various theatres of war
throughout most of the year. Inevitably these operations had an impact on
life in Australia. Operations began on 3 January 1941 when the 6th Australian
Division successfully attacked the fortified town of Bardia in Italian Libya.
On 21 January, the division captured the port of Tobruk, and after a daring
advance seized Benghazi on 7 February. Some 10 000 Italian soldiers were
taken prisoner, and the Australian government agreed to accept custody of
many of them.

By the beginning of April, the 6th Division was arriving in Greece to
support that country against an expected German attack. But the Empire
forces were no match for the German blitzkrieg and by the end of the month
they were being evacuated. Meanwhile the German Afrika Korps, under
General Rommel, had attacked the 9th Division in Libya, driving it back into
the fortress of Tobruk. There the Australians under General Morshead
mounted an aggressive defence which became a thorn in the side of the
German advance across northern Africa, and put the siege of Tobruk into
Australian history. The Australians held on until relieved later in the year.

Some of the Australian troops evacuated from Greece helped defend Crete
against a German airborne invasion in May; most were evacuated but large
numbers were captured. Meanwhile, the British high command had become
concerned at German interest in French-ruled Syria. Since the armistice in
June 1940, France had been ruled by a neutral government that was sympa-
thetic to Germany. On 8 January 1941, the 7th Australian Division took the
major role in an invasion of Syria. After a hard-fought but successful
campaign an armistice was signed on 12 July.

After the successes in Libya in January and February, the defeats in Greece
and Crete came as a shock to the Australian public. Not only did the

campaigns reveal a lack of strategic wisdom, but, for the first time, Australian casualties brought the full effect of war to Australian homes. During 1941, the Australian divisions in the Middle East suffered over 13 300 casualties— 2098 killed, 5175 wounded and 6094 captured. The vast majority of the casualties took place in the first half of the year. At one stage during June the casualty lists totalled up to 700 names a day. In addition, Australian ships were under air attack in the Mediterranean, and German surface raiders continued to operate in Australian waters. Australian aircrews were flying over Britain and Europe, and during the year they suffered about 400 casualties, 349 of whom were killed in action.

In May 1941, Menzies returned to Australia after a lengthy overseas visit to Britain where he had unsuccessfully sought reinforcements for Malaya. He had visited Australian troops in North Africa, had experienced the London Blitz, and had sat in the British War Cabinet during the fighting in Greece and the siege of Tobruk. Bolstered by this experience and his understanding of how Britain was organising its economy, he was determined to step up the Australian war effort. His government decided to send another brigade to Malaya, home defences were to be reorganised, new departments of Aircraft Production, Transport, War Organisation of Industry, Home Security and External Territories were created, and he called for 'an unlimited war effort' throughout the country. The list of reserved occupations would be overhauled and the government would direct where manpower would be used.

About the same time, the government appointed a Director of Manpower Priorities to make use of all available manpower. In September, the War Cabinet received a report claiming that the three services plus Munitions and Aircraft Production would require a total of 794 000 men and 52 400 women up to 30 June 1943. This assumed that the armed forces would not expand further, but even to maintain the AIF overseas would require 280 000 men to volunteer during the next twelve months. Yet it was estimated that the total manpower available between eighteen and sixty years of age was only about 1 140 000.

One answer to this problem was to make further use of women—both in the services and in industry. In all areas there was an initial reluctance to use women, and it was the women themselves who often formed voluntary quasi-military organisations. In due course women were admitted into the three services. For example, the first service to admit women, the RAAF, was authorised by the War Cabinet on 5 February 1941 to form the Women's Auxiliary Australian Air Force (WAAAF) with an establishment of only 308. By war's end 27 000 women had served in it. On 30 June 1941, there were only 1400 women in the three services and 11 500 in civilian employment for the services or in munitions factories. It was planned to increase the numbers of women in the services and munitions factories to 52 000 in two years.

Manpower was also a problem for those planning the defence of Australia against a possible Japanese attack. By August 1941, almost 190 000 men had volunteered for the AIF but most were overseas; only 36 000 were training in Australia. At the same time, the remaining Army which had to defend Australia, comprised 173 000 members of the militia, but only 45 000 of these were full-time. In addition, the Permanent Army numbered 5000, while there were a further 13 000 in garrison battalions, which were filled with old soldiers from the First World War and manned the coastal defences. There were almost 44 000 in the Volunteer Defence Corps (VDC), which had been formed by the Returned Servicemen's League in mid-1940 and was taken over by the Military Board in May 1941. It was a voluntary, part-time unpaid organisation composed mainly of mere boys, old diggers or men rejected by the Army.

The German attack on the Soviet Union on 22 June 1941 affected Australia in a number of ways. Domestically, the Australian Communist Party no longer opposed the war and generally supported the Australian war effort, even if it continued to disagree with the government on many issues. But it remained banned until December 1942. There was widespread sympathy for the Soviet Union even among some conservative Australians.

The invasion of the Soviet Union altered the strategic situation not only in Europe but also in the Far East. Britain sent munitions to the Soviet Union which it might otherwise have sent to Malaya, and Japan now felt free to advance into South-East Asia. When Japanese forces moved into southern Indochina, the US froze Japanese assets and imposed an oil embargo. War with Japan seemed likely. The only encouraging sign was that the US might also be involved, but this was not certain.

Faced with this increasingly dangerous situation, Menzies wished to return to Britain to put an Australian point of view to their War Cabinet. He lost the confidence of his party, and on 28 August he resigned in favour of the Leader of the Country Party, Arthur Fadden. During the Budget debate two Independent Members of Parliament sided with the Opposition, and on 3 October 1941 the Leader of the Labor Party, John Curtin, became Prime Minister.

For the next two months the new government maintained the policies of the previous government; for example supporting General Sir Thomas Blamey, commanding the AIF in the Middle East, in his determination to relieve the remaining Australian battalion in Tobruk. But the new Prime Minister was soon faced with the responsibilities of his position when on 19 November the German raider, *Kormoran*, fought a battle with HMAS *Sydney* 150 miles south-west off Carnarvon, Western Australia. Both ships were sunk, *Sydney* losing its entire crew of 644 virtually without trace. *Sydney's* fate was not known until survivors from the *Kormoran* were picked up on 24 November and the Prime Minister announced its loss on 30 November. This shock, however, was to be outweighed by the Japanese attack on Pearl Harbor a week later.

Australia was vastly better prepared for this new challenge than it had been a year earlier. Its armed forces had gained valuable operational experience, even if they were still largely deployed in the Middle East. At home the economy was switching effectively to munitions production, more women were employed, and home defences were being strengthened. Under the threat of invasion the new Labor Government was to build on these considerable achievements.

Left *Italian POW Pasquale Matera, captured in Libya.* Right *Gunther Bahnemann, Deutsches Afrika Korps, Panzer Unit, captured in North Africa.*

1 POWs

I was taken prison of war in Benghazi and from there I was sent to Egypt. One day they marched us to the wharf and there was the great *Queen Mary*, 2000 of us they put on the *Queen Mary* bound for Australia.

We got to Australia, we didn't know what to expect of course and I never forget the first few days they sent us a lot of mutton. In Italy we didn't eat mutton and we didn't like mutton, so we said to the Captain, 'Never mind about mutton, macaroni OK, take the mutton back', and we got all the macaroni we wanted.

When we arrived in Australia they sent us to a camp in Hay [NSW]. What we used to do in the camp really, was play cards all day long and go round the camp about ten or fifteen or twenty times a day which was one kilometre in circumference just to keep fit, and play soccer. That was our life, we had it very easy.

Ric Pisaturo, Italian POW

We'd been captured in Libya and sent to Alexandria and then they start to send POWs away from Egypt—some went to England, some to India, some they come to Australia and I was in the third expedition 'cause we was 25 000 when they captured me. So we finished up in Australia.

The British soldiers said, 'No go to Australia, no go to Australia,

Italian POW Ric Pisaturo aged ten. 'We were very much indoctrinated from the Fascists as children and that's all you knew'.

Australia no good, they cut your head off, they eat you', and we didn't know what to do—we have to go where they send us. And we come here under the Australian guard and they were very very good people. We used to sit all in the same dining room, have the same food and the same service, everything.

We finish up in Cowra [NSW] POW camp. It was a new camp, there was nothing, we sleep in a tent. But after nearly a year we saw grass three feet high, which in Libya you don't see—all dry, all sand. We duck down like sheep and start to nibble the grass, we were so pleased to see the green.

Pasquale Matera, Italian POW

I came here, I was a prison of war. We were about 53 German prisoners and there was over 15 000 Italian prisoners, we all went on the *Queen Mary*. I remember when I got into Sydney there was a sergeant standing at Circular Quay. And I said to that sergeant, 'How many people in this country?'.

Now this was on 14 December 1941—I remember that date—and he said, 'We are 8 million in this country'.

'Oh yes' I said, 'How many in Sydney?'.

And nearly the button busted on his shirt, he said, 'One million.' He said, 'Where did you come from?'.

I said, 'Hamburg'. I said, 'three million'. But then he told me how many sheep they had in this country and that left me speechless.

I ended up in Murchison East [Victoria] but I was not put in the prisoner of war camp. I could speak Italian reasonably fluent, I could speak German and English, and they had a lot of civilians there, they came over from Palestine, they came from Malaya, from Persia, and they were all shipped to Australia—Germans, Italians and God knows what, they were all put in camps here as internees. And I was asked would I operate as interpreter for them. They had a lot of Germans there from Palestine, Jaffa and Haifa, and they couldn't speak English.

So I did all the paperwork for them as well as for the Australian government.
Gunther Bahnemann, German POW

2 A Knock at the Door

In those days one of the most frightening things to see come to your door used to be a telegram.
Brian Loughry, schoolboy, Sydney

I came home this day and my father-in-law was there and he had the telegram from the Air Ministry to tell me my husband had lost his life. My husband's choice was the telegram to go to his father—to save the shock. Two weeks later he was buried in Devon. And our local minister, knowing the Air Ministry told me he was being buried at ten o'clock, our minister held a service in our church at midnight so that the two burial services were conducted at the one time.
Lillian Malcolm, airman's widow, Sydney

The minister arrived first so I knew then. By the time the boy came with the telegram I was so upset, I just wouldn't accept it. I was home with my parents at the time, so my poor old Dad went out and I think he tipped the chap and signed and that's how the telegram was accepted.

They were flying this night over France and dropping their last bomb I think. The pilot came to see me after he came back to Australia and he said he made sure Cliff was dead—he said, 'I shook

Left *Lillian Malcolm's husband Pilot Officer Reg White, killed flying Beaufort Bombers for Britain.* Right *French villagers inspect the wrecked plane in which Margaret Hopgood's husband was killed while flying for Britain.*

Bob Taylor (third from right) wearing his telegraph messenger's hat and coat, returning with his mates from a cycling exercise.

him very hard before the plane went down,' he said, 'so reassure yourself that Cliff was dead'; because the news the RAAF tell you is that they don't know whether they're missing or dead.

Our son Robert was only about three-and-a-half. The hardest part was, every night of course you prayed and you taught the child to say, 'God bless my Daddy send him safely home to me'. So when the telegram came, what could you say?—he seemed just too young to tell him. He had a lovely knitted toy called Airforce Bluey and he just took that doll to bed every night, and I tried to be brave.

Margaret Hopgood, airman's widow, Brisbane

My mother and father were married in August 1939 and my father left for overseas in April. I was born the following August and then he was at El Alamein and all the battles over there, and he was killed in the following November when I was fifteen months old—so I never saw my father.

Christina Mowbray, war baby, Millicent, South Australia

We were helping a neighbour one day, Mr Clark, and we were walking back to the house and we looked down the driveway and there was a minister of religion walking up the driveway and the minister paused at a break in the silver-leaf hedge where there was a gate. And Mr Clark saw the minister and he straightaway realised what he had come for. He came to tell him that his only son had been killed at Tobruk. And when Mr Clark saw him he said, 'Come on, I can take it'. He knew what the minister had come for.

Charles Janeway, schoolboy, Mt Gambier, South Australia

Christina Mowbray and her mother Molly Hemmings. Christina was born after her father's departure for the Middle East; he was killed at El Alamein when she was 15 months old so she never met her father.

When someone was lost or wounded in action the relatives got a telegram and it was delivered by a telegram boy on his little red bicycle. And one day the knock came to our door. We had several relatives and friends in the forces and Mum opened the door and here's the telegram boy with the telegram. And she blanched white and she put her hand out to take the telegram and she dropped it and she said, 'Ken, you pick that up and read that'. And I can remember her leaning back on the door wondering what the heck it is and I picked the telegram up—I was just as white as Mum and just as trembling—and opened the telegram and there was a birthday greeting from my uncle who happened to be in camp in Greta [NSW].
Ken Haylings, schoolboy, Sydney

I was a 14-year-old lad walking the whole square of Adelaide delivering telegrams, up until eleven o'clock at night. And I remember the first death telegram I ever delivered. I remember being instructed, 'Whatever you do, make sure the woman signs the bit of paper first, to show she's received it'. The first one was in Athelton. And I went in, knocked on the door, handed the slip of paper, would you sign this please, she signed this slip of paper. I handed the telegram and by the time I'd turned around to go out of the gate, which was three or four feet away—bang! she'd fainted. And I turned around and she'd hit her head on the rung of a chair. And I sang out, 'Is anybody there?'. And there was a neighbour having a cup of tea with her. So the two of us lifted her up and put her on the sofa. And I remember her coming to, crying.
Bob Taylor, Post Office worker, Adelaide

Vi McLauchlan, Melbourne, (second from right) *with some of the many helpers in her scheme to send food parcels to Britain. This photo appeared in the Melbourne* Sun *in December 1945 by which time she had already received more than ten thousand letters from Britain.*

3 The Average Person Couldn't Do Enough

We were well aware of the rationing in England, and we used to send off food parcels and stuff occasionally through the Red Cross to go to England. We didn't know anybody to whom we could send them directly, but the Red Cross would distribute them.
Maurie Jones, schoolboy, Perth

They'd have big dos in the area to raise money and the womenfolk used to send parcels. A lot of the wife's people were English, and they were in a desperate position over there with foodstuffs so we used to make a food parcel and send it away every week to England. They used to write back to us what they really needed and we used to send whatever we had on the farm. We used to send eggs—we put them in dripping and they'd come out over there perfect—it's amazing what you could do.
Harry Seis, farmer, Gulgong, New South Wales

My husband was in Britain, he was sent over to England to get the gen for the aircraft which was all hush hush at the time, and he wrote home to me and said, 'Can't you do something about rustling up some food parcels? Because these people are starving but they don't know it'.

As I didn't have many names and addresses, I wrote to *Good Housekeeping* magazine [in Britain] and they put my letter into their magazine and before I knew where I was I had all these letters

'You just felt you wanted to do the utmost': Joy (Attwater) Boucher, Adelaide, later worked assembling aircraft in Sydney.

coming back to me, just thousands of them. So I called up friends and different people volunteered to come, and the manufacturers were very good, they used to deliver tins of all sorts of food. We had our garage stacked up with cases of stuff to send, fruit and meat in cans, and we'd have packing day two or three times a week and the girls would come. We were only allowed to send I think it was three or four pounds in weight and we'd pack a bit of this and a bit of that and a bit of the other, and honey and fruit, then the tins were sealed and off they went.

In time the letters accumulated and when it reached about eight and a half to ten thousand we stopped counting, but it was quite a massive thing it developed into. It was a terribly busy time, the phone rang constantly and it was almost a full-time job really. The postman used to stagger in every day with a great bag of mail and he'd tip them all out on to the floor and we'd have to go through them and put them into their shoe box files and have another broadcast for helpers.

A lot of friendships developed because people here in Australia kept the same families that they originally started with and they got to writing and sending further parcels to them and when the war was over, there was a lot of visiting and real friendships made. I heard of a lot of people that travelled after the war and made contact with those who were in England and received the parcels.

Vi McLauchlan, housewife and mother, Melbourne

There was always something going on that just kept you busy and
you were saying goodbye to men, they'd say, 'I'll come round, I'm on
my final leave'. And you were busy writing letters or you were
making cakes and sending them over to them, or knitting socks. In
the meantime, we were studying first aid and learning all about
mustard gas and doing anything that we could—we didn't know what
we were to prepare for.
Patricia Penrose, dress designer, Melbourne

Well the average person couldn't do enough, it was a very very strong
feeling especially when things were really going bad there for a long
time, you just felt you wanted to do the utmost.
Joy Boucher, café worker, Adelaide

My mother and sisters were perpetually knitting and crocheting scarves
and so on, to send off to the Red Cross. You were urged all the time
to give to the war effort in one form or another, and there were lots
of avenues that you could contribute to, the Red Cross being a
particularly strong one of course, being an international organisation.
Maurie Jones

I was working as a secretary then and I used to go up to Central
Railway after work and serve the troops that were coming down and
wanted refreshments and I'd do that until nearly midnight and then go
home.
Joy Boehm, Sydney

The home front was most supportive and I had a girlfriend at the time
and she kept writing to me of course, plenty of letters, and I had her
photograph stuck up on the wall of the bunk. We were always talking
about our girlfriends, and there was always somebody knitting socks
and balaclavas and scarves and sending you over little things, so we
were constantly in touch.
Sandy Rayward, 6th Division

When you got to places like the Middle East and so forth there was
no one that you could talk to really apart from your mates and you
relied on a letter from home and it was great and I suppose you
would read them half a dozen times when you received them.
Alan Low, 6th Division

We had one old dear who made pyjamas, she cut out hundreds of
pairs of pyjamas and sewed them up, and people helped her. And
one lady had a very large kitchen and about six of us used to go
every week and make these fruit cakes, beautiful mixtures, and they
were put into special tins which had lids. My mother and I used to
take them down to the baker's wife, he was away at the war and she
baked all these cakes after the bread came out. And then the next day
we'd go and pick them all up again, and take them down to the

Alan Low, 6th Division: 'When you got to the Middle East you relied on a letter from home.'

plumber and he would put the lids on and solder the tins. Then we'd take them into the CWA [Country Women's Association] and cut out calico and cover the tins and then sew it all up and put on the names and addresses of all the local boys.
Betty Cox, Gulgong, New South Wales

Some of the young girls used to write notes, and especially if they knew them they'd send a tender loving message. And of course the boys'd love that, and they'd mention that when they were writing back to thank us, they'd mention that they appreciated the loving message.
Kathleen Loneregan, store proprietor, Gulgong, New South Wales

My youngest brother was away and we would put a bottle of wine inside two loaves of bread so it wouldn't break, send it away, and send him cakes. Half the time he didn't get them but the wharfies were playing football with them down on the wharves—it was as rough as bags as far as I was concerned.
Ray Blissett, policeman, Sydney

I had a thing about asparagus and I used to ask people to get it and they'd tell me, 'It's like trying to get gold over here in Australia'. So people hunted everywhere and they used to send me tins of asparagus—it was marvellous!
Alan Low

There were all sorts of Comforts Funds and I used to knit socks for them on a knitting machine. Miles of these wretched khaki socks.

Then we did spinning for seaboot stockings for the soldiers. We'd spin the stuff and then knit it up. And we used to do apples. People would give us great boxes of apples and we'd make four gallon drums of apple pulp, cook it and send it down to Sydney—to make into pies for the soldiers on leave.

Then there was the Voluntary Aid Detachment, we used to all march around in blue uniforms and do voluntary work at the hospital and first aid and home nursing courses. I hated nursing, I loathed it. But I went every week to that hospital, and it wasn't my favourite time.
Betty Cox

My mother used to billet out the Air Force. They'd come down at weekends and my father would pick them up from the bus and bring them home and we'd have a dance in the hall for them and they'd play billiards and we weren't the only ones that had these boys—there was a lot of them and they were very homesick. Mum would always cook them a country dinner and then on the Sunday night we had to put them in the car again and take them back.
Melba Janeway, schoolgirl, Tantanoola, South Australia

Dad knew a lot of the young lads very well and they would come home on long service leave before going overseas and they would be invited to our place for lunch and they would come and spend some time. And three or four got killed that had been home for lunch and I remember Mum saying, 'Oh, I hope that I haven't put a jinx on those fellows!'. It worried her that it seemed like if they came to lunch with us—that was the end of the story.
Charles Janeway

4 Dad's Army

The Volunteer Defence Corps, or VDC, was started here as a civilian defence corps by the old diggers of the First World War. Each town had their own branch. They all had a commissioned officer from the First World War as the head—their OC. We trained every Friday, Saturday and Sunday all through the war, and we had mostly farmers and graziers and people that were exempt from going to the war. Also some young ones that were seventeen and put in a year with us before they were old enough to be called up. And we trained all the time. Some of the old fellas, I don't know how they kept up, but they did. The Army equipped us, a lot of the stuff was the old stuff from the First World War, but they made a special uniform for us—dark green, and they issued us with the uniform—shirts, military boots and socks, braces, and odds and ends.

I joined the VDC because I was turned down for the Army; and I enjoyed it—it was certainly better than sitting doing nothing and thinking about the war.
Ray Adams, farmer, Gulgong, New South Wales

I can remember the Sunday parades were something to behold. All
these chaps would come into town and form a parade, and then
they'd go up on the Common and shoot rabbits or whatever. They
were getting ready for the invasion. Most of them were well beyond
it—they were probably ex-'14–'18 blokes, so they're getting on. Or
very young, too young for the Army. And the parade was always
worth looking at. There were no two guns alike. They had shotguns
and .22 rifles and no two had the same uniform. And they always
seemed to come into town just that little bit early so they could have
a pre-parade over at Matt Crow's Hotel, and by the time the CO
turned up they were ready for anything.
**Brian Loughry, speaking of wartime holidays in Gundaroo, New
South Wales**

My father was very much involved in the local VDC. He was 38 when
war broke out and he enlisted but he had a steel fabrication business,
he had five children, he had a small dairy farm and so I guess it was
probably thought he was more important at home. So he put his
whole effort into the Defence Corps.

There was a call nationally for people to invent things—for
weaponry or anything at all, it could have been clothing—anything to
help aid this great war effort, and he developed a machine gun, and
he made grenades and he invented a grenade-thrower so you didn't
have to throw it by hand. In the VDC they used to have lots of
bivouacs and practise with all these weapons, and on occasion they
would do themselves an injury. They used to camp in the old
racecourse buildings and have their meetings under the rooms at the
Grandstand and apparently they nearly blew themselves up there one
night—the whole thing nearly came down around them.
Rosemary McCourt, schoolgirl, Millicent, South Australia

The local VDC was mainly run by my father but he had two offsiders
both of whom were mad keen dynamite people. And in their
manoeuvres they'd have homemade land mines right across where
they had to go and it was lucky they didn't have people with their
legs blown off.

One particular group who came back said that they had done a bit
of work in the VDC in Millicent and then had gone overseas and had
gone to Tobruk, and they felt the VDC was far more dangerous than
the whole of that period in Tobruk and the Middle East.
Ren deGaris, schoolboy, Millicent, South Australia

5 Bring the Women In

In the same month I joined up, three of my cousins did, of the same
age, born within a few months of one another and eventually there
were eighteen people from our family, young people—they just
rushed. And I would think each one of us rushed for the same thing.

The Depression had been repressive for us, and here was excitement. It's not only men that get that excitement—it's something foreign to you, and that's where it's at. Women were no different from men, we were ready for anyone who'd let us get in the services.
Patsy Adam-Smith, VAD nurse

I was only seventeen-and-a-half then but I felt I had to be part of it. My father was Army, my brother was in the Middle East and I felt that there had to be something I could do other than just be at home.

I worked at Peak Freans which made biscuits and of course there was a great change, they went from all these fancy biscuits to army biscuits which were very hard, solid biscuits to be sent to the troops. I still didn't feel that that was enough so I joined a voluntary service called the WANS, which was the Women's Australian National Service and two or three times a week we went to town, we wore a uniform that we bought, and we learnt blackout duties and air-raid duties, first aid, all these things that could be handy. We had to know all the points of Sydney—like where you would get an ambulance, where you would get a fire brigade, where you would usher people to. We were taught all this sort of thing and you felt you were doing something.
Peggy Williams, Sydney

The WANS held a meeting I recall in 1940 where ten thousand women turned up at the Town Hall to join—ten thousand women trying to get into Sydney Town Hall, this is how keen and how adamant women were that they could help in the war effort. Of course they were helping already in all the other voluntary organisations as well, but there was a constant enthusiasm with them to get in and help the men, to join the forces. But prior to this time, women who'd served in the defence forces of Australia were mainly in the medical services, so the government itself was not very keen to use women in defence. But eventually they did decide to have a women's army, and AWAS—Australian Women's Army Service—was formed on 13 August 1941.

I had joined the Red Cross as a transport driver but when my husband went into the forces, I was free to do something which totally took my time, so I joined the AWAS. We were replacing the fit males, of course, freeing them to go ahead and volunteer for service in the fighting units, and the three women's services—the WRANS, the AWAS and the WAAAF—were all formed along those lines, to replace men where possible and allow them to go and fight.

The rate of pay was two-thirds of the equivalent male rate. But the women who were going into the services were mainly doing it because they wanted to do a job, they wanted to help the war effort, they wanted to help their country. I don't think many of them would have ever thought about the pay, they wanted to go and help. Many

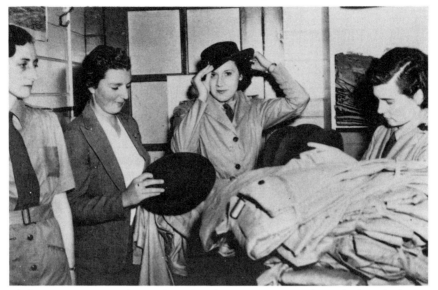

Thelma Long, second from left and still in 'civvies', wonders whether the hat will fit. She is with other AWAS recruits in Melbourne in early 1942 being fitted out for their new life in the Army. (Photo courtesy AWM, P 784/214/088)

of them were very young—two-thirds of them when they enlisted were under the age of 21.

Thelma Long, AWAS

I went into the WAAAF and I joined it simply because it was the first of the women's services and there was nowhere else to go, so it was the WAAAF. I was nineteen. It was for the same reason the boys wanted to join up: you felt that you had to do something for your country. It was something entirely different and I was young. Women were stepping into these roles simply because we were a small country, they needed so many, they were committed to send so many of the young men away and the only way to handle everything was to bring the women in.

When we first joined up, uniforms didn't exist as such because they hadn't been able to plan everything, and it was a bit makeshift at times. We were given jeans—and they were men's jeans. The crutch was between our knees, we had to roll up the bottoms, roll up the sleeves, and we were dreadful. But we were part of the service and that was the main thing. By the time we wore those and we had our berets on—and some of us looked dreadful in berets—I'm sure our mothers must have wondered why we'd ever left our nice homes to go and do that kind of thing.

I came from a home where my mother did practically everything for me. I went into Bankstown camp and we were the first of the WAAAF in New South Wales. Now just imagine coming from a home where

Left *'You felt that you had to do something for your country': June (Garside) Stone in January 1942.* Right *'When we first joined up uniforms didn't exist as such . . .': June with fellow WAAAFs in October 1941. She is second from right in second row.*

you never cleaned anything, your main job was to mend your stockings, and to find out that you had to clean everything you used, including the toilets and the showers, the duckboards—everything. Believe me, that was a culture shock! And to think you had to share a bedroom—it was only a hut—with all those women and you'd never even undressed in front of others before. It was so entirely different. It didn't take us long, though—it was a case of survival of the fittest and you had to be fit so we survived.

Very early in the piece there were some servicemen who rather resented us being there but I think in the main most of the men accepted us, they couldn't have handled it without us or a lot of the men wouldn't have been sent overseas. So we were very necessary.
June Stone, WAAAF

When war was declared I'd just finished my training so I immediately put my name down to join the services. I thought it would be just a wonderful adventure, to go with the troops wherever they went. I found out that the Army was staffing the hospital ships, so I put my name down for the Army, and had to wait until 1941, when I was called up and sent to Bathurst, working with the 2/10th Field Ambulance looking after the 8th Division who had already started moving to Singapore. But to our horror, four of us were sent to Darwin, which we weren't very happy about because we wanted to go where there was some action and we didn't think we'd ever have action there.
Meg Ewart, Army nurse

Of course the women had to go into industry, it happened in the First World War too, because the men were going overseas or were in the armed forces. The problem arose then of conditions—say in the textile industry—which were terrible, they were real sweated workshops. So to attract women and to keep women in such industries, it was necessary to fight the employers for higher wages and better conditions for them. But it was also necessary to fight attitudes among many men workers. For example, there was a lot of opposition from men who worked in the tramway industry and on the buses, to women coming on even as conductors. There were often quite intense arguments and conflicts in the union movement about it. And above all, the employers were dead hostile to paying equal pay.

Laurie Aarons, factory worker and Communist Party member, Sydney

I got a job at De Havilland Aircraft working in the office. When I went into the Inspection Department, to interview for the job, there weren't any women there at all, it was all men. So they hired me and there was some silly stuff about it because the guy whose job I took over didn't want to teach me too much about it because they had never had women working there before and whether they thought it was threatening to their jobs or what, because later on the place was full of women, even women working out in the factory part.

Margaret Blair, office worker, Sydney

The men started to disappear and by necessity—and it was very successful—women were put into men's departments. So you saw women selling in the men's shoe department which was most unusual. They were on men's wages—the store protected the job of the man who'd enlisted, so that their job wasn't downgraded in any way as far as salaries were concerned.

Florence Paterson, department store clerk, Sydney

I worked for G. J. Coles Ltd and about July 1941 I was made manager of a small store in Middle Brighton. There was another girl and myself and this was a first, but naturally it was because of the war that women were put into these jobs, and because Coles had a very big percentage of men who joined the services and they were getting

Beattie Crawford in her office in the Coles store, Brighton, Melbourne, where she was promoted from clerk to manageress during the war years.

short of trained personnel and people with the knowledge to manage the stores. And so this was a test to see if the girls could do the job. Though even before then, there were girls doing lots of heavy work that previously had been done by men; they didn't object, they were pleased to do it, and felt they were contributing their effort.
Beattie Crawford, Melbourne

6 About Face

One of the leading members of the Communist Party, Dick Dixon, had been at a secret conference of the party in I think Adelaide and he said, 'There are reports that Hitler is going to invade the Soviet Union and they're absolutely wrong'. And of course it was a surprise to most of us, I can still remember the night that the news came across. It was I think a Saturday night, the 22nd June, in 1941.
Laurie Aarons

And I can remember that overnight these Commo friends of mine, they changed—from saying that it was a phoney war and we shouldn't take part in it, to saying oh no, it's really workers and all unite. And of course from then on they were pro the war.
Margaret Holmes, pacifist, Sydney

There was a remarkable sea change took place in Australian politics. For example Frank Packer's *Sunday Telegraph*, one of the most violent, anti-Communist, anti-Labor newspapers in Australia at that time, shortly afterwards came out and called the Russians 'our gallant allies' and how great they were, and how they were tearing the guts out of the German army and so on and so forth.
Laurie Aarons

Immediately after Hitler invaded the Soviet Union, the Communist Party threw its full weight into the war and organised huge rallies in town halls throughout Australia. I can remember having been at such rallies in the Sydney Town Hall, and the hall holds 3000 and there were overflow audiences outside.

There was definitely a strong about-face. It was most amusing—I mean the *Sydney Morning Herald* was carrying huge articles about how good things were in the Soviet Union, all the progress that had been made in health, education and what a wonderful life it was for the people. It was really most surprising. And of course all sorts of people who had never been involved in any Left movement became great supporters of the 'sheepskins for Russia' appeal and various things like that.

I remember at one stage we had the hammer and sickle flying on the Sydney Town Hall which of course was the official flag of the Soviet Union, which was rather surprising and brought great joy to people in the Left who thought it was wonderful and thought, 'Oh one day we'll have it flying there all the time!'.

Quite a number of Communists joined the forces after the Soviet Union came into the war and I can remember one friend who was stationed in Darwin and he told me that when they had the open air films in the theatre there, they played 'God Save the King', as was usual in Australia then before the programme, and the troops used to call out, 'We want Uncle Joe, we want Uncle Joe' . . .
Joyce Batterham, Communist Party worker, Newcastle, New South Wales

'Joe for King', 'Joe for Pope' even—a rather unusual sort of demand I guess. But this was an illustration of how people thought about it. Of course not everyone in Australia thought that way. Menzies of course never changed his attitude. And even those who gave lip service to support our glorious Soviet allies, often did it through clenched teeth as one might say.
Laurie Aarons

7 A Change of Direction

I think the feeling amongst people was that it would be impossible for Menzies to remain as Prime Minister because he would never get the co-operation from the working people and the trade unions that was needed to help Australia win the war, that he just would not be able to—he was no Churchill.
Joyce Batterham

Menzies was a most ineffective prime minister in his first period. He was not seen as an effective leader, he could easily make a lot of enemies, he had a very sharp tongue and he antagonised a lot of people, possibly without meaning to do so.
Ralph Doig, Premier's Department, Perth

Menzies was so utterly British, bowing the knee and touching the forelock and all that stuff. We were already a nation but Menzies didn't want us to be a nation, he wanted us to be an appendix of the British, which was all wrong for policy. Menzies was ousted because people recognised he could never win a war, they threw him out and he was replaced by a man for whom I have the deepest admiration, that's John Curtin, a quiet man, a silent man, a sincere man.

When I first met Curtin, the Department of Information brought him out to the studio and he wanted to make a national speech. I instinctively took a liking to the man because he was so quiet, he wasn't throwing orders about, he was unostentatious and with a great deal of charm. He was conscious of the fact that his right eye turned out somewhat and he said, 'Could you do something about that?'. And I said, 'Of course sir' and took care of it as anybody could. But he

Matron Connie Fall with Prime Minister Robert Menzies during his stopover in the Middle East in February 1941, en route to England.

came over on camera with a great sincerity that most politicians lack—you know they're phonies all the time. But this man was not a phoney, he was an honest-to-God sincere man and what he said came from his heart. He was pleased with the result that he got and from then on he wouldn't have anybody else to make his statements and he made many to the country, to the public, to lift morale and tell them to do this and do that. And he still remains in my mind as the best character to emerge in Australia out of the war.
Ken G. Hall, managing director, *Cinesound Review*, Sydney

I had a very high opinion of Curtin. He was quite a remarkable man really and he was a delightful companion. I think his outstanding qualities were his honesty, his determination and his sheer capacity to master a situation and to feel what was the right thing to do and stick by it.

He was a man of great strength. It's general knowledge that he earlier had a very serious drinking problem which he mastered completely, and never touched liquor again. And he had a great power to convince people and persuade people, and he had a power of not making people hostile to him.
Ralph Doig

He always seemed to me to be a slightly drab figure, efficient but drab. I don't think Curtin would have lasted long in television days, which is rather sad to think of.
John Hinde, ABC war correspondent, Sydney

In November 1941, not long after he had become Prime Minister, Curtin had the most melancholy duty, which caused everyone of us who heard it pain. He had to announce the loss of *HMAS Sydney*. The *Sydney* had gunned down the German raider *Kormoran* and the German raider had then gunned her down—it was a most remarkable, hideous thing and the awful thing was there was not one of those boys saved. Not one. And all I could remember was having seen them in the streets of Sydney—they'd been given the freedom of the city of Sydney and a great ticker-tape welcome, and marched up to the Town Hall because they had sunk the Italian cruiser *Bartolomeo Colleoni* and they'd come home to Sydney to a heroes' welcome and I'd managed to get up right near the Town Hall and they were all going to be marching in there. There was a boy from our town but I didn't see him; I'd expected to, but there were about a thousand boys and they were all dressed beautifully and the Sydney crowds had turned out and we were yelling out, and I was shouting, and you were so close you were touching them and I was nearly jumping the damn rails. It was so exciting to see these beautiful boys who'd had this great victory. And then you suddenly learnt only a few months later that every one of them was under the water. They were all dead, every one—including the boy from our home town.
Patsy Adam-Smith

One morning we heard that the *Sydney* had been sunk and my sister and I were both devastated because a lot of the boys we knew from Collaroy [a Sydney suburb] were on that boat and especially, the daughter of the very nice grocer we had was engaged to one of the boys and we were really sad about it. And then we heard afterwards that people had said, 'There they were rejoicing in their national costumes'—well, we had these dirndls which we had been wearing quite a bit, so after we found that it was not well looked upon, we wore different things.

I had three children, and my sister helped me with the children. Then she was interned and that was pretty ghastly; and when I wanted to visit my husband, he was at Long Bay [a Sydney gaol]. And the worst was that one didn't know what was happening to the family in Germany. I come from Wuppertal and the city was bombed and I remember the day when I saw the headline—'Totally Destroyed'—and I felt my knees knocking, and there was nothing at all that you could do.

Right in the beginning of the war we had been to a party and somebody I'd never seen before and have never seen since said, 'If ever you want to be interned you can contact me', and gave me his card. I thought what an odd thing to say, who wants to be interned, but then after the war looked as if it would drag on, after I was without my husband, my sister and without all our friends, I thought well, probably better to be interned—which it was. I was much happier there because if the war news was good for Germany one

could talk about it, it was different where you had to be careful what you said to people, so I didn't mind being interned at all.
Irmhild Beinssen, German-born resident

3

The Darkest Hour

This is our darkest hour for the nation itself is imperilled . . . Men and women of Australia, the call is to you for your courage, your physical and mental ability, your inflexible determination that we as a free people shall survive. My appeal to you is in the name of Australia, for Australia is the stake in this contest.

The Prime Minister, John Curtin, broadcasting on the radio on 8 December 1941, after the attack on Pearl Harbor.

The news that Japan had attacked Pearl Harbor and landed at Kota Bharu, Malaya, on 8 December 1941 came to most Australians and their government as a tremendous shock, but initially there was little dismay. Singapore was thought to be impregnable; two large British warships, *Prince of Wales* and *Repulse*, had been sent as reinforcements to the Far East; and the attack on Pearl Harbor assured the USA's entry into the war. The Prime Minister, John Curtin, immediately declared war on Japan, but he realised that Australia would soon be fighting for its life in the 'gravest hour of our history'. He spoke of 'a complete revision of the whole economic, domestic and industrial life' of the country, and declared on 16 December that the government would act ruthlessly.

The public might have been shocked, but the Japanese attack came as no surprise to Australian defence planners. Like their counterparts in Britain and America, they had been well informed of Japanese intentions throughout 1941, and the threat of Japan had formed the focal point of Australian defence planning since federation in 1901. Realising that Australia had neither the population nor industrial strength to defend itself adequately, successive governments had relied on what was called the Singapore strategy. Under this strategy, Singapore was built up as a naval base and fortress to which the main British fleet would be sent in time of war. Australia provided naval forces to operate with the Royal Navy, while preparing to deal with only minor raids against Australian territory.

Critics, including senior army officers, pointed out that Japan would not attack until Britain was occupied in Europe, and that therefore Australia had to build up its army and air force. Short of money, and reliant on British advice, Australian governments in the 1930s continued the policy of imperial defence.

Although the Menzies Government continued this policy after the outbreak of war in Europe, sending forces to the Middle East and Britain, it did not blindly ignore the Japanese threat. The government knew it had to help Britain which could not assist Australia or deter the Japanese if it were defeated by Germany. In turn, the government expected the British to fulfil their obligations in the Far East.

The Australian public was broadly aware of these factors. From the time of the Japanese victory over Russia in 1905, they had seen the expansion of Japan; they had read of Japan's seizure of Manchuria in 1931, and had seen newsreels of the rape of Nanking in 1937. The fears of the 'yellow horde' which had existed in Australia for decades, were quickly brought to the surface by the events of December 1941.

The attack on Pearl Harbor and the landing in Malaya were followed by a series of hammer blows. On 10 December *Prince of Wales* and *Repulse* were sunk by Japanese aircraft. Within a few days Japanese forces had moved into Hong Kong, had landed in north Borneo and had begun an invasion of the Philippines. As early as 4 January 1942, Japanese planes bombed Rabaul in the Australian-mandated territory of New Guinea.

There was little that Australia could do about this relentless advance. The government called up 114 000 men to bring the Home Army to 246 000, but these men had to be trained and equipped. The few remaining AIF battalions in Australia were deployed to Ambon, Timor and Rabaul to secure forward air bases, but the RAAF units lacked modern planes and even their obsolescent planes were few in number. Militia troops were rushed to Darwin and Port Moresby. At home, preparations were made to deal with Japanese air raids. The best hope for the government was to persuade Britain to give higher priority to the defence of Malaya, but it was realised that in the long term Australia would have to rely on the United States.

On 27 December, Curtin wrote in an article in the Melbourne *Herald* that Australia looked to America 'free of any pangs' of kinship with the United Kingdom. The importance of this article has been exaggerated, but it was seized upon by many as signalling a new direction in Australia's foreign relations. Certainly the article annoyed the British Prime Minister, Churchill who, in a bitter cable to Curtin, spoke of Australia's 'mood of panic'.

Australia had not yet reached this stage, but as January unfolded the strategic situation declined rapidly. By mid-January the Australian 8th Division in Malaya was in action against the Japanese, and after initial optimistic reports that they had defeated a Japanese thrust, the Australian commander, General Bennett, reported that the British and Indian troops there had not fought well, thus causing two Australian battalions to be cut off by the advancing Japanese. On 23 January, the Australian representative in Singapore advised the government that the position there was 'desperate and possibly irretrievable', and that same day a powerful Japanese force landed at Rabaul and quickly drove back the Australian defenders. A week later another Japanese force overwhelmed the Australian battalion at Ambon, while in Malaya the Empire forces had been chased down the peninsula and across the causeway into Singapore island.

However desperate the situation might appear, while Singapore held out it seemed that the Japanese would not mount a major attack on Australia. In reality, of course, Singapore had already lost all but psychological importance. The British could not send a fleet to operate from it, any more than the Americans could send naval forces to operate out of the Philippines, where General MacArthur's American–Filipino army was also facing defeat.

Contrary to popular belief that Churchill refused to allow the AIF divisions to leave the Middle East, in January he suggested that the 1st Australian Corps, comprising the 6th and 7th Divisions, be sent to the Far East, and by early February the convoys were setting sail. Their final destination had not yet been decided, but it was possible that they might join the combined ABDA (Australia, British, Dutch, American) command then being set up under General Wavell with its headquarters in Java.

ABDA command was responsible for the defence of all South-east Asia down to and including Darwin, but it was a forlorn hope. On the night of 8 February the Japanese army crossed the Strait of Johore and rapidly pushed into the centre of Singapore island. It was not true, as many supposed, that Singapore's guns could not be turned to face inland, but they did fire armour-piercing rather than high-explosive rounds. On 15 February the British forces there surrendered. It was the most humiliating defeat in British military history and smashed the reputation of British power in Asia.

During the advance down the Malaya Peninsula, a Japanese army of about 35 000 had defeated a force of some 60 000 Indian, Australian and British troops. Over 85 000 Empire troops defended the island, 70 000 being combat troops, while the Japanese attackers were much less in number, and yet the battle for the island lasted only a week. During the whole campaign, the Japanese took about 130 000 prisoners. The Australians lost 1789 killed, 1306 wounded and 15 395 captured. Those captured suffered terribly, with about one third dying in captivity.

With the fall of Singapore, Australia's military leaders faced a situation which they had long predicted—Australia would have to prepare to resist an invasion of its own shores. On 15 February the Chief of the General Staff, General Sturdee, submitted to Curtin a paper in which he argued that Java would also probably be lost and that Australia should be built up as the base for an Allied offensive against Japan. British and US forces should be sent to Australia, and most important, the 1st Australian Corps, then heading towards the Far East should return to Australia. Without consulting the Australian government, Churchill had already directed that the leading convoys carrying the Australians should proceed towards Burma; but steeled by Sturdee, Curtin demanded that they be sent to Australia.

In two bewildering months the Japanese had dealt a heavy blow to the US Pacific Fleet, had smashed British power in the East, and had seized most of South-east Asia. Within days their bombs would be raining on Australian soil. For the first time since white settlement, Australia faced the real prospect of invasion.

1 Pearl Harbor

I remember my father coming home with the *Daily News* with letters the biggest I've ever seen, saying 'Pacific War', and we really got a fright then.
Maurie Jones, schoolboy, Perth

I can remember feeling first of all horror, then a feeling of what does

it mean to us? The Japanese are now on the rampage, the American navy is destroyed. What stands between Japan and Australia? And people were very apprehensive indeed immediately, and there was a feeling of great fear, almost approaching panic.
Ralph Doig, Premier's Department, Perth

I can remember what an outrageous thing we all though it was, Japan attacking a power like America. It wasn't very long before we realised just how well organised they were, and just what damage they *did* cause, at Pearl Harbor. But initially we thought that it was almost a comedy that they'd even attempt such a thing.
Brian Loughry, schoolboy, Sydney

Pearl Harbor was numbing and I'm not sure that we knew how to react to it, because it was a completely new situation. I don't think a lot of us knew how to cope with it, it was just such a shattering new experience.
Niall Brennan, university student, Melbourne

2 Not many facts and a great deal of fiction

The Australian people knew very little about the Japanese culture or anything else. All they knew was the propaganda that was printed in the paper about them being the 'yellow menace' and very derogatory things and there was no attempt to give an understanding of what the Japanese people really were.
Joyce Batterham, Communist Party worker, Sydney

Ignorance of the Japanese was total. But we knew they'd committed unspeakable atrocities in China. We knew that they had conquered Nanking and that they had slaughtered 300 000 civilians and there was newsreel of that and newsreel showing children sitting there in the midst of mountains of bodies, crying. So we knew that much.
Bob Bahnsen, machinist, Sydney

For years and years the Left movement had been saying that Japan was a danger to Australia—we go right back to the wharfies refusing to load pig iron for Japan, because they said we'd be getting it back in bullets and bombs. So that we weren't exactly surprised by the attack on Pearl Harbor but it did make us very very fearful
Joyce Batterham

And apart from that, there were people like Billy Hughes [former Prime Minister], who believed in White Australia, which the Communists didn't, but nevertheless, he also perceived the threat that Japan represented to Australia.
Laurie Aarons, factory worker and Communist Party member, Sydney

We knew practically nothing about the Japanese as people. All our upbringing had been directed to the belief that we were basically a European outpost, we were a European country, we knew nothing about Asia at all. We had no contacts with Asia, we had only the most tenuous contacts with the Dutch East Indies—that became Indonesia—and as for visiting Japan, I don't know that anybody ever gave that a thought.
Niall Brennan

We got not many facts and a great deal of fiction: they were pictured as being small, unable to see very well in the dark, all this sort of thing—undernourished.
Maurie Jones

We hadn't even imagined Japan coming into the war—after all, we'd looked on Japan as a second-rate nation right from the end of the First World War. If something was made in Japan it was inferior—tools, for instance, and any of their mechanical work—it was all second rate. Cutlery and crockery—you turned it upside down, teacups for example, and if they were made in Japan you put them back on the shelf because they had a reputation for the handles falling off them. And so we looked on Japan as an inferior sort of nation.
Bill Graham, wheat farmer, Gulgong, New South Wales

Then we were confronted with the situation where the Japanese have got a fleet, they've got a massive air arm, they've got a huge army, they're capable of making aircraft and guns and motor vehicles and tanks. It just didn't seem possible, it was just unreal.
Robert Squires, schoolboy, Warwick, Queensland

We'd learned a little about Japan at school and none of us paid much attention because we weren't interested. We were all for Britain and the Empire.
Margaret Maxwell, schoolgirl, Swan Hill, Victoria

Of course the 'yellow horde' thing had been so much part of the whole Australian mythology for so long—we were always being told that the yellow hordes would arrive from somewhere and take over the whole of the country. And it looked as if it was on the agenda at last.
Dorothy Hewett, university student, Perth

3 A Bit of a Bash

By the time the Japanese were in the Pacific and they were coming down towards Australia, we had nothing. Anything, all the best of

what we'd had, had gone to Europe—including the best of our
fighting men.
Brian Loughry

So we got up and girded up our loins or whatever it is they do in the
Old Testament, and realised that we had to act for ourselves, no
alternative. So that's what we did. I think that fundamentally we were
united as a nation. We had to be. There's nothing like grim reality to
bring these things back.
Nell Stronach, AWAS welfare worker

On the Sunday I had gone up to my girlfriend's home in the
afternoon and I hadn't been there very long when an army truck
arrived. The chap had come to pick me up, he'd been to my home
and had been told where I was. He'd been sent out to get me and
take me back to camp and I remember I said, 'I'll have to go home
because I'll have to get my pack and bits of gear'. And he said, 'I've
got it'. I went straight back to camp because they were recalling
personnel and they were preparing to move quickly to Darwin to
relieve another battalion, though we didn't know at that point where
we would be going.
   I felt some apprehension then as to what's going to happen—I
realised that I was really going to be off.
George Telfer, infantryman, Adelaide

I thought surely this can't be happening, one hadn't had enough time
to adjust, it was only the night before when the news hit of the
bombing of Pearl Harbor, and we hadn't thought the impact would be
quite as sudden on us personally. I was a bit selfish I think, there
were lots of Australian young men away already by then. But it hit me
with a big shock, I felt devastated.
Betty Telfer, radio station typist and programmer, Adelaide

I went AWL. We were at Wallgrove Camp [in western Sydney] and
they stopped all our weekend leave, gave us no reason whatsoever.
So we went on strike for two days—the only brigade in the whole
Australian Army that went on strike. Officers and all went. We
marched out of Wallgrove, all the way down to Parramatta station, we
commandeered trains from there, just went onto the trains and took
'em over and went wherever they were going to. A Friday afternoon
that happened, Sunday afternoon we all rolled up back in camp again
and they charged us two days AWL.
   Well we found out later the Japs were starting to come into the war,
that was the reason they cancelled our leave. It was just after Pearl
Harbor.
Hilary Hughes, infantryman, Sydney

Those who didn't support the war shut up like mousetraps the day
the Japs bombed Pearl Harbor. From that day on you never heard

'Those who didn't support the war shut up like mousetraps the day the Japs bombed Pearl Harbor': Bob Bahnsen, who was in a reserved occupation in Sydney.

another word about not supporting the war because they understood that this was a matter of survival for Australia.

I tried to join up then. I volunteered for the Air Force and I was rejected on medical grounds. They wouldn't let me go in the Army, they wouldn't let me join the Air Force ground crew, so I was forced to stay where I was. I can't say that I was sorry, but I felt that all my friends had gone and that I really ought to make the effort to go. And that was brought on by the Japs entering the war.
Bob Bahnsen

I decided to join up because the Japanese were coming and it was time for the patriotic war. The defence of Australia for everyone—it was a time when our own country, our own people were involved and we didn't have much in the way of army or strengths or anything else, and required everyone in the field. So there was nothing else for it but to be ready to have a bit of a bash, go out there with bow and arrow–the old service rifle from the First World War, that didn't throw true any longer, that's what we had.
Merv Lilley, rural worker, Queensland

When we heard the news of Pearl Harbor, I was working in a boot factory and a mate of mine, also a left-winger, he and I immediately

said, 'Well, this is it, we'll go down to the recruiting depot in
Woolloomooloo and we'll join the Air Force'.

So we did very exhaustive tests, including general knowledge. I
remember one of the questions that was asked, which I was the only
one to answer correctly, was, 'What is the meaning of the word
"toxophilite"?' [A lover of archery]. This somehow helped me to get
into the Air Crew Reserve. But a few weeks later, I was surprised and
shocked to get a letter from the Air Force to say that it had been
decided that you are not satisfactory, not suitable to become a
member of His Majesty's Royal Australian Air Force. We kicked up a
bit of a stink about that, but quite unsuccessfully, and we knew it was
because I was a member of the Communist Party. And I was probably
saved, since we had very few aircraft and most of them got shot
down in the first period of the war in the Pacific against Japan.
Laurie Aarons

We knew then straight away that Australia would be the target and
everybody realised that we were going to have it on our own shores
if we didn't defend them, and everybody responded to whatever was
asked of them. We didn't want them to be ruling us.

I felt that I had a responsibility to join, but I really had two
responsibilities, I was on the land and they were wanting as much
food as we could possibly do, and to keep food supplies going was
going to be serious. So I thought I was playing my part. Quite a few
went away at that time and we used to look after the women, trying
to run their places, and we used to go and help wherever we possibly
could and do any of the hard work for other people.
Harry Seis, farmer, Gulgong, New South Wales

When Pearl Harbor was bombed, we had the job to round up
Japanese business people, and there were quite a lot of pearling
luggers in the harbour, and these people were taken to Adelaide and
put in a compound.

The only photographer in Darwin was Japanese—Morikami.
Everybody that had a camera, they were taking photos of whatever
was round about, and he developed them—I've got photos taken that
Morikami developed. Anyway, he got rounded up. I don't know
whether he was a spy or what he was, but he was certainly in a good
position to find out a lot of information.
Col Nowlan, infantryman, Darwin

4 Lights Out

That was a really terrifying time because we lived in Mosman and it
was declared to be a target area and that's why we had an air-raid
shelter built in our backyard because my husband thought that he was
going to be called up any time and he was, soon after that, and he

didn't want to leave me and the three kids there unprotected if we were going to be bombed.
Margaret Holmes, pacifist, Sydney

A lot of air-raid shelters were built in Perth because we were expecting to be bombed and machine-gunned. Business premises which had basements fortified those for their employees. Any large parks, such as the one down on the Perth foreshore, which were big enough for, say, glider planes to land foreign troops on, were ploughed up or, more often, had slit trenches put across them where people could shelter as well, at least from machine-gun fire.

A lot of people built their own. My father and my brother Des and I built one, starting immediately after Pearl Harbor on 7th December, and it was ready by Christmas time. It was the best we could do—it was made out of half an old corrugated-iron water tank, cut down the middle and a hole dug in the ground lined with wood. Mum was out in the garden, watering, one day and there were two council workers outside, and they couldn't see Mum behind the hedge, and one of them said, 'Bill, come and have a look at this' he said, 'an air-raid shelter'. 'God,' he said, 'I'd rather get under the bloody gas stove, I'd feel safer there'. That rather dampened Mum's confidence in the defence of *her* realm at any rate.
Maurie Jones

Of course we had tremendous preparations, all the windows had to be shatterproofed, it was called the brown-out, it wasn't a blackout, but you weren't allowed to show any light at night and cars had to have little louvre sort of things over the headlights to stop light showing so that Sydney shouldn't be seen in the sky for Japanese bombers to come and easily target it. And preparations in case your house got bombed—we had buckets of sand around and buckets of water and little pumps and things.
Margaret Holmes

At school, we pasted Xs on the windows to stop the bomb blasts or fragments of glass going in, and we had a call for volunteers and we had to pretend we were bomb victims or wounded in the war. We had a little ticket on us and we lay on the floor of the Town Hall and I was allotted to my mother and she came over with bandages and splints and she read the little notice and it said I had two broken arms and flying glass fragments. And she looked at me and I could see for a moment that she was really disturbed; and then she started to bandage—but she was disturbed, that perhaps this sort of thing might really happen one day.
Ken Muggleston, schoolboy, Katoomba, New South Wales

I went to the council to see if I can do something for the war, and they wanted air-raid wardens. They gave us this enormous book and enormous maps, all the electricity, and all the water and gas, and you

'You felt you had to be brave and you hoped you were going to be': Anne (Duley) Pellew became an air raid warden in Sydney.

had to get screwdrivers and all sorts of things for turning off and fixing up and joining up, and it was an experience for a man I thought, but then I had nothing better to do so I loved it.

They gave you one particular area, maybe two or three streets, and you had to study and study them 'til you knew how everything worked, where everything was, if the water main broke you knew where the next part was that you could turn off temporary and things like that, and where you had to phone to get through to the power station or whatever—depended where the bomb dropped. The ladies worked from daylight 'til dark, and the men from dark 'til daylight. And you felt you had to be brave and you hoped you were going to be.

Anne Pellew, ARP warden, Sydney

I went down to Sydney, to my uncle's place at Annandale, with a whole library of books, and I thought, 'Oh gosh I'll be able to read till midnight'. And I heard stomp stomp stomp up the stairs and Uncle George burst through the door and he said, 'I'm the warden in this street and the only bloody light in the street's in *my* house!'. And boom!—out went the light.

Ken Muggleston

One day there was an old lady standing at the bus stop, and this unidentified vehicle started to approach and she stopped me and said, 'Tell me, is that a bus?'. And I could tell her, yes, it was a bus, but I couldn't tell her where it was going because they blanked out any sort of destination sign in case the enemy knew where they were going. The buses were completely camouflaged. The glass was taken out and

they had metal sliding pieces which were the same colour as the
camouflage. And every street sign was taken down or covered or
painted over, so there was a lot of confusion. If you were a stranger
in town, you'd be just as lost as the enemy who'd just landed.
Brian Loughry

I remember twice in the middle of the night, or the small hours of the
morning, the alarm went and we hopped out and we went into the
air-raid shelter, taking biscuits and cat and dog. Cat escaped
immediately of course. But then after a while the all-clear sounded, so
we went back inside. I don't know, they might have seen a plane, or
there might have been an aircraft carrier sighted somewhere off our
coast.
Maurie Jones

I was working at the AWA [Amalgamated Wireless of Australasia] in the
canteen there and they had enormous air-raid shelters under their
gardens at the front, and they gave us practice perhaps once or twice
a week—it would suddenly go off and we'd all have to rush down to
the air-raid shelter. And there was always one person standing at the
top while everybody shot past—that was me. I couldn't go down in
that air-raid shelter if they'd have come and bombed me to death. I
suffered terribly from claustrophobia. So I couldn't tell you what the
inside of one looked like.
Anne Pellew

We did have a false alarm one day but we really thought it was an air
raid. And we all rushed into the trenches, teachers too. And it'd rained
the night before and so we were all up to our hips in water, and we
sat there in the mud with our air-raid bags.
Helen McAnulty, schoolgirl, Canberra

We were having this practice down in Burwood Park and they said,
'We're going to let off an incendiary bomb.' Anyway, we got down
there and when they get it all ready to let it off, he said, 'We're going
to have a countdown, from ten down, and then it will go off, but
when we get to about three, everybody open their mouths really wide
so the concussion from the ground goes through you and it won't
hurt your jaws'. Well, we all stood there with our mouths open like
billygoats and as soon as it went—bang! out went my bottom plate. In
all the darkness, in all the people, I'm screaming out, 'Don't walk
don't walk'—my bottom plate was floating around in the park.
    We got it.
Anne Pellew

The appearance changed of Australian cities. Window displays
disappeared because of the danger of flying glass and a lot of the
display windows were themselves converted into air-raid shelters, at

street level. So there was a generally drab appearance about everything.
Maurice Jones

People were sending their wives to Katoomba, a number of my friends sent their wives away—mine wouldn't go, she just stopped here. We were only half a mile from Bondi where they were going to land.

I lived in Bellevue Hill and there were a lot of European settlers, they were out with carts and piling their bedding on it. People were rushing to the mountains. The New Australians ran but not many Australians did. I mean the people who had been in Europe who knew what war was—we didn't know anything about war but they did and there were a great many Germans here at that time who'd flown away from Hitler.
Ken G. Hall, managing editor, *Cinesound Review*, Sydney

Our three children went to a nursery school in Mosman and the whole nursery school evacuated; they went to Blackheath [in the Blue Mountains, New South Wales]. We stayed in Mosman. My husband had his practice there and so the people that stayed behind had to be looked after by doctors and you just couldn't help but stay really, but we'd been told though that if the Japs did invade, Mosman would be a compulsorily evacuated area.
Margaret Holmes

5 Free from any pangs . . .

Of course over the next few months we were absolutely astounded at how successful the Japs were, getting closer to Australia all the time.
Brian Loughry

Margaret Holmes' husband, Dr 'Tag' Holmes, with children Eleanor and Bill and nephew Allen outside the concrete air raid shelter in the garden of their home in Mosman, Sydney, considered a target area should the Japanese attack. It was used once, on the night the Japanese submarines entered Sydney Harbour in 1942.

And there was a general feel of real terror because they were just sweeping south so fast. We thought well, we're next. And we were fully expecting Western Australia to be invaded.
Maurie Jones

The press and the newsreels were invited by the government to come to a meeting every Friday where they sent a man from Canberra to give us the real background on the war. This particularly began with the débâcle in Malaya when we were really going down the drain, and they told us things that scared the daylights out of us all because top editors were there, but we were sworn to secrecy of course, and nobody blew the gaff.

It was a disaster, complete and utter, and by this time the government here was getting terrified and they wanted to keep us all informed, so this guy from Canberra made it look bloody bad, he didn't pull any punches. And at this period, when everything looked damned dangerous, Curtin made an appeal and said Australia looks to America, he had no option but to say that because where else could they look? We were scared, scared for our country and for our women and for all the dreadful things the Japanese had done already. We had every reason to be scared, and we had no troops here.
Ken G. Hall

'. . . free from any pangs of loyalty to the old mother country, we look to America'—that made an impact. I think it was seen as a fairly obvious thing in the circumstances, that we were on the same side as the Americans. Britain didn't have much part in it. A lot of us had felt for a long time that we had been misled, that the whole idea of supporting the Empire during the war, any war, because Britain would come to help us if we needed it, that that was hogwash. We knew that Britain would not come to help us and in fact that was demonstrated—she was too busy looking after herself, so this angled us towards the Americans.
Niall Brennan

I remember Curtin's speech about this for a rather special reason. I was on the early morning shift on the ABC news, and alone in the office, and we were at that time getting all our news from the paper. And it was a weekend, a Sunday, and I went through the *Telegraph* and well into the paper there was a single column, possibly on the leader page, and it wasn't a place where I normally looked for news, and I looked at it and I looked back and I thought, 'Good God, this is news'. And so we led the bulletin with it, but it could easily have got lost. It's very strange to think that now: this sudden shift in policy, practically lost in the papers. And certainly not a page-one read.
John Hinde, ABC war correspondent, Sydney

In some quarters there would appear to have been considerable concern when Curtin said, 'We look to America'. They're always

there—the old diehards, 'Well, I'm British, thank God, I'm British'—that's been going on for two hundred years, but we all must take into fact the circumstances of the time. What good of appealing to Britain—they couldn't do another thing, they were at their wits' end to save themselves. Hitler was just across the road with a vast army and a vast air force and all the things that they had to withstand.
Ken G. Hall

6 Facing the Music: the Fall of Singapore

We always thought that nobody would take Singapore. It was a bastion in the Pacific, it had been written up as this and pictured as this for many many years. And we were confident that Britain would defend Australia.
Bill Graham

The entire defence of Australia and New Zealand was predicated on a British battle fleet being based in Singapore in the event of war with the Japanese. And it was to protect the Western Pacific, the northern approaches to Australia. The Australian, British and New Zealand governments had paid for the construction of this huge naval base, and in the event of hostilities the big battle fleet was to be there. It never appeared. The Brits said they couldn't spare it when the time came, so they sent the *Prince of Wales* and the *Repulse* out and of course they were sunk immediately at the outbreak of the Japanese war.
Ken Cunningham, seaman, RAN

There was very little understanding at that time of the necessity for air cover. When the *Prince of Wales* and the *Repulse* were sunk off Malaya by a few Japanese planes, this was really our first confirmation that a fleet was dead unless it had air cover, and of course the British fleet had practically none.
    And it took a few days, but the Japanese swept down and we had these mad stories about these bicycle platoons covering a hundred miles a day down the peninsula towards Singapore. But then of course Singapore was impregnable, we knew that.
John Hinde

You've got to get back to the basic fact that in the 1930s the community was anti-war, so they were eager to swallow the story that Singapore was impregnable, that no one could capture Singapore. This is what we all wanted to hear. The last thing we wanted to hear was that Singapore wasn't really impregnable at all, that Singapore couldn't be relied upon, and when Singapore fell—we were devastated.
Bob Bahnsen

The dear old British always thought, 'Oh well, they'll come from the

sea, old boy'. All the guns were pointing out to sea, but these nasty Japanese decided to come down through the jungle where everybody said it's impenetrable, you can't pass it. Well, the Japs could pass it and we lost a division, they were butchered and taken prisoners.
Ken G. Hall

My mother was notified that I was missing, believed killed, and then was informed that I was dead, and with typical feminine perversity decided that I wasn't and she continued to send letters which the Japanese continued not to deliver. She received nothing from me, like the parents of many men who were in the 8th Division, no word at all, and had to await our return with faith, no more than maternal faith. Funny people, mums, they really are.
Russell Braddon, POW Changi and Burma Railway

The fact is that when Australia was threatened, myself and hundreds of others were overseas in the United Kingdom and various other places in Europe fighting the Germans when we should've been back here combatting the Japs.

And I also knew my father was over there in Singapore, he had joined up and was in the 8th Division, so naturally I became extremely concerned. I didn't know whether he was dead or alive, and it was sort of a peculiar feeling, when you were over there and you couldn't do anything about it.
Gerry Judd, pilot, Empire Air Training Scheme, UK

I was in Portsmouth Barracks, as a sailor waiting to go to sea having done preliminary training, and there were a number of other

'It was sort of a peculiar feeling, when you were over there and you couldn't do anything about it': Gerry Judd was in Britain training to be a pilot under the Empire Air Training Scheme when Singapore fell.

Australians in Portsmouth Barracks at the same time, and there was a great deal of anxiety and agitation about the whole thing and many of them volunteered to go back to Australia because they felt that that's where they should be.
Roy Hall, Admiralty Yachtsman Scheme, ordinary seaman, RANVR

Did we feel that Britain had let us down? Yes, yes absolutely. We'd paid all this money, ever since the proposal was first suggested in 1919 that Singapore Naval Base be built, and every Australian prime minister was sure that we could be protected. The fall of Singapore, its threat to Australia, was devastating. The people of Australia in February and March of 1942— they were devastated. That was Australia's lowest ebb of the war.
Ken Cunningham

I think there was a general realisation at that stage that things had been bungled, that the defence of Singapore hadn't really been properly prepared, and that the whole thing was a shambles. I don't think we were angry that Britain wasn't able to send more actual physical resources out to Singapore at that stage. But there was a feeling of resentment and anger that Singapore wasn't what it had been cracked up to be.
Ralph Doig

The ABC used to play 'The British Grenadiers' as the introduction to its news, and I think it was after the fall of Singapore, they changed it to 'Advance Australia Fair'. That was part of that breaking the nexus with the Poms that went on.
Maurie Jones

Once we heard of the fall of Singapore I decided that's it, I'm going to join up, because that's where my fiancé was, he was taken prisoner of war. But I thought now how am I going to tell the family? So I went into Dad's office and he said, 'What can I do for you, madam?' And I said, 'Dad, I've come to tell you I'm joining the Army.' And—I get emotional still when I think about it—he said, 'I'm so pleased because if I had a son that's what I'd like him to do', and he said 'I'm proud of you'. And so that's how I came to join the Women's Army Service.
Joy Boehm, AWAS, Sydney

After the fall of Singapore the King, George the Sixth, ordered a day of prayer, and the attendance at the church was quite phenomenal. There were several days of prayer during the war, but that's the first time I recall. The thing that impressed me was the fact that it was the only time in my life I'd seen a church so full, that people were standing in the centre aisle, down the outer aisles, it was just an unheard-of-thing. It indicated the depth of anxiety in the community.
Robert Squires

I don't think Australians really understood the implication of war until we lost the 8th Division in Singapore and then of course it became a personal thing with everybody. It brought home to us that Japan was a very very real threat. There were a lot of enlistments from Gulgong [NSW] and quite a few of them were caught up in the 8th Division and were taken prisoner.

And it was a fairly cold sort of a feeling to realise then that Britain was not able to do what we expected her to do—to back up and defend Australia. She was too busy of course defending herself, but it was a bit of a let-down when we found out that Britain couldn't do it.

Bill Graham

4

Under Attack

In attacking the enemy's runways and hangars, these were shattered one by one and the battle sounds were as if heaven and earth were destroyed. The fate of Australia is now in our hands.

Japanese commentary over their newsreel footage of the bombing of Darwin.

Expectations that Australia might be faced with a Japanese invasion reached their height during the six week period following the fall of Singapore on 15 February 1942. From the outbreak of war with Japan, the public had appreciated the possibility that there might be Japanese air raids, but while Singapore and the Netherlands East Indies were in Allied hands there was a thin shield of security.

As mentioned in Chapter 3, about this time the Chief of the General Staff, General Sturdee, had written a paper advocating the build-up of Allied forces in Australia. On the morning of 15 February, he telephoned Curtin to urge him to order that the convoy carrying the 1st Australian Corps be diverted to Australia. Curtin was worried, and in a broadcast the next day described the fall of Singapore as 'Australia's Dunkirk', opening the way for the Battle of Australia. There were further cables between Churchill and Curtin before, on 23 February, Churchill ordered the convoys to head towards Australia. Despite the fact that he became ill from the strain and had to be hospitalised, Curtin saw the arguments clearly, even if at times some of his ministers acted in a less rational fashion.

Australian defence planners had for many years anticipated the possibility of invasion, but they had never been given the resources to prepare adequate defences. Since the Home Army was based on the militia, inevitably the bulk of this force would be located around the main population centres in the south-east, and the training camps were located there. Once they were called out on full-time duty, the militia units had to be equipped and trained before they could be ready for combat.

By the end of January there were two brigades in the Darwin area, and one each in Perth, Port Moresby and the Townsville–Cairns area. By contrast there were some eight divisions between Brisbane and Adelaide, reflecting not only the fact that these forces were raised there, but also that it had long been realised that it was essential to defend this key industrial and population base.

Later, critics were to claim that the Army and the government had pursued a Brisbane Line strategy, whereby Australia defended the area from Brisbane to Adelaide but abandoned the area to the north of that line to the Japanese.

This was a misunderstanding of the true situation. Certainly the units located around Brisbane built defensive positions, causing the soldiers there and the local public to believe that there was a Brisbane Line. But the brigades in the more remote localities, such as Perth, Darwin and Townsville, also built defensive positions.

Furthermore, the government never endorsed the concept of defending only the south-east corner of Australia; the military planned to reinforce the outer areas just as soon as troops were trained, and more importantly, as soon as they could be transported there and adequately supported once they arrived. There was a critical lack of modern fighter aircraft to defend these areas, the RAAF had only a few modern bombers to take the fight to the Japanese, the Royal Australian Navy was small and lacked air cover, and the Allied navies had suffered losses and had been driven from the area.

These military realities were cold comfort to the citizens of Western Australia, Darwin or northern Queensland. And their vulnerability was revealed on 19 February when the Japanese bombed Darwin for the first time. The Japanese attack was part of their campaign to seize Timor, where an Australian battalion was overwhelmed by a Japanese invasion force and an independent company was driven into the hills. During 19 February, there were two attacks on Darwin; the first by 188 aircraft from four carriers of the fleet that had earlier attacked Pearl Harbor, and the second by 54 land-based aircraft from Kenadari and Ambon. Nine ships, including an American destroyer, two American transports, a British tanker and an Australian transport were sunk, and another was beached. A total of 243 were killed, including 191 in the ships and 35 civilians ashore, while a further 350 were wounded. Twenty-three Allied aircraft were destroyed. The extent of these losses was kept from the Australian public, as was the panic and disorganisation that followed in Darwin.

Having secured their eastern flank, the Japanese now turned their attention to Java, landing at three places on 28 February. That night HMAS *Perth* was sunk in the Battle of Sunda Strait, and during the battle for the Netherlands East Indies a total of five Allied cruisers and nine destroyers were lost. As part of this battle, on 3 March Japanese aircraft raided Broome, Western Australia, destroying 24 Allied aircraft and killing about 70 people.

It is understandable that people in Perth would have been apprehensive, but it was more likely that Japanese would attack Australia from the north-east. On 29 January, Japanese Imperial Headquarters had ordered the capture of Lae and Salamaua in New Guinea, and at the proper time Port Moresby. The first air raids on Port Moresby began on 3 February, and on 8 March Japanese forces landed at Lae and Salamaua.

It is now known that on 15 March Imperial General Headquarters debated whether to attack Australia, and decided to capture Port Moresby and the southern Solomons, and then 'to isolate Australia' by seizing Fiji, Samoa and New Caledonia. Japan was now poised to strike at the islands to the north-east of Australia, but events elsewhere were to divert its attention until May. The Japanese high command never really agreed to invade Australia, but this was not known in Australia.

In recent years some historians have suggested that radio intercepts should have revealed to the Australian high command that Australia was not under threat of invasion. But due to code changes, the Japanese operational signals were not being broken consistently during this period, and in any case the Japanese did not actually decide *not* to invade Australia until mid-March. The appreciations prepared by the Australian chiefs of staff during this period reveal that they expected the Japanese to attack Port Moresby in mid-March, Darwin in early April, New Caledonia in mid-April and the east coast of Australia in May. The American high command in Australia expected an attack on Darwin by three enemy divisions before the end of March, and on 25 March there was an invasion scare in Darwin when a Japanese fleet was detected in the Celebes; it went to the Bay of Bengal.

The Australian government and the public were therefore fully justified in planning to repel an invasion, and by the middle of March an air of panic or desperation hung over some quarters of the Australian population. On 11 March Ek Dum of the *Bulletin* wrote: 'War has ceased merely to be on Australia's doorstep. It is on the mat reaching for the knocker'. The Sydney *Daily Mirror* discovered a 'reputed tremor of civilian morale through some sections in Australia', and federal ministers were perturbed at what they considered to be a lowering of public morale.

One aspect of this desperation was the government's consideration of a 'scorched earth' policy. Throughout January it had been under pressure from the public, as well as from the New South Wales premier, to initiate a plan for the denial of resources to the enemy. On 4 February the War Cabinet decided that undue emphasis should not be placed on evacuation measures as this would lower morale, but the State governments were to be informed that military authorities would make special arrangements to conduct operations in Australia. Some State governments continued to advocate a scorched earth policy, and on 1 April the War Cabinet considered a draft directive from the military that stated that 'in cities, towns and localities from which the evacuation of the civil population has been ordered and from which the military forces are about to withdraw, a TOTAL denial policy will be implemented'. The directive was approved at the end of May.

Although the possibility of invasion did not diminish in March, towards the end of the month a number of events caused a revival of confidence in the community. The first of these was the return to Australia of the 7th Division and one brigade of the 6th Division. Two brigades of the 6th Division were detained in Ceylon (Sri Lanka) to defend that island. The returning troops stopped briefly in Perth, and then arrived in Adelaide between 9 and 28 March. One brigade, along with the headquarters of the 6th Division, was hurried north to help defend Darwin.

The second event was the reorganisation of the Australian Army and the appointment of General Sir Thomas Blamey as Commander-in-Chief of the Australian Military Forces. The reorganisation had begun before Blamey arrived back in Australia from the Middle East on 23 March, but his presence, along with other officers who returned to Australia with recent combat experience, helped raise the standard of the militia.

The third event was the arrival in Australia on 17 March of General Douglas MacArthur, who was to command the combined Australian, American and Dutch forces of the newly formed South-West Pacific Area. Already American forces had started to arrive in Australia, but MacArthur's presence underlined the fact that Australia would not be alone in the coming struggle. The threat of invasion had not passed, but the period of desperation was over. This chapter concentrates on the period before MacArthur's arrival, while his impact and that of the American forces will be discussed in the following chapter.

1 Dances at 'The Darwin'

I got a job in the records office at the Barracks in Darwin which was very fortunate for me because when I started going out with the boys I could check their records and find out if they were married or single, so I had a real advantage. There were about 5000 men or more to a girl. I started going out with the Air Force when I first went up there and it was nothing for one girl to sit at a table with ten men, it was just commonplace and nobody really thought anything about it.

The Air Force boys that we danced with, they were screamingly funny, some of them. They'd get a kid's scooter on the dance floor and scoot around on that, or somebody'd bring a crocodile in, sit it on a seat, trussed up of course, about four feet long, and stick a cigarette in the corner of its mouth.

Well, they'd be there and then they wouldn't—they'd fly off in their antiquated planes to Timor and a lot of them didn't come back. Nobody said anything but you knew damn well a plane had gone down and we got to call them the suicide squadron because that's just what it damn well was. It makes me mad when I think of what we had to send out against those Zeros that flew so high like little mosquitoes.

This 'didn't come back' was all around me at the time. I didn't feel it so much then but later on thinking about it—there was death all around.

Toni Mooy Hurley, Army records office, Darwin

My twin sister Toni was working for the Army in Darwin and she invited me up there. And at the time I was doing some freelance work for *Pix* magazine and the editor said, 'Look, when you're up there take some pictures for us'. So I did. Now I didn't have a proper press pass, and no way could I get into the Army camp to photograph the men. So a young chap said, 'Well don't worry, we'll get you a uniform, take the make-up off your face, put your hair up under a hat and we'll get you in'—which they did. Actually I probably looked about an 18-year-old youth, and there I was in the front seat of the truck and we went past, no trouble at all, so I went around taking pictures and nobody stopped me. It was quite remarkable.

I think the morale was pretty low in parts. There wasn't anything for them to do, it was a very small town in those days, dirt roads, nothing

Left *Toni Mooy Hurley in 1941 at a dance at The Darwin Hotel, and* right, *skylarking on Darwin oval with Frank Mooy whom she met in Darwin and later married: 'I could check their records and find out if they were married or single, so I had a real advantage'.*

much going on whatsoever, about three hotels, and of course swimming wasn't very safe, there were the crocodiles, and it was a real outback-type town full of Army—everywhere you went, Army, not a lot of civilians.

Adelie Hurley with some of the hundreds of soldiers she photographed during the war. This occasion was at Ingleburn, Sydney.

The Japanese were in New Guinea and that wasn't very far away, and all through the islands, so I'm sure they expected to be invaded and there were a lot of people evacuated. I was finally evacuated with the police sergeant and his wife and family and a few others—we went off on the back of an open oil truck, they tied mattresses on the top of the oil barrels and we sat on top of those all the way down to Alice Springs, and it was an epic trip.
Adelie Hurley, freelance photographer

There was a coast watching organisation, organised by the RAN, and it comprised 800 volunteers who were mainly missionaries, planters, people who owned cattle ranches, and mining outposts, particularly in the Top End of Australia, and in New Guinea. The RAN supplied them with a radio transceiver. And all those 800 volunteers were of course exposed to tremendous danger particularly those in the very forward areas, not only from being attacked by the enemy—if the enemy suspected they were passing on information— but if they were ever captured, they could be beheaded or executed as a spy.
Phil Chapman, radio operator, Darwin

It was common knowledge for us to communicate with the other Islanders and Aboriginals and we knew that the Japs were going to come. Because they used to be divers up there—hundreds of them. They used to tell our divers, 'We're not coming back to fight youse, we are coming back to fight the whites'.

But the Aboriginal people weren't likely to help the Japanese, they were against them, because Aboriginal people used to slaughter the Japs that came into our waters—unknown numbers, nobody knows how many—and this bit of violation of country carried on and it was

The truck on which Adelie Hurley was evacuated from Darwin shortly before the raid of 19 February 1942.

George Telfer having the army version of a bath in Darwin where he was stationed as an infantryman at the time of the raid.

only more Japanese coming with stronger powers and we had to watch for it.

When we first heard about the war, we were told at the mission station to keep a look-out for the coastwatch, and we used to report every movement of any ships—or luggers—around the islands. We used to have Aboriginals walking around the island and when they come back they tell us—'Oh I seen Japs there, so many boats here and so many boats out there', and there were actually thousands of boats in the tropic part of Australia. Outside our own beach at Emerald River there used to be 29 pearlers every day.

The Japanese knew all our waters more than any other person, more than the Aboriginal people even, who only knew the coast—but they knew the ocean.
Gerry Blitner, coastwatcher, Thursday Island

When Singapore fell we knew then that things were on the go for sure and I think that there's something more should've or could've been done. The Administrator and the civil service—they didn't get on well. For some unknown reason there was animosity. I suppose really each one wanted to be the boss or kingpin, which was wrong—they should have been working together, and I feel they could've got more civilians out before the 19th.
Col Nowlan, infantryman, Darwin

My impression of Darwin was that it was almost what I call a frontier town. There were things that we didn't see in Adelaide—shops run by Chinese, and by Malayan people, Aboriginals about the place. The alerts were already on, I remember if we went into Darwin we had to take a gas respirator and a steel helmet because they were expecting air raids could occur at any time, but business seemed to be as usual for the first few weeks.

The chaps that had arrived a week before I did said, 'We've been out around the area, we are aware of the large area to be defended'. And we were still putting up barbed-wire entanglements and things around the beaches. Certainly the possibility of invasion was there and in fact some of the chaps I spoke to were saying, 'If we are invaded, I don't like our chances very much'.

George Telfer, infantryman, Darwin

We had numerous air-raid warnings, time and time and time again but it went on so often, nobody took any notice of them in the finish because they didn't know—is that just practice for the sirens or was an air raid really coming?

So life seemed to just go on in a merry round of dances at 'The Darwin'. Gregory, who was the Pearl King of Darwin, had cocktail parties every Saturday morning and people went; we had picnics where we used to take all the food in kerosene tins with ice; and I don't think a lot of people had any idea of what could happen.

Toni Mooy Hurley

2 Darwin Attack

The weather was fine, there was no cloud at all, clear blue sky, humid of course but the fellas were working away in the Post Office

'It was horrendous': The ammunition ship Neptuna *explodes alongside Darwin wharf. (Photo: Arthur Oliver, courtesy Phil Chapman)*

and suddenly we became aware of air-raid siren noises and other explosions that could have been bombs or anti-aircraft guns.

Most of us left the Post Office and went across to a slit trench about 50 yards from the office, and on the way across, a few of us looked up and saw these silvery images up in the sky and we realised that they weren't American.
Murray Fletcher, Post Office worker, Darwin

One of my mates called out to me, 'Hey come and have a look at these planes, they're everywhere'. So I strolls out and God, looked up and there was this heap of planes up there and the sun was in a position to shine on them like white dots and you could count them as plain as day. There was nine waves of nine, that's 81 high-level planes. We didn't realise they were Japs even then. And the Ack Ack was firing, the shells were bursting all around—it was a real cracker night and someone said, 'You beaut—the Yanks are here, and they're firing the salute'. And just then—up goes part of the wharf, whoomf. You see flames shooting in the air, about a mile-and-a-half away and someone said, 'Yanks be blowed', he said, 'Japs'.

Well from then on it was about half a dozen Guy Fawkes nights actually—because the bombers done the harbour and the town area over. So we had a grandstand view of what was going on, and we were right in the thick of it.
Col Nowlan

As we went into the trench two of us seemed to be tail-enders and being young I guess I was fleet enough to get into the trench quickly and the other fellow who was close to me waited just that second or

Left *Col Nowlan, infantryman.* Right *Postal worker Murray Fletcher.*

two longer and he was actually blown into the trench as a result of the blast from one of the bombs. He was pretty severely injured and died shortly afterwards.

The Post Office building was fairly badly damaged but other bombs made direct hits onto the area and caused complete devastation. There was a direct hit on a trench or shelter in the Postmaster's residence, alongside the Post Office and the nine people sheltering there were killed immediately.

Murray Fletcher

It was something new to us because we'd never seen enemy action before. And there was smoke, there were explosions, there was flames flying, the air was just full of smoke and dust and you could smell—I suppose it was cordite. And that went on round about an hour and the Zero fighters were just cruising around our area just about the tree-top level. You could see the pilots as plain as day and we had no planes to combat them because the few planes that did, they just got slaughtered on the ground before they even got off. So they just had the run of the roost really, the Japs.

Col Nowlan

It's not true to say there was no defence. There was indeed defence, the anti-aircraft fire was intense but it was largely ineffectual—sixteen 3.7 inch guns and two antiquated 3 inch guns *would* be ineffectual against 188 aeroplanes flying around above a small village.

There was certainly no Allied air defence as such. The American Kittyhawk planes that were there were in the process of being ferried to Java via Timor, and the Americans who died that morning in those

Left *Ken Thompson, anti-aircraft gunner*. Right *Phil Chapman, radio operator*.

'It just sounded as if a bullet was going through you at any tick of the clock':
Meg Ewart (extreme left) *and other nursing sisters of the 119th AGH, Darwin.*

P-40s had in fact taken off to fly to Timor and because of weather conditions had to abort and return to Darwin—unfortunately just at about the same time as the Japanese were arriving.
Ken Thompson, anti-aircraft gunner, Darwin

There was a lot of bravery and the wharfies, they really copped it there on the wharf, and they rowed out and picked up survivors, bringing them back to shore and they were still being strafed and dive-bombed.
Col Nowlan

And I think there were some incredible acts of heroism on the harbour amongst the navy and the merchant seamen.
Ken Thompson

All the patients of course, those that could be, were moved out to trenches and those too ill they lifted, mattress and all and put them under a bed. But it was a very frustrating business being out in trenches and seeing all these columns of black smoke come up from the city and the harbour and feel that there was nothing you could do about it, and we had nothing to stop them. And then all of a sudden, one fighter plane dive-bombed on the hospital and strafed it and it was so low that you could see the pilot and that I think was the first time we felt frightened—before, we were really furious. But it just sounded as if a bullet was going through you at any tick of the clock.
Meg Ewart, army nurse, Darwin

After it cleared off, after about an hour I suppose, we all got together, everybody was talking at once, all keyed up, and the sergeant in charge of the mess said, 'I think we'd better open up the bar, they might need a drink'. So I opened it up and it wasn't long before it was full of sergeants having drinks and there was this explosion, my God the ground shook and I went outside and everyone was looking down towards the harbour, and there all you could see was debris and smoke and flame, and we found out it was the *Neptuna* blew up, and I've never heard an explosion like it since.

Col Nowlan

It was an ammunition ship and it blew up with 200 tons of depth charges, and that shook the town, it was just like an atomic explosion, it was horrendous.

Phil Chapman

The fellas that got out of our trench were wandering around not really knowing what to do, and I remember we walked to the Esplanade about 100 yards from our trench, and when the vessel *Neptuna* exploded, one of the side plates of that ship landed on the cliff, right in front of us.

It was a bewildering time we just didn't know what was going on, I think some of us had the attitude of 'it can't happen to us in Australia'.

There were about 50 people there, working for the Post Office, we worked together, we were all living together. And it was quite devastating really to realise that just one bomb could do away with a handful of people that you knew quite well. I think a lot of us got to the point of thinking we might be next.

Murray Fletcher

3 No Warning

We now know that there was in fact a warning and it had been received twenty minutes before, via the RAAF Area Headquarters in the form of a radio message from Father McGrath, the Catholic priest on Bathurst Island. But we didn't receive that warning. Had that warning been made available to us, we would've had just those few extra minutes and therefore we may have been able to engage the Japanese aeroplanes before they reached their point of bomb-release and the ships in the harbour swinging helplessly on their anchors may have had time to pull their anchors up and get under way, thus making them a more difficult target for the Japanese dive-bombers.

Ken Thompson

As soon as the bombs stopped I went to the radio station, I just had my shorts on, my tin hat, I didn't even have my shoes.

I perused the log as to what had happened earlier and there in Curnock's writing in the log was 9.35 a.m., 8SE—that was the call sign of Bathurst Island and Father McGrath who was the coastwatcher there—to VID which was our call sign, Darwin Radio, and the exact words are indelible in my mind forever—HUGE FLIGHT OF PLANES PASSED OVER BOUND TOWARDS DARWIN, and in brackets RECEIVED. The next entry was PHONED TO RAAF OPERATIONS. So at 9.35 Curnock passed that message to RAAF Operations. Then further in the log were attempts by Curnock where he had on the X frequency called back to Father McGrath without any reply. Nothing happened then at the station of course 'til the bombs started to fall at 9.58.

Words can't describe what an error that was in not acting on that information. For instance there were some 40 ships in the harbour—they could have had steam up and been dispersed. You could've evacuated all the people from the wharf—all the other civilians that were killed, they could have been in slit trenches but nobody was told and it's incomprehensible to the mind that there we have a coastwatching organisation specifically for this purpose, suspicious aircraft, we get a positive warning, a huge flight of planes passed over bound towards Darwin—and they never acted on it.

On the 19th February there were ten American fighter aircraft returning from Java and it was believed by RAAF Operations that they were the aircraft referred to by Father McGrath. This of course is ludicrous in that they were ten aircraft where he specifically said HUGE flight and ten aircraft is not huge by any stretch of the imagination.
Phil Chapman

And yet I believe the possibility of attack was present certainly in the minds of the military people in the area because the previous day, the 18th, a convoy which had been bound for Timor with reinforcements had been turned back by Japanese air action. And we were also aware, as anti-aircraft people, that there had been reconnaissance aircraft over the town of Darwin within the few preceding days. So it was just a question of when.
Ken Thompson

4 Heaven and Earth

About midday they decided to give us another visit—they must have liked it. There was two waves of 27 high level bombers came over and done the RAAF over again.
Col Nowlan

Two formations of 27 each, approaching from different directions and I remember quite vividly looking up at the clear blue sky and thinking there are those planes silver in the sky in perfect formation. Because they didn't have anyone to attack them at this stage. And then as they got right over Darwin there was the loud rumble of explosions.

We watched it all happen, and when it had passed we set off. We got to what is now the Stuart Highway, heading for Darwin in this utility, and of course before long we met the outgoing people from Darwin—motor cars, people on foot, people with handcarts, this mass of people moving south, getting out of town.

George Telfer

All forms of transport were used to get out of Darwin and a lot of people headed for Adelaide River which was the only road out of the town anyway, but the variety of vehicles that went was quite amazing. One of the vehicles was the truck that was used to collect night soil from the township.

Murray Fletcher

We walked towards the dock area and as we were walking into Darwin we saw civilians streaming out by the hundreds, every way, and they were yelling out to us, 'You're going the wrong way, mate'. Anyhow, we carried on down to the waterfront to see the carnage and there it was. All I could see was smoke coming from ships, parties depositing bodies on the beach and there were lots of motor boats going back and forth to the hospital ship, *Manunda*. Even though it had been directly hit and damaged and quite a few killed aboard, they still set a lot of people aboard for treatment.

It was quite devastating. One of course had seen photographs of the bomb damage in London and other European cities; but you must understand that Darwin was only the size of a postage stamp and the amount of planes, as the Japanese commander said, he used a sledgehammer to crack a walnut. Buildings were just blown apart and gutted, the dwellings were just shattered, everywhere was just an awful scene. This was a big air raid on a small town.

Phil Chapman

There were hundreds and hundred of injured, because there were a lot of ships in the harbour filled with troops and of course they sustained terrific burns when they got into the water—the water was all alight with the oil—and so apart from wounds you got all these very severe burn cases. We had to work very long hours, you just worked until you nearly dropped, and nobody worried about time, you just stayed on duty and worked.

Another thing I think too that we did feel, was that there wouldn't have been a raid like that unless the Japanese were going to follow it on and land, and that wasn't a very happy thought either.

Meg Ewart

That night the moral was absolutely unbelievable. We had Army guards at the radio station, and soon after the second raid an Army

Phil Chapman (left) *and a mate after the attack in a crater made by a 500 lb. Japanese bomb. The shadow belongs to the photographer, Arthur Oliver.*

captain with an Army utility pulled up and he said to the two guards that were there, 'Hop aboard'.

And Curnock, our officer in charge, said, 'Where are you going?'.

And he said, 'We're withdrawing to Adelaide River—the Army have been told to evacuate, that invasion is imminent and we're not going to be caught here'.

And Curnock said, 'How about us?'

He said, 'That's for you to worry about'.

We were left with two 303 rifles between the five of us.
Phil Chapman.

Lots of people thought that it was a prelude to an invasion, and that was not an unreasonable expectation at the time.
Ken Thompson

It was absolute pandemonium after the raids, the load of work was enormous, but in between we still kept calling Father McGrath, 8SE, and it wasn't until six o'clock that evening that he responded and his words are again still in my memory. He said, 'I am back on the air. After I passed that message to you, six Japanese planes broke formation and bombed and strafed me and blew my radio off the air and I've been up to now getting back on'.
Phil Chapman

I walked in next day just to have a look at the place and there was a hell of a mess. All you could see in the harbour was boats lying on

their side, upside down, there was fires burning, actually there was
smoke and that flying around for days—a pall of smoke.
Col Nowlan

Food was very very scarce and after the first raid, when people had
run away, we looted, we took as much food as we could out of the
stores, tinned food, all the alcohol we could find, we thought we're in
for a long hard winter. They don't want it, they've gone, and we
gathered together ducks and fowls and put them in a pen.
Phil Chapman

I remember going to civilian houses and seeing the effects of
machine-gun fire which had damaged furniture, cooked food left on a
stove, clothes strewn around. Now some of that was due to people
leaving hurriedly, some may have been due to pillaging, but it was
rather touching to see signs on some of the houses—'Please don't
touch anything, we still live here'.
George Telfer

Censorship was immediately closed down on Darwin—you couldn't
say anything or do anything. We got no footage on that, no footage at
all.
Ken G. Hall, managing editor, *Cinesound Review*, Sydney

The government of the day played it down to the extent that nobody
even to this day I think appreciates the magnitude of the event.
Ken Thompson

When you consider the amount of ships, I think they estimated about
thirty-odd sunk and most of them lost their crews, so that amounts to
quite a few, plus the wharfies—they lost a number—and civilians, and
quite a few at the RAAF. We always said there was close to a
thousand in our estimation and I'd say we'd be very very close to the
truth really, a thousand. And that's beside the bodies that would have
been washed away, gone up in the mangrove swamps, little creeks
full of crocodiles—they'd never find them, no way.
Col Nowlan

All the sailors and soldiers that were on the American ships were
burnt, some of them were saved but most of them were burnt and
they were washed ashore when they died, and they were buried
where they were, where the tide washed them up, in trenches, and
when they were rotten enough and smelled enough the crocodiles
dug 'em up and ate them, and then we'd have to go down and bury
them again.
Roy leRougetel, anti-aircraft gunner, Darwin

I believe that if the true story had got out the civilians in the south
would have panicked so the government just put a blanket over it and

said it was of no consequence. There were lots of people that actually found their way all the way south to all the capital cities, but of course they just weren't believed. People believed the press, rather than those who had been there firsthand.
Phil Chapman

I think by and large Australia just wasn't ready for that sort of thing. Remember only a few days prior, on 15 February, Singapore had capitulated—we had lost twenty-odd thousand Australian soldiers there. I just don't think the government of the day wanted to hear about it and I think that they set about deliberately covering up the magnitude of the damage for fear that the civilian population may panic.

The final report that I recall was that nine people had been killed in Darwin and there'd been something like a hundred or a few hundred injured. There was nothing serious about the whole thing, we had to wait for many years to hear the true story of Darwin.
Bill Graham, wheat farmer, Gulgong, New South Wales

5 Never Any Panic

When Darwin was bombed we felt that the war had come to Australia. I was at high school by then, I can remember going back to school with a friend and we were most impressed because it was the first time that war had been fought on Australian soil.

I always felt we'd win because we won the other war, and I was brought up on that; but I think we were very much afraid that the Japanese would get here.
Margaret Maxwell, schoolgirl, Swan Hill, Victoria

Oh yes, people expected an invasion after Darwin was hit—once they invaded Australia at all we knew anything might happen.
Ray Adams, farmer, Gulgong, New South Wales

I was way up on a coastal patrol the other side of Geraldton and we heard through our wirelesses that Darwin had been bombed. We were on full alert then, red alert we called it, stuck out on the beaches in case they came further. We had the armoured division backing us up behind, with tanks, and there was a full brigade of us which is three battalions, plus our own hospital, and we stood to for about 24 hours expecting them to come further down the coast.
Hilary Hughes, infantryman, Sydney

I was worried as hell about my wife, I was worried about the girls at the studio, we knew what was going on, so it was a frightening period and you weren't thinking about yourself, you were thinking about the women, as you should. So this was a period of great alarm,

Charles Janeway outside the farm homestead where he lived in Mt Gambier, opposite the milk factory which he was instructed to help blow up if the Japanese came.

but there was never any panic, I'm happy to say, never any panic that I saw or heard about—and I had newsreel tentacles out in every area.
Ken G. Hall, managing editor, *Cinesound Review*, Sydney

There was one poster just like one of those Nazi posters about the Jews, it had this great apelike creature with its horrible teeth and its great hairy paw and talons stretching out to Australia, and 'They're Coming South' was the message.
Ted Hartley, conscientious objector, Sydney

Australia in those days because of its isolation and because of its racial mix did think of the rest of the world largely in stereotypes and all over the cities were these posters showing the Japanese as less than human, as fanged animals really, who were sort of coming to rape your sister, your mother, your grandmother or anybody else about the place, and this does have an effect on people of course. And people were very frightened by the whole concept of the Japanese.
Dorothy Hewett, university student, Perth

The Germans seemed to be the same race that we came from, but the Japanese seemed to be a race of their own—they could live in different environments than we could. Where the German needed the same type of food and the same type of cleanliness, the Japanese could live on the smell of an oil rag.
Charles Janeway, schoolboy, Mt Gambier, South Australia

Stories had come in of course from the atrocities that they'd performed elsewhere, and so there was an absolute dread of what would happen if the Japanese took over here. A lot of it came through by word-of-mouth of course—you really had to live in those days to realise what rumours were. Rumours floated throughout the country on every subject under the sun. There were invasions, there were fifth columns, there were all sorts of things. Rumours just spread like wildfire.

Ralph Doig, Premier's Department, Perth

Oh, it was horrifying. I was very pregnant at the time, and you heard stories of the Japs slitting open the pregnant women and things like that. It was terrifying.

Barbara Doig, housewife and mother, Perth

Girls used to talk about, 'If the Japanese come, what will we do?'. And some girls would say, 'Oh well, take a cyanide pill'—rather than be raped by these dreadful little yellow animal bastards. And where the hell they would get a cyanide pill is an interesting question—I don't think they were generally available. I suppose it was partly a dramatic sort of stance: 'I will fight for my virginity against the yellow hordes', and also there were all these extraordinary ideas about racial purity milling in the background somewhere.

Dorothy Hewett, university student, Perth

I had to go to the doctor, and he said, 'If the Japs invade we are going to issue the young girls and women with this particular sponge'—it was for birth control and he said that would stop them getting pregnant with the Japanese, so it really brought it right home to us then.

Mary Comer, soldier's wife, Gulgong, New South Wales

I can remember a conversation in the workshop that went like this: someone said, 'What are you going to do when the Japs come?'—not *if* they come but *when* they come. And someone else said, 'Oh, don't know, go bush I suppose'. And someone else said, 'The Japs won't bother us'—because of course it is all men—'They'll be too busy raping the women'. And this is how it was expected the Japs would arrive in Australia. No-one was under any illusion of what would happen.

Bob Bahnsen, machinist, Sydney

I knew a girl in Geelong who had a pistol that her father had brought back from the World War and she had ammunition and she was quite definite that if the Japanese came to her suburb, she was going to shoot herself, and I think she meant it and a lot of people no doubt felt the same.

John Slee, Army engineer, Victoria

I overheard my mother talking with a friend who had children the same age, they decided if the Japanese got to Swan Hill, they would kill us rather than let the Japanese get us.
Margaret Maxwell, schoolgirl, Swan Hill, Victoria

We weren't given a great deal of instructions if the worst came to the worst about a Japanese invasion. But we were told to hand over our pistols and just do what the Japanese told us to do. As far as civilians are concerned I think that they would have been wise to do as we were told to do—just give in and do as the Japanese requested them. Because the Japanese in those days were ruthless and it meant your life if you resisted them.
Ray Blissett, policeman, Sydney

If the Japs had really come, I had my big brother's Speedwell bike—in case the railway lines had been blown up—and my mother had Dad's rucksack with some tinned food and a tin opener, and a rug, and I was to get to Bathurst and go out to Granny's house which was a sort of a safe haven. Once there I suppose Mum thought there were plenty of rabbits and cream and preserved fruit and all those things that Granny had up there, so she would have looked after me. Or one could always hide in the mountains or kill rabbits, or eat something. I thought it was quite a good idea actually, I was too young to really understand.
Ken Muggleston, schoolboy, Katoomba, New South Wales

We talked about it and we thought well we really better get prepared ourselves. So we decided we'd collect a few guns, which we did, not that they would have been any use, they were .22s, Pea Rifles as we used to call them. And we established a cache, up in the Blue Mountains, of a bit of food, and guns and so on.

What we wanted to do was to have at least the possibility that should the Japanese invade, that we'd have some stores, some weapons, to enable us to conduct a guerrilla war. This was just my brother and my father with a couple of friends of ours, but it was broader—there was a movement to develop what we called a People's War, the idea that not just the armed forces, but also the people should be involved should Australia be invaded.
Laurie Aarons, factory worker and Communist Party member, Sydney

We didn't think of civilian resistance, I'm sure. We didn't think of anything like, say, the Resistance in France, or the various underground movements which fought back against the Nazis. We knew we'd had it. We had less than seven million people in the whole country in those days. We fully expected to be slaves too. Some of the wartime posters showed white people in coolie hats—'This is what's going to happen to you if you don't join the war effort'.
Maurie Jones, schoolboy, Perth

*'Be Prepared': Ken Haylings'
friend Jack Crawley, Sydney, a
scout and member of the
National Emergency Scheme
(NES) ready to make his
contribution to the defence of
his country.*

There was a scorched earth policy, particularly from the Kimberley in
the north, although in Western Australia, scorched earth didn't need
much to put it into effect—it was already there. But all women and
children were evacuated from the Kimberley region, from Broome,
Derby and Wyndham, and they came south, and a lot of the men as
well, and only essential people were allowed to stay up there. There
were certain small Army units in occupation up there, and the Army
really took over control of the area north of Hedland.
Ralph Doig, Premier's Department, Perth

The idea was that everything went up with a big bang and all they'd
be left with was no bridges, no roads, no rails, no factories and they
just had a big blank piece of country with no tucker and no facilities
in it. Don't know what happened to the population, that was our
worry I suppose—get out or wait.
Roger Jones, schoolboy, Mackay, Queensland

And the Army, as part of their scorched earth policy, wired up the
Wyndham [WA] meatworks for demolition. They planted a lot of
explosives in the meatworks and they were very proud of this, and
their fingers itched, they wanted to press the button to see what sort
of a bang it would make. They said, 'It shouldn't be left there,
because if it's left there, we may not be able to send it off when we
want to'. Well, Wilcock as Premier said, 'That's all very well, but that's
a State industry. Why shouldn't we wait until there is an actual threat
of invasion? Surely you can leave two or three men there and when
invasion is imminent, then it's time enough to let it off. Why should it

be done now?'. But they were dead keen on letting it off straightaway, I think they wanted to see the results of their handiwork, and they became very hostile about this, but Wilcock held out and that was how the Wyndham meatworks was preserved and able to resume operations when the war was over.
Ralph Doig, Premier's Department, Perth

I was a lad of about thirteen or fourteen and I lived on a farm across the road from this milk factory that made cheese and butter produce for the war, and a gentleman from the government was sent out to Father and I to get us to go over and destroy the milk factory in case the Japanese army came and he took us over and I was taken into the factory itself, the main room, and told to get in with an axe and punch holes in all the milk vats and just go berserk and break everything so that when the Japs came they wouldn't be able to use the milk factory and I remember I thought—'Crikey, what are we going to do with our milk?'.
Charles Janeway

We were doing such things as travelling around the Victorian countryside and inspecting all the bridges, working out how they could be destroyed if they had to be. One project that our company was concerned with was the wooden bridge over the river at Barwon Heads [Vic.]: the various piles and other sections of the bridge were drilled and gelignite put in place, sufficient to destroy the bridge.

Another job that we had was at two airfields, one at Malacoota [Vic.] and the other near Wilson's Promontory [Vic.] and the job there was to drill bore holes across the runways and place quite substantial charges of explosive. And they were actually connected up and wired to a central bunker or foxhole so that if invasion was threatened and it looked as if these airfields could be used in a leapfrogging operation by Japanese aircraft, they could be destroyed. And these were actually wired and ready to go.
John Slee

Japan only had to control the cities really and they controlled Australia—they didn't have to control the bush, they could do that in their own good time. So I think we were very conscious of that—the scorched earth policy wasn't going to do anybody any good.

And if the Japanese had got this far—to Gulgong or wherever—there was nothing much you could do about it. It was a fatalistic thought, but it was a thought that went through *my* mind, anyway—'What can we do if they do get here?'.
Bill Graham

We took turns at a spotting post for the aeroplanes up at the Town Hall—that was manned day and night. There were charts on the wall

of all the enemy planes and we had binoculars, but I don't know that we took it too seriously.
Roma Wallis, store assistant, Gulgong, New South Wales

All the local VDC had their kangaroo or rabbit guns, and my uncle did a volunteer duty where he had to stand on the side of a mountain while somebody overhead would throw a rock and they had to aim their guns and pretend it was a Jap Zero coming in. And they all had a tree which in the event of the Japs coming, they had to cut down at the crossroads of each particular road. But he came home one day disheartened and he said, 'How am I going to get a Jap Zero with a double-barrelled shotgun?'—which only had a range of 50 yards or so, of course.
Ken Muggleston

Bondi had two marvellous promenade piers that stuck right out into the beach and they blew these up because they felt in the event of a Japanese landing that they'd provide good cover for the landing troops. So to get into the water you had to negotiate these little pieces of concrete that were the remains of the piers, and barbed wire all along—it was pretty difficult getting a swim.
Jack Pollard, cadet journalist, Sydney

What would I do if the Japanese invaded Australia? I was thinking of that all the time and I never came up with an answer. I don't know what I would have done. I don't think pacifists knew how to handle that situation. I'm still not sure in my own mind, because it was a situation that was so totally outside our experience. I suppose we would have resolved it in some way or other, perhaps non-combatant activities of some sort, trying to be nice to everybody—I don't know. But what would I do if a Japanese came at me with a bayonet or a Samurai sword? I suppose I'd have tried to hit him with a cricket bat—or something like that.
Niall Brennan, university student and pacifist, Melbourne

6 Sitting Ducks

A large number of Dutch flying boats landed in Broome one evening with Dutch evacuees largely, from Java and points north. That day a Japanese reconnaissance airplane had been sighted over Broome, and the military authority in Broome warned the pilots that they should not delay but should get out immediately. The pilots and their passengers, women and children, had had a very long trying day and flight. They had to refuel in Broome, anyhow, and so it was decided that they would stay overnight and take off the next morning.

And that was the fatal decision, because before they could get underway in the morning, a flight of Zeros came in and simply sank

all the aircraft in the Bay. Of course all the people who were in the
flying boats were immediate casualties.
Ralph Doig

I looked up and I saw some specks on the horizon and I said to the
attendant who was going to fill the aircraft with petrol, 'Do you have
any aircraft here, is the RAAF here?'
'No' he said.
So I said to him, 'Man, sound the alarm, the Japs are coming'.
And he laughed and he said to me, 'They won't come that far south'.
They did sound the alarm but by then it was too late because the
Japs were there already. Now a week before they had fitted two 303
machine guns to the Lodestars and when I saw them coming I stood
just to the side of the Lodestar and I held the machine gun to my
shoulder, hand on the barrel, and I waited until one came and I gave
him the full burst and my hand got badly burnt but those things you
don't feel in moments like that, and after he passed there was a lot of
black smoke coming out of it and he crashed in the sea. There were
about eight or nine flying boats full of evacuees, women and children,
and they shot the whole thing to pieces.
But there was no defence whatsoever in Broome—they could have
taken it with fifteen men.
Guy Winckel, Dutch pilot of evacuee plane

The people of Broome panicked immediately. Shot straight through
and grabbed any transport they could get. It was mainly men, the
women and children were already gone from Broome. We received
word from the Army that the State public servants who were still in
Broome had left their posts, so a message was sent to them
immediately that they were to get back and stay on the job and await
further orders. Even one of the police inspectors had moved out and
had gone bush as the first step towards moving south. The same sort
of thing as happened after Darwin.
And you can understand the panic. Nobody then in Australia had
previous experience of being bombed like that, and it only wanted
somebody to come in again—they were all sitting ducks. There was
no defence against them.
Ralph Doig

I think there was a distinct change after that. A wave of fear went over
the population of Western Australia because it was so unexpected, and
from then on there was a definite fear that we could actually be
invaded. Here we were, who had always been so safe and so isolated
and suddenly we'd been bombed by the Japanese. Even if it was a
long way up the coast, it was still the Western Australian coastline.
Dorothy Hewett

There was a terrible lot of fishermen on the coast of Western Australia
and they stopped all that, and boats were all confiscated or run up on

slipways and got out of the road and that was actually part of our job, to keep civilians off the coast, they were all shunted back to towns further inland.
Hilary Hughes

An attack by air on Australia was considered very likely and people in Western Australia only had to go down towards Fremantle and they could see over 100 ships in the Fremantle Harbour, holed up there because there was nowhere else for them to go. And that would have presented a very inviting target to the Japanese if they felt like sending some sort of a force down and bombing Fremantle Harbour. And of course if they did that, the people of Perth naturally felt that they were at risk as well. The fear and the dread was there that this was going to happen.

But it was decided that there should be no mass evacuation. There was nowhere to evacuate to. Where were you going to take them? If you took them to Kalgoorlie, it was dependent on a pipeline from Perth. All you had to do was break the pipeline and there was no water. And other centres in Western Australia just didn't have the capacity to support large numbers of evacuees. So people were encouraged, if they had friends and relatives in the country, to make their own arrangements and many many people did this, that was the first reaction of a large number of families.
Ralph Doig

My husband was talking about getting back to the station—his people were on a station, where they had wells. And that's what we would have done if things had been very bad here. He was a bushman, so he knew what to do. Otherwise, it was just hope for the best.
Myrtle Boddington, housewife and mother, Kalgoorlie, Western Australia

I remember my father and mother discussing whether to send us away or at least the two younger children, because we had relatives in the country who would have been happy to look after them. And they came to the conclusion that if we were invaded it might be better to be in a big city where the occupying forces might exercise some control over their troops, rather than be in the country at the mercy of 'marauding bands'. I remember my father using that phrase, 'marauding bands'—Japanese soldiers.
Maurie Jones

In the event of an invasion my job was to stay where I was, but I didn't want my wife to stay, so we had a sort of an arrangement. We had a little Austin 7 motor car and when I gave her the word to go, she was to put the two young children in the car and head for Kalgoorlie, where I had a married sister who could be depended upon to look after her.
Ralph Doig

I was to pack the baby up and put the pram on, plus a box with the wire netting on it with the fowls. And I bought some seeds for vegetables and that, to plant, and tinned foods, and away we were to go, three children and myself, in this Baby Austin.
Barbara Doig

Because there was no alternative really, Kalgoorlie could have existed for a while, the pipeline might have been repaired. See, we didn't know what was going to happen. The government had no idea really of what would happen if the Japanese landed and came into Perth.
Ralph Doig

7 The Boys Come Home

We landed in Perth and one thing I remember about that is smelling gum trees before you could even see the land and that was a wonderful experience. And the first thing we did when we arrived, we went to a football match—and I'm not a person that goes to football matches but it just seemed to be something Australian, something of home.
Betty Oldham, Army nurse, 2/1 AGH, 6th Division

We didn't know they were coming of course because it was very hush-hush but suddenly these soldiers appeared in large numbers in the streets, and there was a general feeling of—'we're a bit safer now'.
Maurie Jones

They came up the Port Adelaide railway line in trucks. And I remember standing at the railway line and it was just full of these soldiers waving to us. We were young lads and we saw the soldiers as great heroes.
Bob Taylor, Post Office worker, Adelaide

Dad was the first one in our family to come home from the Middle East, and when he came home, I very distinctly remember that day because we had over 100 visitors—everybody in the town came to see Dad, particularly ones who had family over there, who came to see if he had any news of their family.
Margaret Burton, schoolgirl, Adelaide

When I arrived at Sydney Station, at Central, my Mum and Dad were there and my brother and of course I'd grown nearly two to three inches since I'd gone in and I suppose they found it hard to believe that that was their little boy. Mum was crying and it was quite a scene—well, we were all crying I suppose.
Alan Low, 6th Division

But there was a feeling rather of discontent in Western Australia because when all these forces came back, including Western Australian men, they didn't come to Western Australia. They were shunted over into the eastern States and put up into Queensland, where the Commonwealth government felt that the greatest fear of invasion existed, and then of course they went into New Guinea.

So that we in Western Australia were still left completely defenceless, and there was nothing to stop the Japanese if they wanted to come down the west coast of Australia, there was nothing whatever to stop them. We had two or three big guns on Rottnest [Island], and we had one or two coastal batteries, but there was no air defence, there was no army at that stage, only the CMF, which had no wartime experience. And so we felt we were completely exposed to invasion because of our lack of defences.

There was no way you could bring forces across Australia, in any case. When we went to a premiers' conference in Canberra, it took us five nights in the train, each way. Now, trying to bring forces across Australia in that time of course was a hopeless proposition, even if they could've been spared. So we were totally and completely isolated from the rest of Australia.
Ralph Doig

A lot of people in Western Australia really felt that if it came to an actual invasion by the Japanese, the Western Australians would be left to fend for themselves and that they would become a vassal state immediately. Though how they thought the rest of Australia was going to defend itself against the Japanese is an interesting question too.
Dorothy Hewett

5

Saviours and Heroes

We shall win or we shall die, and to this end, I pledge you the full resources of all the mighty power of my country and all the blood of my countrymen . . . There is a link which binds our countries together which does not depend on written protocol, upon treaties of alliance, or upon diplomatic doctrine. It goes deeper than that. It is that indescribable consanguinity of race which causes us to have the same aspirations, the same hopes and desires, and the same ideals and dreams of future destiny . . . My presence here is tangible evidence of our unity . . . My faith in our ultimate victory is invincible . . .

General Douglas MacArthur speaking at a dinner at Parliament House, Canberra, 26 March 1942.

The first American troops arrived in Australia almost by accident. During 1941 the US had not planned to send forces to Australia, and in the event of war the agreed British–American strategy was to 'beat Hitler first'. Nevertheless, the Americans planned to hold the Philippines, and they realised that if the direct route from the United States to the Philippines were interrupted by the Japanese, their planes and other reinforcements would have to be sent via Australia. On the outbreak of war in the Far East, an American convoy was carrying reinforcements towards the Philippines and, on the orders of President Roosevelt, it was diverted to Australia.

Thus on 21 December 1941, four transports escorted by the heavy cruiser *Pensacola* arrived in Brisbane with 4600 US troops, including artillery units and air force ground crews. This convoy was closely followed by another carrying 250 fighter aircraft. By this time, the US Joint Chiefs of Staff had decided that Australia would have to become a base for any subsequent operations in the South-west Pacific and they endorsed the build-up of US forces there.

Late in December, Lieutenant-General George Brett was appointed to command the US forces in Australia, and on 3 January 1942 he moved his headquarters from Brisbane to Melbourne, where the headquarters of the Australian services were located. Initially he ordered four US bases to be established in Australia—in Darwin, Townsville, Brisbane and Melbourne— and later bases were established in Perth, Adelaide and Sydney, with sub-bases at Cairns and Charters Towers, 100 kilometres inland from Townsville.

On 14 February, at the time when Curtin was arguing with Churchill over the destination of the convoy carrying the 1st Australian Corps, the US Joint Chiefs ordered the US 41st Infantry Division to be sent to Australia. By the

time of the Japanese air raid on Darwin on 19 February, US Kittyhawk
fighters and anti-aircraft units were operating there.

During January and February, wartime censorship prevented the mention
of US forces in Australia, but by the end of February it was becoming
difficult to ignore their presence For example, on 26 February almost a
division of US troops arrived in Melbourne. They were billeted for a few
days in Ballarat and Bendigo before they sailed again on 6 March to garrison
New Caledonia.

The importance of the US presence in Australia was not fully realised until
General MacArthur and his party arrived by B-17 bomber from the Philippines on 17 March and, when news of his arrival was released the following
day, the newspapers were jubilant. The editorial of the Brisbane *Courier Mail*
said that: 'The arrival in Australia of General Douglas MacArthur . . . is
stirring news, the best news Australians have had for many a day'. The
Bulletin commented that: 'in sending their national hero to Australia [the
Americans] have charged themselves with the responsibility of saving it as
a free white English speaking nation, as far as it lies within their power, for
it is not in the nature of that great people to let MacArthur down'.

After a slow journey by plane and then train, MacArthur arrived at Spencer
Street Station in Melbourne on 21 March, to an enthusiastic welcome from
the Deputy Prime Minister, Frank Forde, and a large crowd. On 26 March,
MacArthur travelled to Canberra to meet the Prime Minister and the Advisory
War Council. It was planned that MacArthur would assume command of all
Australian, US and Dutch forces in the South-West Pacific Area and, with
the co-operation of local authorities, he immediately began to act in this
capacity, but it took a little while for the details to be negotiated by the US
and Australian governments.

In the meantime, on 28 March the US Joint Chiefs ordered the US 32nd
Infantry Division to Australia, and on 6 April the bulk of the 41st Division
arrived in Melbourne. They went by train to a camp at Seymour, 100
kilometres north of Melbourne.

On 18 April MacArthur assumed command of the South-West Pacific Area.
Of his five subordinate commanders, only one, General Blamey, who commanded the Allied Land Forces, was Australian. The other Allied commands
were Allied Naval Forces, commanded by Vice-Admiral Herbert F. Leary;
Allied Air Forces, commanded by Lieutenant-General Brett; the US forces
in the Philippines, which for a while remained under MacArthur's command
until eventually forced to surrender; and a separate command looking after
the administration of the US forces in Australia. In all, by 18 April there
were 38 000 Americans in Australia, while AIF troops under his command
totalled 104 000 and the militia, 265 000.

Not only did MacArthur have command of all the Australian forces in the
area, but he also became the government's principal adviser on strategic
matters. In other words, the Australian government gave up a large measure
of Australian sovereignty. Considering the strategic situation perhaps it felt
that in the emergency it had no other option. Fortunately, for at least a year
or more Australia's strategic priorities corresponded with those of MacArthur
and the Americans.

A key element in MacArthur's conduct of Allied strategy was his complete control over the issuing of press communiqués. Critics were to charge that when Australian forces were involved in operations the communiqués described them as Allied troops, while American troops were always described as Americans.

On 14 May the remainder of the 41st Division and the entire US 32nd Division arrived in Melbourne, and the latter was sent to Adelaide for its initial training. Early in July, in preparation for a planned offensive, MacArthur moved his headquarters from Melbourne to Brisbane, and soon afterwards the 32nd Division moved from Adelaide to Brisbane, while the 41st Division went from Melbourne to Rockhampton. The headquarters of the US 1st Corps was also located at Rockhampton.

While the infantry divisions were training in preparation for later operations, the US air force was already on operations. Fighter and bomber squadrons were based at Darwin, and long-range bombers from Townsville and Charters Towers raided Japanese positions at Rabaul and on the north coast of New Guinea. Aircraft from these bases took part in the Battle of the Coral Sea in early May. US construction units, with large numbers of blacks, were busy building airstrips in northern Queensland, and by July US bombers were operating from those constructed on the Atherton tableland.

The number of US Army and Air Corps servicemen in Australia and New Guinea grew dramatically. According to the Australian official war history, at the end of August 1942 there were 99 000; at the end of November, 107 000; at the end of January 1943, 125 000; at the end of April, 160 000; and at the end of June, 200 000. The US Navy numbered 2000 at the end of 1942, and reached a peak of 14 300 in December 1943. At the end of 1942 there were over 8000 black troops in Australia and New Guinea. Large numbers of US troops were in Melbourne and Sydney but generally they were transients. By contrast, most of the Americans in Queensland were in training or occupied permanent camps or quarters.

Under threat of invasion, Australians were delighted that the Americans had arrived. As one Labor Member of Parliament said at the time: 'I'd rather be pushed off the footpath by a drunken gob [US sailor] than be chased down Martin Place by a Jap with a bayonet'.

1 We almost fell on our knees ...

It would have been late February or early March 1942 and we were absolutely convinced that the Japs would overrun us within a few months at the most. We were outside, sitting on the footpath having lunch and chiacking the girls as they walked past. And four planes flew over and someone said, 'By God, they're Kittyhawks—you beaut, the Yanks are here!' and we almost fell on our knees in gratitude. I've never forgotten that.
Bob Bahnsen, machinist, Sydney

We were coming back on the boat from a holiday on Bribie Island

and we saw the *Pensacola* coming up the Brisbane River with all
these uniforms and somebody said, 'Look at them, they're bloody
Yanks!'—and that was the first time I ever saw an American.
Joan Bentson, office worker, Brisbane

I remember the great relief that was felt in Western Australia when the
first Kittyhawks were seen flying around overhead, and when the
American servicemen in uniform were seen in the streets of the city of
Perth. We said, 'Well, we're not being altogether forgotten. The
Americans are here, people are taking more of an interest in Western
Australia, and things are beginning to look brighter'. And so they were
really welcomed with open arms.
Ralph Doig, Premier's Department, Perth

The ships had come in with American sailors, and everybody was
down there, welcoming them. I didn't meet anyone in particular, but it
was very exciting, I thought. They looked all very young and of
course I was young too, but they were exuberant and cheerful and
we all thought it was great seeing all these American soldiers. I was
very happy that they did come, because things were not good at the
time.
Margaret Blair, office worker, Sydney

You would suddenly become aware that the city was crowded with
American troops. And as young girls, I can remember us all looking a
little bit, and thinking, 'Oh dear, they could've come from Mars'—they
seemed so different to us.
Glenys Kirk, office worker, Melbourne

When the Americans came in against the Japanese the same
confidence I suppose evolved about their participation in the war that
we had about Britain in the European segment of the war. We
believed the Americans were pretty invincible and from what you saw,
the number of troops that they were sending to Australia and this sort
of thing—that gave us a lot of confidence that the Japanese would be
ultimately defeated.
Bill Graham, wheat farmer, Gulgong, New South Wales

People welcomed the idea of the Americans coming into the war, and
so did the left-wingers. Not that we had a great amount of time for
the Americans either, but it was a matter of life and death as it
were—that's how we saw it, and I think it was exactly that.
**Laurie Aarons, factory worker and Communist Party member,
Sydney**

Without the Americans a whole generation of Australian-born people,
if they had been born at all, would have been half-caste Japanese,
there is no question about that. After Singapore fell, no-one was under

any illusions about that, that's exactly what was expected, and you can imagine how that traumatised the entire Australian population.
Bob Bahnsen

2 MacArthur

One afternoon there'd been a nasty little Japanese sneaking raid, and we were still standing to and on our gun position, when the noise of aircraft engines was heard and target duly located, fire control instruments on target, all the necessary calculations are made, rounds are ready, we're only waiting for the rude four-letter word to fire. However the officer exercising tactical control that afternoon, one Mick Phillips, peered into the telescope identification and said, 'Do *not* engage'. The aircraft approaching from the west is a lone American B-17. And that was the arrival in Australia of General Douglas MacArthur—which could have been different, had we fired.
Ken Thompson, anti-aircraft gunner, Darwin

It was MacArthur. Loud cheers all round the place and of course there was the greatest sigh of relief that ever happened in any country, you could hear the nation go, 'Aaaagh the Yanks are here'. We knew that they had enormous power, that they had an enormous navy and while the Japanese had an enormous navy too, the Americans would win, they had to win, they couldn't afford to lose.

So the public were wildly excited about it and MacArthur was taking poses for cameras, he was the greatest actor I've ever known but he was a ham, he really was a ham, he'd take a photo, watching the cameras all the time.
Ken G. Hall, managing editor, *Cinesound Review*, Sydney

People just needed something new. And of course MacArthur was the new thing we got. I was sent down to cover his first Melbourne press relations conference. And I was strangely reassured by this magnificent figure that MacArthur cut. He was very tall and good-looking and he had this sloppy cap and lots of braid and a corncob pipe that he loved and chewed on and actually smoked, and he had absolute confidence in himself and in what he was going to do—which was to beat the Japanese and return to the Philippines.

It had this strange effect on me because, being young and stupid I suppose, I'd been depressed over what was happening. I really had fallen for a lot of the public hysteria, I suppose, that the Japanese would come here and invade the place. But MacArthur just said that he was going to win and he talked to us and just radiated something that comforted me, at least. And I think a lot of the editors fell for him a bit too. That was the feeling at first that he was the thing we needed to turn things around, and he was the symbol of course of the US and we all looked forward to the kindly, helpful US people

coming in here and fixing things up. Typical Australian reaction—we do always seem to expect somebody else to fix up our problems.
John Hinde, ABC war correspondent, Sydney

When MacArthur and his wife came, they'd just got off the submarine from the Philippines, and she was only wearing a snood around her head and a coat which she had clutched around her because she apparently got out in a hurry and didn't bring very much with her. Now, the protocol was that he would not have her introduced to anybody in any sort of position, until she was properly clothed. So therefore she was taken into Isleys, which was a very exclusive costumier's in Collins Street, and she was fitted out. Everything else stopped the whole week while Mrs MacArthur was clad and then by the weekend she was able to be received by the Governor and the Lord Mayor and everyone else of any high priority.
Patricia Penrose, Isley's dress designer, Melbourne

MacArthur was given the royal treatment by the Australian parliament, as part of the American takeover. No Eastern potentate visiting his dominions was ever treated with the royalty that MacArthur got—given a seat in parliament, on the floor of the House, and his word was law, what he wanted he got, and he of course was a bit of a demi-god, he loved the limelight, he loved photographers. The press fell over backwards to give him all the adulation that he wanted.
Niall Brennan, university student and pacifist, Melbourne

Little Arthur was here too with an amah [Filipina nanny] and she used to take him down to the Botanical Gardens to feed the swans. And General MacArthur always had a very good suite right up in Menzies Hotel, which was the best one, and he liked playing the piano so they had to carry a piano up the stairs at Menzies right to his suite. Because MacArthur always got what he wanted, some way or other.
Patricia Penrose

I was with him once and he frightened me to death. I got into this elevator at Lennons Hotel in Brisbane and who was in there but MacArthur and we just stood at attention to every floor. I don't know whether he was approachable or not, he looked very stern at the time.
Roy Parker, pilot, US Air Force

3 The Aussies and the Yanks

They were all conscripts sent to fight here, and they didn't appear in the slightest to resent the fact that here was I, of military age, apparently in good health but in civilian clothes. They never asked me, they were completely tolerant. They loved Australia, they loved the girls, and the girls loved them back. I guess they were noisy, more outgoing than Australians, they were pretty likeable really. But of

course at that stage, very early on, we were very much disposed to like them, they were our saviours you see.
Bob Bahnsen

All of a sudden there were thousands and thousands of Yanks pouring off ships here. Well the girls were very excited about this I can tell you and they weren't backward in coming forward. The town became a riot, an absolute riot, because all the Yanks wanted to come to Sydney, it was even then the Mecca of Australia. Kings Cross was a panic, you kept pushing soldiers away to go in and get a hamburger. But they had great fun.
Ken G. Hall

I think that the first thing that impressed me about the Americans was their demeanour. They were well presented, they all looked like generals. Their Marines in particular with their beautiful dark green top and khaki pants and highly polished shoes and a million medals—they all looked great.
George Kendall, cinema projectionist, Sydney

There were so many things that are different from now and men had buttoned flies, all army uniforms had buttoned flies, and then along came the Yanks and they had zippers—and you found yourself trying not to look. They really made the front of trousers very neat, I tell you, and they really didn't come into the civilian population in Australia, zippers, until the war had ended—but oh, very neat.
Patsy Adam-Smith, VAD nurse

They varied very much in their manner. Some of them were very bold people; they'd say, 'Hey sister', or something like that to any woman. But they varied from that to, 'Excuse me, ma'am', sort of quiet country boys I suppose, in a country as big and varied as that. But we were glad to see them.
Maurie Jones, schoolboy, Perth

The first time I ever saw a man carrying a bunch of flowers was the Americans.
Patricia Penrose

We were fascinated by the accents, formerly we'd only known them from the movies. And I remember seeing things in the shops, beside the cash registers, giving the equivalents in Australian money and American money, and the government said, well, it'll have to be legal tender, because they couldn't suddenly produce enough coins and notes from nowhere to exchange all this money, especially as the Yanks did have a lot of money compared to our people.
Maurie Jones

After I'd met quite a few of them it seemed to me that in the main

'All in all it was a wonderful time': Dulcie Cunningham, Beaudesert, Queensland, with an American friend.

they had a great way of looking at things. They had a wonderful feeling for the joy of living. They were courteous, well mannered in the main, and some people used to say to me, 'Oh I think that's just a big act, they're just putting it on to impress people'. But it wasn't, that was just the way they were.
Joan Bentson

I lived in Beaudesert, which was a country town outside Brisbane, and the troops came there for rest and recreation. There was an American camp, and then there was an Australian camp and the Light Horse, and the American Marines came at one time. And all in all it was a wonderful time, and *they* had a wonderful time and I used to entertain them round at my house, bring them home for dinner, make them feel at home and I think because they were away from home so much they just appreciated it. Of course a lot of the Americans, they were pretty forward, they said if ever they saw a house that had a beautiful green lawn, they'd jump over the fence or over the gate and they'd just lie on this lovely lawn and they said ten to one they'd be asked for dinner. I couldn't see an Australian doing that!
Dulcie Cunningham, housewife and mother, Beaudesert, Queensland

The only American I met was on the train and I was knitting and I ran out of wool and I got the spare skein out and I was holding it on my own hands and winding the ball as well, as you do, and he was sitting opposite me and he presently leant over and he said, 'For Gawd's sake give me that wool', and he took it on his hands and I went on winding.
Vi McLauchlan, housewife and mother, Melbourne

Now I'd heard about Americans but I'd never met them. And they came off the train and one of them came up to me and said, 'Say girl'—what's he want me to say 'girl' for?—and he says, 'Say girl, where's the nearest drugstore?'. And I thought drugstore, drugstore, now I have heard of that, that means buying sweets and we had two what we used to call sweet shops so I said, 'Up the road'. I often wonder what happened up there because we didn't have sweets at that time, with sugar rations and everything.

Margaret Burton, schoolgirl, Adelaide

Our town was a quiet little town and all of a sudden the Yanks arrived and what a cloudburst—they came out of the sky, they came down the streets in four-wheel drive jeeps and of course real typical Yanks—some of them was even smoking big cigars—I'll never forget that. Long-legged fellas they were and drove down the street and our town, it just came to life.

Well, they got out in the country in their planes and they really showed off, and the cows jumped fences and went into the neighbours' paddocks and that night when we went to milk our dairy cows—well all they would do, it was like we gave them a packet of Laxettes.

The Yanks had plenty of everything, they had cigarettes, they had money, and they were very kind-hearted people, they'd give you anything and they used to give us Pall Mall cigarettes. They were quite a lot longer than Australian cigarettes and very mild, I know we used to love to get hold of these Pall Mall cigarettes, we were just learning to smoke in those days.

Charles Janeway, schoolboy, Mt Gambier, South Australia

They did things very very nicely, but then of course they had the money. They had a PX store and there were things in it that Australians had never seen—Carnation milk that we used for cream as a substitute; Nescafé, which was instant coffee which had not come into Australia before; and other things—sweets, nylon stockings—so they had a great advantage in many, many respects.

Toni Mooy Hurley, Army records office, Darwin

They made an R & R Centre here and they took over half the town and unless you lived there or had kin there, you couldn't come home on leave to Mackay, it was a closed town. It was Yanks, Yanks and that's it, and they had a whale of a time.

They used to fly them down, and they were here for ten days and they'd have at least a hundred quid in their pocket when they got there and they all went back broke so somebody got a big slice of that. The taxis would take them via the moon to go round the block if they could scrounge enough petrol, and the publicans were charging five quid for a 17s 6d bottle of Scotch and one reputable firm used to hire out push bikes to them with a quid deposit and five bob a day, and they'd have the local kids going to pinch the bikes back. Another old fellow used to put about six straws on an old wagon with a

*Lillian (Clark) Harding, aged
10, with her mother Ethel in
Adelaide. A pound in the
Parklands turned into a new
pair of shoes for a friend.*

burnt-out horse and the Yanks would hire this to take the girls for a
hayride down the beach of a night-time. And after the war there was
a lot of people had a lot of money—black money—salted away and
they were very quiet about it, but these new rich appeared.
Roger Jones, schoolboy, Mackay, Queensland

I remember a friend of mine found a pound note in the South
Parklands once, and it had been used as toilet paper so—I mean, a
pound note was a lot of money to a child—so she took it home and
showed her mother and they washed it and ironed it and then
sprayed a bit of perfume on it and her mother bought her a pair of
shoes, probably the first new pair of shoes that she had ever had.
Lillian Harding, schoolgirl, Adelaide

Of course the American not being familiar with the Australian
currency, he was very easy sheep to shear and they really fleeced
them, same as the nightclubs and that, they used to double and triple
what we'd pay in a nightclub for the same reason.
Athol Meers, aircraft construction supervisor, Sydney

A friend of mine was carrying a baby in her arms, and a Yankee voice
stopped her and said how old is your baby? And she told him and he
said, 'Oh I've got one that age at home, could I hold her?'. And he
held the baby for a while, just to get the feeling of what his baby was
like.
Vi McLauchlan

They were always so charming. Australians were very modest people
and our standard of morals, I think were very high compared with
people from overseas. I mean the things that they would talk about

kind of at times shocked me a bit, and I think they rather fascinated us.
Dulcie Cunningham

4 The American had a way about him . . .

One very big factor which stood out, the first thing you noticed when you met an American, was their manners. They had very good manners with women. A woman likes to be spoken to properly and treated properly, and naturally when they were treated so well by the Americans, the reaction was quite profound. Almost everyone went out with some Americans, because they were just everywhere and we had no Australians to dance with.
Joy Boucher, aircraft construction worker, Sydney

All life changed radically in Perth from then on because suddenly you had this influx of American airmen—on Catalina boats mainly—and American army personnel, but particularly American sailors and submarine ratings. And the streets of Perth suddenly became this R and R joint, with all the girls rushing round after the Americans because they'd never been treated like this in their lives, with orchids and lots of money and fur coats and nice speeches. Australians didn't really go in for those things very much.
Dorothy Hewett, university student, Perth

They seemed to treat you more like a lady. That's how we felt. They had very good pay, so they had a lot of money to spend. They were quite gentlemanly, most of them, that my friends and I met. Very well-spoken. We brought them home to meet our mothers, and of course they came with flowers for our mothers, which *they* were thrilled about. So we had a wonderful time.
Nora Symonds, textile worker, Sydney

Overnight there were a lot of women sort of came out of the woodwork or wherever they came from, I don't know, but they stayed for the duration of the Americans being here. They had orchids, they had nylon stockings, they had coffee, they had cigarettes, they had all these things that the ordinary person couldn't have had.
Patricia Penrose

I used to get the *Herald* every day just to see where they were going to berth and I would rush to the Quay or wherever the ship was coming in and we'd stand there and there'd be taxis waiting and when they come down the steps, 'Hello babe, can you show me a good time?'—grab 'em up and in the cab and up to Kings Cross.

   The American—he had a way about him, he was warm, he was wonderful, now even as I talk it makes me feel young again. The

American really had IT. I wasn't interested in Australian men any more, the American had me, right on, I was really rapt.
Pat Grainger, prostitute, Sydney

My sister was in a concert party that used to go round and entertain the troops and she came to me one day and said would I mind if she brought two or three of them home to our place? She said all they want is to be in a home and to have the home foods and to potter around. And they used to come and bring all sorts of goodies and have parties, we used to have a wonderful time with them, they were a marvellous bunch of men.

They were much more polite to you than the men here were, and they were very generous too. They used to bring wonderful stuff—cigarettes and grog and coffee, and all sorts of extras that they got, they would bring along for us.
Barbara Doig, housewife and mother, Perth

It was nothing for me to go home and find my parents at the weekend had two or three Americans to a meal, and sometimes they'd have nurses. There was a number you could ring if you wanted to give them hospitality, and they'd come out and have a meal Saturday or Sunday evening, whenever they had leave.

And it was quite commonplace to ask them if they'd like a bath, because they never got baths in camp and if they could wallow in a bath and just slosh around in it–my mother'd give them some very nice soap, not scented but quite masculine soap—they thought that was wonderful and there was no hurry for them to come out. They usually said, 'Oh yes thanks!'. My mother got used to cooking hot apple pie and putting ice-cream on, something that she'd never heard of before. But they were extremely nice and I think my mother felt that if the occasion ever arose she would like somebody else to be doing that for her son. She felt that they were a long way from home and it was nice for them to have hospitality and learn something about us.
Patricia Penrose

We entertained some Americans, but we entertained the Negro soldiers. There were always appeals for people to entertain American servicemen and we just specified yes we'd like to do that but we would prefer black Americans. There was a bunch of them, I'll never forget it, we got to know a Sergeant Bazza and he'd organised within the armed forces some friends of his into a choir, and we had them out at home singing and they were wonderful. They sang quite a number of the old spirituals mostly—'Sweet and Low', and all those sorts of old Negro songs and they sang without accompaniment, they harmonised, and they were really beautiful to listen to.
Joyce Batterham, Communist Party worker, Sydney

All our female cousins and people that I'd grown up with made acquaintances with the American servicemen and I guess I was really shocked and really impressed, being a 15-year-old girl and seeing all these American photos all round the house and seeing flowers delivered to the door, florists actually coming to the door with bouquets, and this kind of thing we'd never experienced before. We really felt a little bit of Hollywood came to us at that time. There was lots of money and they used to get taxis everywhere and they introduced a lot of music and dance to us and different styles of foods and they seemed to have an abundance of everything, and we of course had very little. We were very, very impressed by them.

They used to come to Redfern [a Sydney suburb] and come in and out of our houses of a day and of an evening, and we'd go to ships' dances and it was a very, very happy time with lots and lots of music and activity and laughter and fun.

What I'd known about black Americans prior to the war was only what I'd seen on movies, and they were the servants. That was very obvious. The other thing that made an impression was that they used perfume and talc powders and the old Aussie, he didn't go in for that type of stuff so we were a bit puzzled about that for a while. I guess they also introduced us to chewing gum cause they always chewed gum. But of course the dancing was the thing that we were impressed by and there was a club called the Booker T. Washington and it was exclusive black and we used to go to in there to the marvellous band and that marvellous jitterbug and the dancing. So it was really exciting because we'd not had anything like this before in our lives.

They made us feel like we were someone, because they said wonderful things to us, like we had eyes like the stars—they sparkled like the stars. They said lovely words of endearment that the Australian man didn't do and called us 'honeychild' and always told us we were beautiful and it was just what I think Americans called the jive and we call bulldust, so a lot of that was around too and it was really nice.

But we were two totally different races. The American struck you as being a very overconfident person, who was a skite as we'd call it, a showoff, terribly sure of himself. We were very different in that sense.

They were really out to impress people, and they were very overconfident and we certainly were not.
Pansy Hickey, textile worker, Sydney

We used to laugh at the dances because sometimes the lights would fail and the boys would take that opportunity to give you a kiss and a cuddle, and I remember once a soldier wrote to me and he said he had pleasant memories of the Beaudesert blackouts. My husband got this letter and he said, 'What does this mean?!'.
Dulcie Cunningham

The women said the Americans knew how to treat women and the

Australians were a bit flabbergasted by this, they didn't know where
they were going to get this sort of tuition in a hurry. When I was
home on leave my father used to have Americans in, and women
would come down for weekends, and I listened to all this palaver and
it was a bit amazing, but I got a bit of firsthand tuition there,
something to carry on with.
Merv Lilley, artilleryman, Torres Strait

When the Americans arrived, this changed the whole aspect of our life
in Canberra. We were living this puritanical sort of nunnery-type life
there, with no dancing, and suddenly here were all these Americans
with their Hershey bars and silk stockings and cigarettes and motor
cars—they even had enough money on their salaries in Australia to
buy motor cars. So we all got American boyfriends, you were mad if
you didn't because it just made such a big difference to life.
Shirley Fenton-Huie, WRANS, Canberra

My sister had an apartment in Vaucluse [a Sydney suburb] and a
girlfriend of hers rang her and said would it be all right if I bring up
some American servicemen, just looking for some place to go to feel
at home, and she said OK so five of them knocked at the door. They
just walked in and I remember I was standing at the sink washing
dishes and Fred came over and said, 'I think that I'll take this one',
and I said to myself, 'Oh fresh Yank!'.
Margaret Blair, office worker, Sydney

And about three days later I called her up and said I'd like to take
her out for a date, and she's been my girl ever since.
Fred Blair, US Air Force

He actually proposed the first time I went out with him. He told me
in a taxi that he loved me and that he knew that I was the one and
he wanted to marry me and I said, 'You crazy Yank'. But he kept it
up and I just weakened and when he came on the second leave, I
said yes.
    Of course my parents were not thrilled about me getting serious
with an American serviceman, which was natural. Then I brought him
home and they met Fred and they just loved him. They said if this is
the guy for you, then you go with him to America, and they never
gave me a hard time about it, and within a year that we met we
married.
Margaret Blair

Actually in order to get married at that time I had to get permission
from my squadron commander, but also from the 5th Bomber
Command, who was a General Ramey, and he was pretty rough. He
said we had a war to fight and this was no time to get married or
even think about it. And I told him I was quite determined, that I had
planned on it, and he said, 'Your plans are no good, our plans are to

'He actually proposed the first time I went out with him': Margaret and Fred Blair after their marriage in December 1943.

win this war and we need you and I'm not going to sign any papers for you'. But I said, 'I'm not going to leave here until you sign them'. So he did.
Fred Blair

We met at a dance at the City Hall, and I was with a group of girls who'd been asked by the Red Cross to go to the dances.
Joan Bentson

And I just sort of picked her out and danced with her and we danced real well together and she was quite attractive and I took her home on the tram and as usual I went to kiss her goodnight and she said, 'Oh no, my mother might be looking!' so we didn't kiss goodnight. But after that we became very friendly and I met her folks and one thing led to another, and four months later we were married.
Bill Bentson, staff sergeant, US Army

My mother felt that if I went to America she'd never see me again, and I was only 17, but I just told her that if I had to wait ten years I'd marry him, so she may as well give me permission right now. But some people were critical and I didn't know until some years later that one of my mother's best friends was quite amazed that I was allowed to marry an American.

But it wasn't a lavish wedding by any means, and after the reception we left the church and went to the honeymoon hotel in the tram.
Joan Bentson

One of my mother's best friends was quite amazed that I was allowed to marry an American': Joan Staines on her wedding day in March 1943, when she married US Army staff sergeant Bill Bentson (right).

5 It took us a while to catch on . . .

Well we knew the language, English language, but it was the slang that got us—'sheila' for girl and 'knocked up' and things like that, 'fair dinkum'—and it took us a while to catch on to all these colloquialisms but it didn't take us long.

They gave us a booklet which we were supposed to read, about Australia, but we didn't pay much attention to it. We knew there were kangaroos and ostriches, or emus down here. But Cola-Cola was available and produced here and you had American signs, like Kodak, Ford, and Shell Oil Company, than we knew in the States, and it was recognisable that the Australians knew a lot more about the Americans than we knew about them, and also they saw the movies and travelogues and everything on the United States.

Australia I think was quite isolated and the American influx during the war put Americans in nearly every hamlet, city and town in Australia, and they were the first foreigners that the Australians had met. And of course they took us into their homes and we learned a lot from them and they learned a lot from us.
Bill Bentson

It was a bit old-fashioned. My first impression was seeing some of the old cars—you had 1933 Studebakers and 1934 cars and you had the burners on the back with the charcoal to save on the gasoline. It just seemed old-fashioned. And the women, they wouldn't go to town

without a hat and a pair of gloves, they were so much more ladylike, where the American women had gone through that bobby-sox stage, wearing beer jackets and saddle shoes. The Australian woman, to me, was like the type of woman my mother was when she was young—that's the impression I got of the Australian women.
Donald Sauer, sergeant, US Army

The Americans thought that the Australian woman was really downtrodden, and we'd go to functions that were put on by the different organisations and the Australian men would be at this end of the floor and the Australian women would be at the other end of the floor and it seemed like the women were being overlooked and not catered to, and segregated. It seemed like the men didn't want to have too much to do with them—they'd be having a joke and yakking amongst themselves in a sort of a man's world and the women were just sort of left to dance with, and things like that.

And there were other things the Americans couldn't understand. In America you get on the train, you go from New York to San Francisco without changing trains. But when we got on the train in Sydney, to go to Melbourne, we had to change at Albury because of the different gauges.

Well, after we were here a while, the American engineers made a plan that they could change the track over so that they could go from Sydney to Melbourne without changing trains. And there was such a fuss about it by the unions, saying they would put all these baggage handlers out of jobs in Albury, that the Americans didn't push it. Headquarters didn't want to cause any animosity with the unions or the Labor Government, so the Americans had to go along with the routine that was normal, even though it did slow things down.
Bill Bentson

The first sergeant came up to me one day and he said, 'Get a hundred men'. I got a hundred men, arranged for trucks from the motor pool and went down to Glebe Island [Sydney]—the wharfies were on strike, they wouldn't load the ships for the United States Army or for their own Army. I had a mobile kitchen down there for two or three weeks, and we loaded the ships and unloaded the ships and as far as the wharfies were concerned, I thought it was a dreadful thing. You had men up there getting shot at, getting killed, waiting for supplies and ammunition and everything else like that—and they're going on strike. I lost respect for the wharfies' union to be honest. How can you forget a thing like that?
Donald Sauer

The Yanks got things done. If something had to go through channels, it didn't go through channels, it got done before that, and that's one thing I think the Australians noted—when the Americans would come in and for example build a complete airport in a part of Queensland overnight.

'The women were so much more ladylike': Donald Sauer, US army, with Daisy Fahey, the girl he met and married in Sydney.

They had some difficulty at times with the city council about getting something approved. Out in Toowong there was a park there with two brick pillars up on both sides, and they weren't wide enough to get the military trucks through, so they went to the city council and this went on for a while. It went on so long that the Colonel came down one day with a detail and he just moved this one pillar over so the trucks and things could get in, and there was a bit of a ruckus about that.
Bill Bentson

I can remember the Americans set up a headquarters in Prahran, in Melbourne, and they applied to the PMG which at the time was telephones and post office, for some telephones. And they said, 'Oh yes, how many do you need?'. And they told them how many and the next day they didn't arrive. So they called up and said, 'These telephones haven't arrived'.

And he said, 'Oh it's going to be two or three months'.

'But we need them now'—oh they were sorry, but you can't get them before that period of time.

So the Commanding Officer dispatched some of his signalmen, and they just started removing public telephones from everywhere, brought them into headquarters and he had his men climb the telephone lines and install them themselves, and so they had telephones in two or three days. I don't think they were very popular with the PMG though.
Roy Parker

Another thing the Americans weren't used to—when we got to Melbourne the pubs all had closing time at six o'clock and I

remember the first time we were in the pub there, we were having a few beers and then they said, 'closing time in five minutes', and everybody's buying as many drinks as they could to put away before they had to be booted out at six o'clock and this didn't go over very well.
Bill Bentson

Typewriters were at a priority in those days and in the built-up areas like Melbourne you just couldn't come across a typewriter for sale. So they just grabbed an old C47 and went to every country town in Victoria and picked up all the typewriters—there were none left—and they came back with an aeroplane full of typewriters.
Roy Parker

They were very critical of Australia, and they were very insular people—Americans do tend to be almost as insular as Australians, I think, and talk about it more, which is more of a problem.
John Hinde

6 A boy from Alabama

We tried to develop, particularly, good relations with the black soldiers and encourage them, so we used to invite them to various functions. Because they really were treated very badly by the Command and by the white American soldiers.

I can remember for example talking to a very nice young American soldier, white, from the south who said, 'Well, negroes are not really people, they don't have a soul like you and I'. And it was very hard to comprehend even, let alone accept such a concept.
Laurie Aarons

They didn't have black Americans in this part of the world, that I know of, in combat outfits. They were mostly in transportation and labour organisations, quartermaster and the like, which was very demeaning.
Roy Parker

The coloured troops, as they called them in those days, were segregated and in most instances there were coloured troops and white officers. The Australian government of course had the White Australia policy at the time and they weren't too keen on American Negroes being shipped here and this was another touchy political situation that MacArthur's staff had to put up with. The Australian government at the time, I think the Queensland government, suggested that the American Negro troops be put out on St Helena Island which lies off in the bay there, to segregate them.

The troops that arrived originally were all service troops—like engineers and quartermaster truck companies—and the quartermaster

truck company was sent up to Mt Isa to get them out of the
populated areas, and the engineers were sent north to Queensland to
build airstrips, so in a sense they were a bit isolated, and there was
one town up north that was set aside—I'm not sure where—where the
coloured troops were allowed to go on leave. Again, they were
segregated as to where they could go, they couldn't spend their
weekend down on the Gold Coast or something like that.
Bill Bentson

Black Americans were definitely the lower caste of the US armed
services. My home town, Brisbane—I'd go home on leave and they
were kept south of the river over at South Brisbane, they weren't
allowed to cross the river where the central business district and the
social centre of Brisbane was, on the northern side. All the coloured
people were kept on the southern side, and of course that was
Aborigine territory there too. And so they were left to cohabit with
each other—the Aborigines and the black Americans. They got on
quite well together, but naturally the Americans thought that they were
superior to the Aborigines, who were a very depressed, shy
community at that time.
    But separation of the races, this was an edict of the United States
administration, not the Australian government.
Ken Cunningham, seaman, RAN

Another thing that I remember was the harshness of the military
police—there was an occasion where they shot an American Negro
who was associated with some Aboriginal people in Surry Hills and
they called him to come out of the toilet and he did, with arms up,
and they just shot him down. Even the Australian police were really
shocked at the American military police attitude towards their own
servicemen.
Pansy Hickey

The American troops, the Catalina pilots and others, were stationed
out the back of the university and we used to have dances every
Friday night, and I remember these black guys used to come and look
in the window and sort of tap their feet to the 'Dark Town Strutters
Ball' or whatever we happened to be jitterbugging to, and look so
much as if they wanted to be part of it all that I remember one night
a couple of us went out and said, 'Why don't you come in?'. And they
said, 'Oh no, ma'am, we couldn't do that, we couldn't come in to join
in with you people'. And I'm sure that lots of black servicemen must
have been incredibly lonely in that society because Australia was a
very racist society and Western Australia perhaps more than most,
because of the Aborigines, and I imagine they must have had some
very unpleasant experiences in that little city then. Some girls went
out with black servicemen but they were shunned and talked about as
if they were the lowest thing that crawled.
Dorothy Hewett

'We really felt a little bit of Hollywood came to us at that time': Pansy (Lester) Hickey (right) with friends Barbara, Christine Hinton (second left) and an American serviceman known as 'Slim' at the Booker T. Washington Club in Surry Hills, Sydney.

The thing that just sort of blew my mind was the segregation between the black and white servicemen. 'Course we as Aboriginals had experienced racism ourselves and segregation—I had lived on Aboriginal missions and reserves under managers and wasn't able to go to secondary school, and things like that so I'd actually experienced that but I had nothing to draw comparison with and when the American servicemen came out, this was one of the things, the blatant segregation.

With the Aboriginal people, there was so much paternalism there, and some subtleties, so to a degree it was a soft kind of racism I guess, but with the American servicemen, the black and white, it was just straight down the middle with them. Navy men that served on the same ship walked past each other, never spoke, wouldn't even look at them. We had dances on aircraft carriers, we went there as visitors, and that was one of the things that's always stuck in my mind.

But they had such freedom here in this country, and we were just so friendly and we were the right type of people for them when they came on furlough, in the sense that we did open our homes to them, we were very impressed by them and we made them feel very welcome. They were very good for us as well and even our Aboriginal men were impressed by the American servicemen and they made friends of them and I don't recall any kind of jealousies at all by the Aboriginal men towards the Americans, I think they were as impressed as anybody was.

Pansy Hickey

Some of them were very surprised to find that they'd been accepted.

At first they were a bit on edge—would it be all right?—but after a while they just relaxed, used to walk anywhere and there was no trouble. And everyone just got to know them, different ones that came through and they were very friendly, very happy, we never had no trouble, not in Redfern. Children used to chase them for money, and they always had money for the little ones.

Christine Hinton, textile worker, Sydney

6

In the Balance

Today Port Moresby and Darwin are the Singapores of Australia. If those two places fall then, inevitably, we are faced with a bloody struggle on our soil when we will be forced to fight grimly, city by city, village by village, until our fair land may become a blackened ruin . . . Our fate is in the balance as I speak to you. The Battle of the Solomons is not only vital in itself, but, as part of a continuing action which will go on, it represents a phase of the Japanese drive in which is wrapped up invasion of Australia.

The Prime Minister, John Curtin, in a national broadcast, 3 September 1942.

Although the arrival of General MacArthur in late March, and his assumption of command of the South-West Pacific Area the following month, raised public morale, the Japanese threat had not disappeared. For the next six months the strategic situation would be in the balance, Allied successes being countered by new Japanese initiatives. And these events would have a direct effect on people in Australia.

Pursuing their plan to isolate Australia, in mid-April the Japanese decided to attack and land at Port Moresby in Papua New Guinea, and as a preliminary, they seized the island of Tulagi in the Solomon Islands. Then, to protect their landing at Port Moresby, the Japanese sent a fleet with three aircraft carriers into the Coral Sea. In the famous Battle of the Coral Sea, the Japanese fleet was intercepted by a combined US and Australian naval force including two US carriers, and on 7 May US and Japanese carrier-borne planes attacked the opposing fleets. The Japanese secured a slight tactical victory, losing one small carrier with another damaged. The US also lost a carrier with the other being damaged. But strategically it was a major Allied victory as the Japanese Port Moresby invasion force returned to Rabaul.

MacArthur still expected another Japanese attack on Australia, and his expectations seemed to be confirmed during the following month. On 20 and 30 May 1942, Japanese aircraft were detected over Sydney, and on the night of 31 May Japanese midget submarines entered Sydney Harbour. They tried to sink the US cruiser *Chicago*, missed, and sunk an Australian barracks ship instead, killing nineteen sailors. On the night of 7 June, large Japanese submarines fired several shells into Sydney and Newcastle. Meanwhile Japanese submarines had been conducting an effective campaign off the Australian coast, sinking three merchantmen during a period of nine days.

While these submarines were operating off Sydney, the main Japanese fleet was sailing towards Midway in the central Pacific. The US Navy had broken the Japanese codes and three US carriers intercepted the Japanese on 2 June. In one of the crucial battles of the war, the Japanese lost four aircraft carriers while the US lost one.

For a few weeks it seemed that the defence of Australia was assured, but for the troops in northern Australia and New Guinea the situation looked less encouraging. Darwin continued to endure periodic air raids, and although an Australian Independent Company was continuing a guerrilla war in Timor, the Japanese forces were nearby and could easily have crossed the Timor Sea to land on Australia's unprotected coastline. Unable to deploy major units across this vast area, in March 1942 the Australian Army initiated a plan to establish a surveillance unit that could report Japanese landings and carry out guerrilla war against them if they did land. The North Australia Observer Unit was formed and it began operations in August 1942.

In New Guinea, the Japanese at Lae and Salamaua were starting to move inland, and they were countered only by commando-type units. Following the Battle of the Coral Sea, additional militia units were sent to Port Moresby, but MacArthur had his eyes elsewhere, and kept back the veteran AIF units which had returned from the Middle East.

Buoyed by the Midway success, he now planned to mount an offensive with the aim of recapturing Rabaul. The Japanese beat him to the punch, and on 21 July a Japanese advance party landed at Buna on the north Coast of Papua with the aim of preparing for a major advance over the rugged Owen Stanley mountains to seize Port Moresby. Neither MacArthur nor Blamey had believed that the Japanese would attempt such an advance, and had failed to provide sufficient defences for New Guinea.

To coincide with this new offensive, the Japanese renewed their submarine activity off the Australian coast and between 20 July and 3 August sunk three Allied merchantmen. On the night of 25 July, three Japanese flying boats bombed Townsville, with a single plane returning on 28 and 29 July. There was little danger, but it was salutary reminder that Australia was still under threat.

Meanwhile the Japanese offensive in New Guinea had developed momentum, and towards the end of August they landed troops at Milne Bay and began a major attack on the Kokoda Track. After several days of hard fighting, the landing at Milne Bay was defeated by Australian troops and fighter aircraft, but the poorly supported Australian forces on the Kokoda Track were forced back by superior numbers. There were signs of panic among some senior members of the government, and troops were rushed to New Guinea. As an indication of the anxiety in Australia, MacArthur asked Curtin to order General Blamey to go to Port Moresby and personally take command of the operations there.

When the Americans landed a marine division at Guadalcanal in the Solomons, the Japanese had to divert resources to counter the American initiative at Guadalcanal. As a result, in mid-September the Japanese high command ordered a halt to the forces advancing on Port Moresby. Already their troops were desperately short of food and other supplies, as they had not expected the fierce rearguard action fought by the Australian troops over the Kokoda Track. Australian reinforcements were arriving in Port Moresby and the tide of battle turned.

In another month of fighting the Japanese were forced back to Kokoda, and by mid-January 1943 they had been eliminated from the north coast of Papua. After their defeat on the Kokoda Track the Japanese were never again able to pose a direct threat to Australia. But this assessment was not clear to the commanders at the time, and in the latter months of 1942 the Australian government continued to warn the public of the possibility of facing a Japanese invasion. The balance had tilted towards the Allies, but a maximum effort was still required.

1 Day of destiny

I was sowing wheat actually. My brother-in-law was in the VDC as well, and he came racing up in the car and he said, 'Just got word, be ready to be picked up at a moment's notice. Destination unknown'. So I went back down with him and we got all ready. We had all our battle gear on and everything, and we walked about there all day with our packs up till about seven o'clock that night, when they rang up and said we wouldn't be needed.

They were fighting the Coral Sea battle and if they'd lost the Coral Sea battle the Japs would have come into Australia somewhere up there and we were to be the first ones there if they came in. There were trains waiting down there to pick us up, we were 90 000 strong in NSW and they were to pick us up and take us north immediately so we would be gun fodder for the first Japs that came in.

We'd trained, we had the men that had been at the head of the First World War army, we had them training us right through the piece. I think I could have hit a man with a bayonet pretty easy if he came at me.

Ray Adams, VDC Gulgong, New South Wales

My outstanding recollection of the Battle of the Coral Sea was that it took place during the course of one of our frequent premiers' conferences, and we were sitting in Parliament House in Canberra and Curtin was obviously ill at ease. He wasn't giving his usual concentration to exactly what was taking place and eventually he realised that this had become noticeable and Curtin said, 'Gentlemen, I apologise for any feeling of lack of concentration which you may have perceived'. He said, and I've forgotten the exact words, but they were to the effect that, 'There is at this juncture taking place a large encounter which may well decide the destiny of Australia'. And that was the Battle of the Coral Sea.

Ralph Doig, Premier's Department, Perth

One of the things our group had to do was monitor Japanese stations and of course the Japanese morse code is dots and dashes anyway, we didn't know what they were sending but we could put on paper

what they were sending, and that'd be transposed by the experts into
the Japanese code. And we virtually followed the Coral Sea battle. I
don't think Australians at this stage realised how very close they were
to a landing in Australia by the Japanese. The Coral Sea battle was a
lot closer to an invasion of Australia than most people even now
accept.
Ren deGaris, wireless intelligence, RAAF, Darwin

I remember, it might have been after the Battle of the Coral Sea when
we owed so much to the Americans, there was a rumour that went
around, and I don't remember ever seeing it in print, but it was
certainly buzzed around by word of mouth, that the Australian
government was going to agree to be the 49th State of the United
States. And I remember hearing people discussing this with some heat,
because some people thought it would be a good idea. I remember
toying with it myself and thinking, well, at least that navy would be
around all the time, or part of it.
Maurie Jones, schoolboy, Perth

But there was no immediate feeling when the Coral Sea battle was
over, 'Oh well, that's the end of it, there's no more danger from the
Japanese'. Oh no, there was not the faintest suggestion of this.
Because they still had this powerful navy, almost on the foreshores of
Australia, and America of course was still feeling the deficiencies
following the destruction of their navy at Pearl Harbor. There was still
a threat, there's no doubt about that. This was only one encounter.
Ralph Doig

2 Under the bed, quick!

My girlfriend and I were on the Harbour that day, we went across to
Manly and we got home fairly late in the afternoon. And of course
that night, the air raid sirens sounded.
Nora Symonds, textile worker, Sydney

And we never heard anything like that in our lives before, these
blessed sirens. I lived in Five Dock and everyone rushed around and
our instructions were to go to the local police station, muster there, all
that sort of thing, but I said to my wife, 'We'll make a cup of tea first'.
Ray Blissett, policeman, Sydney

We were coming across the harbour that evening and just off Garden
Island the first torpedo hit and the boat went up and then of course
all hell broke out—searchlights and depth charges and all that.
Athol Meers, aircraft construction supervisor, Sydney

They blasted them out of the harbour, they give 'em the works, we

heard all the depth charges going off, oh it shook everything, all round.
Alan McMillan, dockworker, Sydney

There were air raid wardens everywhere in the streets. Immediate blackout. Searchlights all over the sky from Rosebery Racecourse where the Army were, and Kensington Racecourse, La Perouse. And we were frightened, we didn't know what was going to happen, whether it was going to be by sea or air.

My mother and I and my sister-in-law were home at the time and we went under my mother's dining-room table with a heavy cloth over it. My sister-in-law was a heavy smoker and she began to smoke and my mother really told her off—'I can't breathe! Put that cigarette out!'.
Nora Symonds, textile worker, Sydney

It was my birthday and I thought it was a terrible night to come. But I rushed over and I pushed the windows up—they were enormous windows—so there wouldn't be too much glass shattered in case it landed in Burwood. And looking out, these people across the road, every light went on and of course I forgot that I was supposed to be a lady and I screamed at them, 'Turn all your . . . . . lights off!' and they didn't want to be friendly with me ever again.

It was utter panic because even though we were close to the harbour we didn't know where it was of course, we had the radio on but they weren't telling you too much because nobody knew anything, it was panic and hell let loose, actually. I don't think we could've felt worse if we'd been right in the middle of it—it's the anticipation of 'Ooah, ooah, what's going to happen?'. But I thanked God up there that it was at night-time and I didn't have to go out and do things—I was a real coward.

But when the siren first went I didn't care about anything but jumping out of bed and opening the wardrobe, and my husband said to me, 'What are you getting in the wardrobe for?'. I said, 'I'm getting my coat out'. And I put it on over my pyjamas and I said, 'If I'm going to die, I'm going to die in this fur coat because I've loved it and it took such an effort to get it'. Oh that fur coat was beautiful, I had it for years.
Anne Pellew, ARP warden, Sydney

Before I went into the Navy I was living at Rose Bay with my mother and I had a boyfriend who was in the navy, and he was a sailor on HMAS *Kuttabul* which was moored near, at Garden Island [Sydney dockyard], and he came and had dinner with us and I remember my mother said, 'Oh don't go back, you don't have to be on duty till eight o'clock, why don't you stay the night, then you can have breakfast with us and get back to your ship early in the morning'.

Well of course that was the night that the *Kuttabul* was sunk by the midget submarines that came in through the net to the harbour, really

to try and sink the big American warship—missed that, and sank the
Kuttabul with all these sleeping sailors on it. So my dear friend
Dudley would have been on board and quite easily could've been
killed I suppose. He was saved by his girlfriend and her mother
prevailing on him to stay the night.
Shirley Fenton-Huie, schoolgirl, Sydney

It wasn't until later we listened on the radio and heard that the
Japanese subs had come in under the Manly ferries. And of course
when my friend and I heard that, we thought, 'Heavens, it could have
been *our* Manly ferry!'. I think people began to see what war was all
about then. Because I think a lot of people don't think terribly much
about it as far as them coming to Australia. It really hit home when
that happened.
Nora Symonds

After two days they brought up one of these Japanese submarines, I
remember the wires trailing from it and it had been blown in half by
a depth charge. And it was incredible, the whole of Sydney was
fascinated by this. And when the Japanese bodies were taken out
there was some dispute over whether there should be a funeral—or
what sort of funeral. And finally they gave them a decent army burial
with some honours, out at Rookwood [Sydney cemetery]. I rang Frank
Dixon, in charge of ABC news, and I said, 'Could I be there to cover
it?' and Frank said, 'Oh I don't think so—it'd be alright if they were
Christians'. And so we didn't actually cover the funeral.
John Hinde, ABC war correspondent, Sydney

About a week later we were going to bed and all of a sudden gunfire
broke out all down along Middle Head and all around, guns going off
willy nilly and I got up and became very abusive, I said 'What a hell
of a time to have gunnery practice, the middle of the bloody night
and they're going with gunnery practice, this is the Army all over', and
all that. Then all of a sudden something went boom! just up the road
from us and I said to my wife 'Under the bed, quick!'—but she
couldn't get under it because the bed was too low! The war really
came to Australia that night.
Ken G. Hall, managing editor, *Cinesound Review*, Sydney

I lived in Balfour Road Rose Bay and I'd just got into bed one Sunday
night, it was twelve o'clock, and then we were shelled from the
submarine and the shells were going right over our house and some
landed in the street, broke all the venetian blinds on a block of flats a
block away from us, blew the leaves off the trees, a lot went into the
bay and a lot into houses opposite us but you could hear them all,
right over us—it was frightening.
   Some people had air-raid shelters, but we didn't have one and I was
just walking around listening to them all—they were going right over
our house, and we said to my father, 'You'd better get into the hall, or

under the table'. But my father said 'If they get me they can get me in bed'—he wouldn't get out.
Daisy Sauer, Army records clerk, Sydney

The whole thing was a nine days wonder, people were swapping stories about the shells that had whistled just past their heads. There were only two or three really, but it was a good story.
John Hinde

I remember seeing in the paper a shell that hadn't gone off—it lodged in somebody's wardrobe. So you really knew that the Japs were not far away.
Jack Pollard, cadet journalist, Sydney

I was really quite frightened at that time I can tell you. I was only a very young girl and I remember having dreams about Japanese coming over the cliffs and coming in to us. I didn't know what raping was really but I knew it was something pretty horrible, and we were really quite frightened at that time. My father was away at the war and my brother was away at boarding school up in the mountains—there was just mother and I together. I think people have forgotten how frightened they were, really.

I don't think we ever thought to run away because we didn't know where we could run away to really. I think we just kept our fingers crossed and hoped for the best.
Shirley Fenton-Huie

People were leaving their homes, selling them for a song and moving up to Bourke to get away from the Japs. They panicked and away they went, couldn't get out quick enough.
Alan McMillan

My brother rang me up and said there's this huge house vacant, the tenants have just fled, which we can have for 25 pounds a month and it's big enough for all of us to share, two couples. It was in Castlecrag [a northern Sydney suburb] and it looked straight down the harbour. It had great big picture windows where you had the whole of Middle Harbour in front of you, so it was a beautiful location even if some people thought it was a bit risky.

We did have one funny experience there because the bedroom my husband Bob and I had upstairs, it had wardrobes with mirrors on the outside and we got a call from—not the ordinary police—the Special Branch. They visited us because they said that it had been reported that we had been sending out messages through the Heads. And of course what it was, as we finally managed to convince them, when we opened our wardrobe doors to put our clothes away at night, the lights flashed out way over to North Head or somewhere.
Joyce Batterham, Communist Party worker, Sydney

Joyce Batterham with husband Bobby and baby daughter in Sydney in May 1942. The police thought that they were sending messages down the Harbour to waiting Japanese submarines.

3 Having a go at us

At the coastal radio station we were listening on the frequency used by merchant navy ships and they only broke radio silence if they were attacked. I have records of many many attacks but the crunch really came with Japan's entry in the war, when submarines and aircraft were attacked around Australia. Submarines operated all around the Australian coastline and accounted for the loss of some 50 ships.
Phil Chapman, radio operator, Darwin

At one stage when we were in our training battalions in Melbourne, we had a stand-to-one night because a submarine had been spotted down off Balcombe in Victoria. There was a lot of shipping sunk off the Australian coast all the way round through to Adelaide, so the Japs knew all about where our shipping was going, and everything else.
Peter Huskins, North Australia Observer Unit

The Japanese subs were picking off ships and you didn't know how many and where they were, and that's why the convoy system was initiated. You got more protection—if you're on your own, you're a sitting duck.

On June 4th, we'd left Melbourne, we were running coal from Newcastle to the gasworks in Melbourne, and we were empty, light ship, returning to Newcastle for another load. I was in my bunk, it was about 5.30, dawn, and I heard this explosion and I got out of my cot and raced up on deck. We saw the mess of the hatch covers,

*Merchant seaman Barney
French whose ship was
torpedoed by a Japanese
submarine in 1942.*

where the shells had come back and split them in two and obviously
it didn't take us long to wake up that they were having a go at us.
And the fact that we were light ship, that's one of the reasons that
saved us—when they were shelling, the torpedo went under the ship;
but if we had've been carrying a cargo or if we'd had any draught at
all, well I don't know whether I'd still be here.

Of course we knew the subs were out, we'd heard the previous day
of the *Iron Chieftain* [sunk by Japanese submarines]. We had heard by
radio the SOS and mayday calls, we were aware of the fact that it
happened, but when it happens to you, it's a different story.
Barney French, merchant seaman

We could hear muffled booms, and then at approximately 2.17 a.m.
the alarm sounded and we took up our posts on the guns. The
battery commander ordered us to load high explosive shells, as we
were being attacked from the sea. The first two rounds were fired,
then we loaded again and just then the light from underneath Fort
Scratchley illuminated the target and the gun crew could be clearly
seen on the deck of the submarine, which was a large ocean-going
submarine. It was as clear as day, then it disappeared.

He would have had no trouble finding Newcastle whatsoever
because his ultimate aim was possibly to attack the powerhouse and
BHP and the whole of this area was lit up like a Christmas tree, he
could have lobbed a shell anywhere he liked.

There was a total of 24 shells fired from the submarine and you had

to see it to believe it, and following one week after the Sydney attack, it gave people something to think about—there was an exodus from the city the next day.
Jim Cannon, gunner, Fort Scratchley, Newcastle, New South Wales

Brisbane and Townsville were very heavily sandbagged, all through the centre of the city—public buildings, shopfronts, that sort of thing, because there was a great expectation of air raids in both cities.
Robert Squires, schoolboy, Warwick, Queensland

They dropped three or four bombs in the sea but of course the sirens went off all up and down the coast including Mackay and at that stage I was a runner for the ARP [Air Raid Precautions]. So the siren went off and I got out of bed very sleepily and switched the light on and Mum jumped right down my throat, so the light went off and I went round to the wardens' post and they had to race round with their little bags of sand and what have you and put out fires—anyway nothing much happened and that was the first and last go at Townsville they had.
Roger Jones, schoolboy, Mackay, Queensland

We were on a troop ship, about six days out of Sydney, and we spotted a submarine. We were unescorted but the ship was fairly fast, and we zigged and zagged for two or three or four days and evidently we lost them.

But I think the Japanese officer must have figured we were going somewhere round Sydney so he must have been going straight while we were zigging and zagging and he evidently caught up to us because a day or two out of Sydney, the submarine was spotted again. And I looked up to the horizon and I saw two ships and they happened to be the Corvettes, and all I could hear was hooting. Now whether they sunk the submarine or not I don't know.

I heard several days later that there were eight ships sunk on eight successive days off the coast of Australia and that was the ninth day—so thank you, Corvettes, we lived to fight another day.
Donald Sauer, sergeant US Army

4 First line of defence

When we were told about the advance of the Japanese in New Guinea—they were almost in Port Moresby, they were only 30 miles away—I really thought they were going to come, it was only a matter of where.
Amory Vane, North Australia Observer Unit ['Nackeroos']

The 'Nackeroos' were to act as small units, three or four men with a wireless set, spread throughout the whole of the Northern Territory, little groups scattered round the coastline and up through the rivers and in observation areas. It was thought that the Japanese were going to invade the northern part of Australia and come up the Roper River and the Ord River and other places like that. Our role was to let them overrun us, and we were to stay behind and report through on our sig. sets their strength, position, and whatever else they were doing; also to harry them and cause them strife. We were fairly heavily armed.

It was pretty much a top secret unit. They were looking for a special unit to work from that area and you were quietly asked would you like to join it. I was nineteen at the time.
Peter Huskins

Hazardous duty—those were the words they used. Our role was not to fight but to live off the land and follow the enemy. If we lost communications with our radio, then the obvious thing was to fight and act like a guerrilla force. We became very self-reliant.

We were going to act like the Boer troops—a hundred Boers could hold down a whole army and our job was to just hit and run, never to stand and fight. We were watching the rivers and the beaches and if anything moved we'd immediately report it by radio, but then we'd do patrols along the coast or inland and we'd also look for Spitfire pilots or Japanese that crash-landed from dogfights.

We were the first line of defence and they never anticipated that we'd last more than 24 hours.
Tip Carty, North Australia Observer Unit

Tip Carty makes friends with a local in Katherine, soon after arrival in the Northern Territory as part of the NAOU.

Aboriginal women near the NAOU Forrest River camp, north of Wyndham, come to say goodbye to their men who were about to go out on patrol. The Aboriginal people were indispensable to the work of the 'Nackeroos' in the harsh and often uncharted country of the North. (Photo: Amory Vane)

We relied on the Aboriginals tremendously. I don't think we travelled anywhere without at least one black tracker and sometimes we ended up with a number because you looked back and you'd find there'd be quite a group of Aboriginal women with their babies—very secretly coming along under the trees because they were trying to catch us up.
Amory Vane

One night we spotted this flare in the sky and then I spotted another plane signalling, but we couldn't hear them. It was obviously Japanese—we couldn't read the Morse code, anyhow. So we immediately signalled Darwin and we had direct contact with the Spitfires there, and they'd known there were Japanese in the air, but they didn't know which way they were coming because they'd gone beyond the radar screens. So they converged on this flare. And they got seven bombers that night.
Tip Carty

The isolation part of it was very severe because the rest of the country was empty behind us. Looking southwards, there was nothing until you got down to Broome or Derby, hundreds and hundreds of miles away. The first year, apart from large numbers of Aborigines, I think we only saw the other sixteen members of our platoon.
Amory Vane

Our rule was never to kill a crocodile. I had a very good friend who was a bushman up there and he said, 'Don't kill the crocodiles and

don't go into the water at night—if the Japanese come in and they want to get at your place, they're going to have to get into the water and there's so many crocodiles in there that they'll be lucky if they survive'. So they were our first line of defence really.
Tip Carty

Every night and every morning we had to report to platoon headquarters and also to north-west headquarters and naturally all the messages were sent in code. But if the Japs had their listening post out or submarines or something they would hear all this wireless chatter going from all these different areas and it would sound like there were thousands of men there instead of only a matter of a few hundred men. Which would have given the impression that they would need a lot more troops to come and take that area than what they really would've needed—because we were very thin on the top.

From what there was up there, I think they could've easily walked in.
Peter Huskins

7

Everyone Must Fight or Work

The Government . . . cannot permit anything to stand in the way
of placing the nation on a full war footing . . . To that end,
Cabinet has made decisions which will be the Government's lead
in the austerity campaign which is opened as from tonight.
Austerity means a new way of life; a new spirit of action to do
the things a nation needs and not to do the things that weaken
the nation.

**The Prime Minister, John Curtin, in a national broadcast 3
September 1942.**

The previous four chapters described how a series of external events affected
people in Australia. First there was the shock of the Japanese attack in
December 1941; then, with the fall of Singapore and the attack on Darwin
it appeared likely that Australia would be facing invasion. At this time of
anxiety, US forces began to arrive in Australia until in April General Douglas
MacArthur assumed command of the South-West Pacific Area. And finally,
from April to September 1942, the strategic situation hung in the balance,
oscillating between the Allied victories in the Coral Sea and at Midway, and
the Japanese submarine attacks on Sydney Harbour and on merchant ships
in Australian waters, followed by their ground offensive in Papua New
Guinea.

This chapter is concerned with how internal events in Australia affected
the public during this time of stress. Soon after the outbreak of war with
Japan, the Prime Minister, Curtin, gave notice that the government was
planning 'a complete revision of the whole Australian economic, domestic
and industrial life', and a little later he added that to achieve defence
requirements the government would act ruthlessly.

The following month, on 29 January 1942, the government established a
Manpower Directorate and appointed a Director-General of Manpower. The
directorate would have exceptional powers, in effect controlling all manpower in Australia. It would decide what every person should do in the armed
forces, war industry or civilian industry. It took several months for the
regulations to be framed and promulgated, and in the meantime a range of
other measures were begun.

Between 12 February (three days before the fall of Singapore) and 19
February (the day of the first attack on Darwin), the government instituted
a series of National Security Regulations. One regulation gave the Minister

for the Army power to declare an emergency in any part of Australia should that be required for defence purposes. Another regulation required any person resident in Australia to perform any specified services for the nation. On 16 February Curtin said: 'It is now work or fight as we have never worked or fought before'.

The details of the government's economic plan were co-ordinated by the Production Executive, which was a committee of nine Ministers chaired by the Minister for War Organisation of Industry, John Dedman. On 18 February he announced the first of a series of measures prohibiting the manufacture of a wide range of non-essential products.

The government's plans were designed to achieve a number of purposes, all of which were connected. First, they had to manage the nation's manpower efficiently. Between December 1941 and June 1942 the number engaged in civil production (excluding rural and domestic work) fell by about 140 000 while war production went up by 70 000 men and nearly 40 000 women. At the same time, 228 000 men and 12 000 women enlisted in the services.

The government also had to build the infrastructure necessary to conduct the war. Camps, airstrips, roads and ports had to be constructed, often in remote areas of Australia. In February 1942, the Allied Works Council was established to supervise big construction jobs for the war effort, and in April a Civil Construction Corps was set up. By June 1943 it had a strength of 53 500 men, 16 600 of whom had been conscripted. Some of these were men who had a conscientious objection to serving in the armed forces.

It was important to make best use of the nation's transport network. Railways were vital for transporting troops and war *matériel*, and soon regulations prohibited civilians from moving from one State to another without a permit. Meanwhile petrol and tyres for civilian vehicles were rationed even further.

All the while, the country needed to maintain food production, not only for home use, but to feed the thousands of American troops in Australia, and also to keep up vital exports to the United Kingdom. After May 1942, men in rural industries were no longer called up for the Army, and in July the Women's Land Army was formed to provide additional workers on farms, particularly where the original workers had joined the Army.

While men were required for the services, and food production had to be maintained, there could be no let-up in war production. The Menzies Government had already begun the production of weapons, planes and ships, but hundreds of other items were necessary. In particular, Australian factories had to produce uniforms, small arms, artillery, and ammunition for use by Australian troops fighting in New Guinea. Small ships were needed for operations in waters near to Australia, and there was a limit to what could be supplied by allies. To preserve industrial stocks and make best use of factory machinery, non-essential products were not to be made, and other items were rationed. For example, in June 1942 clothing rationing was introduced and quotas for cigarettes and tobacco were reduced by a quarter. The following month tea was rationed.

Additional money had to be found to pay for this war effort. Taxes increased, and in May 1942 the Commonwealth took sole responsibility for collecting income tax. The increase in numbers of people employed and in the level of their salaries and wages resulted in a much larger government income from taxation. For example, between 1939 and 1943 the total wages and salaries paid in factories almost doubled. On 15 April 1942, profit margins were pegged at the level applying on that date. But taxation could not pay for the war, and the public was constantly exhorted to contribute to War Loans, or to buy War Bonds.

All these measures were initiated during the first half of 1942, and by September 1942 people were beginning to feel shortages. However, the government felt that more needed to be done, and on 19 August 1942 the Prime Minister asked the Australian people 'to reconcile yourself to a season of austerity, to make your habits of life conform to those of the fighting services'. His austerity campaign was designed to support the raising of a loan of £100 million on the home market; to announce a series of decisions, such as restrictions on horse and dog races; but also to strengthen moral standards in the community. This latter purpose was emphasised when in a national broadcast he called for 'clean and honest thinking . . . By so doing we will be a nation which is morally and spiritually rearmed'.

However high-sounding these sentiments might have been, the public was soon confronted by the reality of the austerity campaign. Regulations required tailors to make only single-breasted suits; dresses had less pleats; and icing on cakes was prohibited, except for wedding cakes when only white icing was permitted. The press stretched the regulation restricting Christmas advertising in late 1942 into a story that Dedman was trying to abolish Father Christmas. The introduction of these austerity measures is touched on in this chapter, but their effect on individuals will be described in greater detail in Chapter 9.

While most Australians made a reasonably honest effort to pull their weight, a number became wealthy from black market trading. And some unions took the opportunity of the war to press for additional wages and better conditions. With the entry of the Soviet Union into the war in June 1941, Communists-controlled unions became more co-operative. Regulations were introduced to control strikes, but stoppages still continued. For the six quarters from March 1940 to June 1941, Australia had almost 600 disputes and lost 1.7 million working days. In the six quarters from March 1942 to June 1943 there were over 1000 disputes, but the number of days lost dropped below 1 million. It was an improvement. Although there were less days lost through strikes in 1942 than in any other year of the war, they were still more than in 1931, 1932 or 1933.

If the government was to show that it was serious about the war effort, a crucial issue was the deployment of conscripted soldiers overseas. Contrary to popular belief, the Labor Party had never really been opposed to conscription for home defence, and large numbers of the militia had been conscripted. But reflecting the attitudes of the great conscription debates of the First World War, the party was strongly opposed to their use overseas.

During the early fighting in New Guinea, this distinction did not matter because although conscripted militia battalions fought at Milne Bay and on the Kokoda Track, this was Australian territory. But should the campaign eventually move northwards, perhaps into Dutch New Guinea or the East Indies, the militia units would not be able to take part. Furthermore, by November 1942 US troops, who were mainly conscripts, were arriving in New Guinea. The charge could be laid that Australia's battles were being fought by US conscripts but Australian conscripts were being held back.

Curtin courageously faced this issue, and in a series of federal Labor conferences between November 1942 and January 1943, persuaded his party to accept a proposal for Australian conscripts to serve outside Australia. In February 1943 parliament passed an Act permitting Australian conscripts to serve in the South-West Pacific Area up to the equator.

By early 1943 Australia was working at a level it had never previously achieved. But it was already clear that the competing demands for manpower from the services, war production and rural industries could not be met. The time was approaching when the government would have to make reductions in one or more of these areas. However, the government hesitated to act until it could be sure that the threat of invasion had passed. Rapidly, following the Japanese attack in December 1941, the nation's economic, industrial and domestic life had been brought to a 'total war' footing. It was an experience few Australians who lived through it would forget.

1 The Manpower

Civilians all had to have an identity card and without that they couldn't have got their rations. And of course you couldn't cross State borders without written permits. You had to have a damn good reason to do that.

The identity card was not only necessary for labour purposes, but—although it might sound a bit hysterical—you do need to know who's who in wartime in your country. It also let the government know which boys were growing older, to be called up. It was a necessary evil, totally necessary though.

Everyone was registered. They'd go to the Post Office, get the forms, and there were big signs up everywhere so nobody could say, 'Oh I didn't know I should have an identity card'. And also letters to every household: 'You must get your identity card by such and such a date', and everybody got them. Nobody kicked about it, to my knowledge. It was just—when you're in war, you're in total war, it's like being pregnant, you can't be a little bit pregnant.
Patsy Adam-Smith, VAD nurse

You needed to carry your identification card on you at all times because the Manpower would pull you up and ask for your identity—the police would do it too, anyone in authority could pull you up for your identity.
Pansy Hickey, textile worker, Sydney

Under the National Service Act you all had to do something unless you were bedridden or had half a dozen little children, so the young

women would have been called up to work in the factories. And I
think some quite young women over that period started working as
prostitutes, around the Kings Cross area, because they preferred that
to working in a factory.
Joyce Batterham, Communist Party worker, Sydney

They brought in total Manpower—conscription—and you had to go
where you were sent, but the problem was then to get yourself into a
good position as quickly as possible, 'cause that's where you'd be for
the duration of the war.

A dear friend of mine, very early in the conscription period, told
me, 'I got up early one morning, I visited 26 friends, and finished the
day as a captain in the Legal Corps'. Now most of my contemporaries,
having some sort of modicum of education, got themselves curious
jobs as navy officers at Victoria Barracks. They became, overnight,
paymasters sub-lieutenants and they remained in that gorgeous
uniform for the rest of the war. But that was the thing that I think
concerned most of us—what should we do? We didn't know, and the
Manpower dragnet was such that we tended to go where we were put.
Niall Brennan, pacifist, Melbourne

One of the experiences I remember really clearly was the Manpower.
They used to get around in a car like police officers and we were
very afraid of them—they used to carry a lot of power. If you were to
have a day off from work, you had to have a very good reason to do
that, and people were really too scared to have time off from work
without just reason.

I remember once I had to go down to the Taxation Department and
I had a day off from work, and I went down with some friends and
we ran up lanes and back streets, hiding and running from these cars
that we supposedly thought were the Manpower people, so all
through Darlinghurst we were ducking and diving because we were
really afraid of being caught.
Pansy Hickey

People were conscripted to work in the munitions factories, and it was
an offence, unless you were sick, to have a day off. But I had a date
with this fellow and I wanted to go home early to get ready, and we had
this awful Sister at work, she was a big frightening woman, and I said to
the girls, 'What can I say?'—to get a certificate. And they said, 'Tell her
you've got piles'. So anyway out I go and she eventually sent me home,
and I'm halfway through getting ready and a government car pulls up
outside the house. And I said, 'Oh my God, they've found out I
haven't got piles and they've come to arrest me!'. I said to my mother,
'Tell them I'm not home' and she was disgusted. She said, 'No, you've
told them lies, now face up to them'. So out I go in my red dressing
gown. And it was the guard from work—he'd come to get the address
of a friend from work who'd been involved in an accident.
Edna Macdonald, munitions worker, Melbourne

I was largely Manpowered. I found myself in a curious organisation called Department of War Organisation of Industry. I had something to do with research and public relations and I spent most of the war there, looking very much like an able-bodied man who should have been doing more active service. But it was a mildly interesting job. We were concerned with civilian supplies and in that sense, my pacifist tendencies came to accommodate this particular job because it was useful up to a point to the civilian population.

One of our biggest activities was in controlling all sorts of building and manufacturing to see that as far as possible materials and resources were directed to the war effort. You had to have a permit to do any sort of building—the place was absolutely thick with permits. You had to have a permit to buy a stove, and people couldn't set up in business with a new manufacture without a permit. Clothing, fabrics—all that sort of thing was under some sort of control.
Niall Brennan, Department of War Organisation of Industry, Melbourne

All of the young people in Redfern enlisted and were in the Army. My brother was sent to New Guinea to serve over there, and I was Manpowered to work in a rag factory. We prepared all the rags to be baled up and sent over for the artillery and the Air Force to clean the machinery.
Pansy Hickey

I'd got chucked out of university for failing French two times, I'd got the sack from a couple of jobs, and there was the great terror of the Manpower who had enormous powers to draft you into any industry that they felt needed you. At university we always used to make jokes—because we were all Arts students—that we'd all end up in the pickle factory or the jam factory. So I went off without telling anybody and joined up with the WAAAFs but I had to get my parents to sign the papers and they refused. I didn't feel violently enough about it to have an enormous family row, just a little bit of a one, but they wouldn't budge an inch so that was the end of that.
Dorothy Hewett, Perth

People who turned eighteen during the war years had to register and the policeman came and saw me, he'd known me since I was a little girl, and said, 'Frances, of course you know that when you are eighteen, you'll have to register'. And I said, 'I'm not going to register and work for a government that has taken my father away'. I said, 'You arrange to have my father sent back home and when my father comes home, then I will register'. So he went away. And I was eighteen in the September and in October my mother and I were both interned, so I feel that was the reason.
Francesca Merenda, Australian-born Italian, Tully, Queensland

'*At university we used to make jokes that we'd all end up in the pickle factory*': Dorothy Hewett (centre) *and First Year students at the University of Perth, 1941.*

2 The patriotic thing to do

Many people were brought into the labour force by the Manpower regulations, but I think women also came in because their husbands were away or their boyfriends and so on, and they just felt it was the patriotic thing to do—and there was work for them, whereas previously they'd be home.
Mary Miller, union representative, munitions factory, Adelaide

Well of course many women got jobs which they would never be able to do normally. In a small way so did I—when I got the job on the *Daily News* [Perth] it was because the male journalists were away at the war, and this was a very common occurrence. There were women working in munitions who had never had jobs like that, and there were many women I'm sure, married women too, who had never had jobs in their lives before, only been housewives and mothers, and suddenly they found themselves Manpowered into jobs.

I think some would have thought this was just a thing which happens during the war and we'll sort of pitch in and help because there's no men here to do it, but I think others would have seen their contribution as much more important than that.
Dorothy Hewett

I decided to go to the Footscray ammunition factory. I worked at Myers for four years as a salesgirl, and one thing that attracted me was the money. I was receiving 26 shillings a week at Myers, working from 9 to 6, four days a week, 9 to 9 on Friday and 9 to 1 on Saturday, and when I went to the ammunition factory my salary was 2 pounds 7s 6d which was marvellous. And people started to flock in, they were employing by the hundred every week and we had all types of people—sports teachers, prostitutes, you name it, they accepted anyone and it was absolutely packed to the hilt.

We were making small arms—7.2 and 9 mm—and it was horrifying for the first few weeks. We had women in their sixties working there and I remember one night I caught this old lady having a swig of gin and she was an examiner—she examined the bullets, so it was very important that there weren't any defects because they could explode and I said to her, 'You're not allowed to drink alcohol'. And she said, 'Look love, I couldn't keep going otherwise'. Of course I didn't report it, but I don't think she lasted too long.
Edna Macdonald

I didn't plan to work in munitions, I was rather looking forward to working in the Land Army, and so was my sister. But when we went to see the lady who ran the Land Army she wasn't there, but there was a welfare officer from munitions and she said, 'Oh don't go into the Land Army, think of it, picking grapes, think of the flies and the spiders and then you come across snakes'. She absolutely terrified us, so she persuaded us to go into munitions. We went into Hendon Small Arms Factory [in Adelaide] where they manufactured 303s and it was terribly boring so I decided to apply to go into something more exciting like the explosives factory. So out I go to Penfield explosive factory [north of Adelaide] which was new and I went into a section called cartridge bundling. Now that was more boring than the small arms, it was sheer hell. And they hadn't really got organised on conditions and so we were all grumbling and I said, 'Let's do something about it'. So we set up a welfare and production committee.

From this committee we improved conditions—and production—and from that I went on to all sorts of other committees: the canteen committee, the Red Cross committee, the war loans committee, the social committee and the munitions club committee, and within three months I'd worked myself right out of cartridge bundling and then I was asked to be the shop steward for the munition workers' union.
Mary Miller

The facilities were terrible. There was nothing. The work was dirty and there weren't any conveniences at all, you had to walk about 200 yards to the outside toilet and they used to allot one bucket per ten people to wash our hands, there were never any wash basins where I worked. It was a huge place, just made of tin, and we'd be freezing, we'd be there with overcoats and scarves, sitting there for all those hours, and on foggy nights you couldn't see beyond 30 feet for fog, it just came in. For about three or four years, I regularly had bronchitis,

which I've never had since, and everyone had flu and heavy colds. It was terrible. And you had bright lights about a foot above your head and I suffered very badly in those days with migraine and I used to nearly pass out, in face I did once—I fainted. And I suppose that was partly the reason, sitting there all those hours.
Edna Macdonald

Of course most of the workers in the factory were women. There were thousands—I think there were about 13 000 at Penfield—so they had to have a woman organiser, or rather it was more a token thing than want, they didn't really want a woman. So I was nominated to be a union officer. The women who were in the factory, some had been in industry before, and others were waitresses, shop assistants and so on and the Manpower regulations had said they were unnecessary and had to come into war work. And a lot of women who'd never worked before, who were housewives.

I would say 20 to 1 were women and a number of them worked alongside men. They did exactly the same job and they received approximately 54 per cent of the male rate so there was irritation there and I thought, 'Well, why can't we get the same as them? This is unfair'. And I think the whole thing about equal pay came from the vast numbers throughout Australia who were in munitions.

We started the campaign for 90 per cent of the male wage and eventually we were successful, but it was a long process.
Mary Miller

The first real move towards equal pay for women certainly came as a result of the war, as a result of the fact that women were in the metal industry and the munitions industry and lots of other industries. So that in some industries women who'd previously got about 53 per cent of the basic wage, got 90 per cent. It's something that went backwards after the war and of course then many women were thrown out or eased out of industries that were previously, and then subsequent to the war, regarded as exclusively male industries.
Laurie Aarons, factory worker and Communist Party member, Sydney

Most of the women had never been in a trade union before, as I had not, and a number had sons who were in the forces and they were worried about them. These women wouldn't take their morning tea break, they wanted to work through it. Now that was a condition that had been fought for and the rest of the workers felt they were breaking down conditions. We almost had a strike on our hands on that, and I had to go and talk to them and they explained to me their sons were there, they felt they had to do the best they could all the time. And I said, 'No, the best you can do is to make sure that your health keeps up, and you need that break, you really do and if you want to help your son, well then save some of your salary and take

out war bonds or things like that to help'. And they could see the logic of that, though in a number of cases it took some convincing.
Mary Miller

One night in winter we went on strike. The management said we couldn't have any more hot bricks. They used to heat the bricks up in the acid room and we'd have a hot brick to put our feet on. I think I started the strike—'Right, we'll lay down arms until we get our hot bricks'. And anyway it lasted for about three hours and they decided to accept our conditions, so we got our hot bricks back, so at least you could warm your feet, if not the rest of you.
Edna Macdonald

I don't recall any strikes in the Commonwealth munition factories because in these factories the conditions were comparatively very good but there were a lot of private heavy industries and their conditions were not good and they really had to fight for them. I can remember a number of factories where they went on strike, just downed tools. The women who'd been working for a couple of years in munitions were quite militant, some of them, by then.
Mary Miller

I got upset one day when the union rep. told us to down tools, they wanted to go on strike. I stood up and I told her I wasn't going on strike, that it was wrong, that there was a war on and I wanted to go on working but she said that I had to stop because everyone else was going to. So I had to, but it was very upsetting.
Joy Boucher, aircraft construction worker, Sydney

In some of the private factories I went to, they worked in horrifying conditions. In munitions factories using a particular acid, people turned yellow and you had yellow arms and yellow face, and then there was another section where you had a sort of rash all over you. And you did have accidents, you could lose a finger, and I think we had a couple of deaths—you had to be very careful in the explosives section.
Mary Miller

There were some very bad accidents happened—they didn't have any guards on the machines and I saw a woman have half her hair dragged out with a drill, she happened to lean over and it happened in a few seconds. Of course that was the normal thing in those days, they didn't look after the worker at all.
Edna Macdonald

The women who did come in from their homes, who'd never been in industry of any sort, they were marvellous—some were very young but some were grandmas. And there was a feeling that you were contributing, you were part of the war effort, and that was important. And personally, sad as it was, most of us quite enjoyed the war—the

conditions of working and so on. It was a happy war to some extent
for those who worked in munitions and factories except of course if
you had the sadness of losing someone.
Mary Miller

Everyone was very close and friendly, but anyone with any authority
wouldn't even speak to you. You might address someone, say 'Good
morning' and they wouldn't even answer you. That was the set-up
there, the higher authority you had, the less you communicated with
the workers.

But of course you realised that they were depending on you. We
were working eleven hours a day, seven days a week, and then they
started shift work and when you were on night shift you couldn't
sleep during the day—but you needed your sleep so *badly*. So as well
as boring and depressing, it was extremely exhausting.
Edna Macdonald

Of course those that were married with children had a problem
because of childminding. There were very few childminding centres.
In munitions you worked three shifts, the day shift and two other
shifts. You had to get either grandmothers or people who were not in
munitions to help, or you had to try and set up childminding centres,
and a number were set up, and various women were very active
during the war years, setting up kindergartens. But it wasn't part of
the government policy.

You were encouraged to come into munitions but nowhere did they
say, 'At this munitions factory there is a child-care centre, you can leave
your children'. Not at all. So they are very peculiar, governments, how
they just don't think through the problem. They did, finally, by the
end, but at the beginning it was just not on their agenda.
Mary Miller

It was a very difficult struggle for the women, I mean not just because
they had their job—and they'd work twelve hours a day sometimes, in
many instances—and had to look after the family, but also their
husbands were away. And so as I suspect as in most wars, women
bore a very heavy burden, that was not always seen or recognised.
Laurie Aarons

It wasn't easy—just running a house and going to work wasn't easy,
with all the restrictions that were on at that period, the difficulty of
transport, all those things. But women didn't complain. They just got
on with doing it and it probably never even registered, because if
you've never known anything much else, you don't think about not
being appreciated.
Sally Bowen, armaments worker, Wollongong, New South Wales

I went into aircraft, and that was interesting because they taught us to
be second-class sheet metal workers, we had to take the place of men

in the aircraft industry. I started off on the production line getting to know the bits and pieces of parts of an aircraft and then I was transferred to subassembly which did the wheel doors or cowlings of the Mosquito bomber. That was much more interesting because we did riveting and drilling and it was more satisfying to do a complete job. It was a challenge too to see that we could use a drill, and could handle the tools just as well as the men. We learned how to countersink and drill and dolly and rivet, all those things which women had never touched on before and it was interesting to know that we could do them well, and to see a finished product—to know that they were actually the wheel doors of a Mosquito bomber.
Joy Boucher

I worked in a factory at Lysaghts assembling the Owen gun. I saw an ad. in the Wollongong paper for workers and I was from a farm and didn't have many skills except cooking and I liked the idea of being able to do something about the war effort. The women who worked there were very sincere about what they were doing. A lot of them had loved ones overseas, and there was a great fear in the community—it's very hard to translate nowadays the fear that was around, with Japan coming closer and closer all the time, and that set up this sort of feeling that you had to do something about the war effort, and you were really keen to do your job properly and get the guns out and get them away. That was the main feeling behind it, to do something to help the soldiers. I was never very fond of weaponry but I felt it was a very necessary job. And lots of women worked after they left there for the day, they went and made camouflage nets and there was a lot of work put into raising war loans.

Of course the men didn't get a very fair go where we were. Some of the women liked to have a smoke and they'd go to the toilet and have a smoke. They didn't waste time, but the management put locks on the toilet doors so that the women had to go and ask for the key when they wanted to go and have a smoke. That lasted exactly one day. We went and got a special screwdriver made and we took the hinges off and laid the doors in the aisles. So they didn't bother putting them up again.

We didn't take any lip from them, and in the end we were all very good mates. They used to chiack and have a lot of fun and we had a lot of fun too. They didn't complain about having us there because they knew there were no men to take the jobs anyway.

The Owen gun, which I worked on, was unique. It was invented by an Australian, Evelyn Owen, and it turned out to be superior to all other weapons. It could fire under all sorts of conditions and proved to be the ideal weapon for the jungle warfare that we were in at the time with Japan. My job later on was to take soldiers and visitors through the factory and many times one of the soldiers just stood there looking at the gun and said, 'Well, if it wasn't for that, I wouldn't be here today'.

Sally (Phipps) Bowen (second from right) *and fellow workers from the Owen Gun Factory on an outing in Sydney in 1943.*

Well of course the women there had a great pride in it and we were very happy to be hearing how well the gun worked after we'd produced it.
Sally Bowen

We were on night shift this particular night and it was about two in the morning, and I noticed this elderly very well-dressed gentleman come through the door, he had a big grey Stetson and a pale grey suit. He came up to me and said, 'Good morning, how are you?' and I said, 'Good, thank you'. And he said, 'How do you like night shift?' and I said, 'I hate it'. And he said, 'Do you ever get tired' and I said, 'Yes' and he said, 'What do you do?'. 'Oh', I said, 'we sneak out and we have a little sleep'. He said, 'Where's your foreman?' and I said, 'I'm keeping an eye out for him now, he's just having a sleep over in the corner'. Then he said, 'Well, do you know who I am?' and I said, 'No', but I started to go goose-fleshy; and he said, 'I'm a factory inspector'.

He told me if it happened again there'd be big trouble. Then off he went and I ran and woke Leo the foreman and told him what had happened. He called me a bloody idiot, but that was the end of it.
Edna Macdonald

3 The enemy was always there

I worked in fighter control, and fighter control was actually underground, in the tunnels under the city. In the operations room, we were plotting anything that was foreign that was along the coastline, any shipping or planes. Reports were received from radar stations which were right down the coast, and also from civilians who were members of the volunteer Air Observer Corps, and they were also working all along the coast of New South Wales. If anything unusual happened, they reported it back to base and we would plot the position on the plotting tables, and the controllers would if necessary be able to send out planes to intercept.

It was very busy along the coast especially in 1942 and 1943 and there were lots of ships there that shouldn't have been there, enemy ships—German and Japanese. It was a stressful time, we were facing a situation that none of us had any experience in. The enemy was always there, you knew about him, everyone was conscious of the fact, civilians too. It was just not talked about. I don't think people realise these days just how close the enemy really came to Australia.
June Stone, WAAAF, Sydney

We monitored the navy ships of all the Allies but we also monitored merchant ships who would be in the area too. In fact they were the ones who would most necessarily call in because they would be on their own usually or had got behind in a convoy and been left behind and were maybe being followed by a submarine and could see torpedoes coming. Sometimes they would call actually for help: they would send out plain language messages if things really got serious, and then of course they would be given high priority.

That's why we took it so seriously, because we felt we really were in touch with where people were in danger of being killed—our side.
Shirley Fenton-Huie, WRANS, Canberra

There were 37 or 40 ships that were attacked and some were sunk, with a huge loss of life. I think something like over 4000 merchant mariners from Australia were lost. But the general population at the time in Sydney and elsewhere had no idea, because of the rigid censorship, of the degree of what was going on out there.
Barney French, merchant seaman

When I went to join up, in May 1942, they said they wanted people for the Australian Corps of Signals. I didn't exactly know what that meant but the man went into what I was good at school and it turned out to be mathematics so he said, 'You will be in cypher'. But he said, 'We have to have references and we have to check your background for security'. So when that was all done I found out that I was going to be a cypher operator and I had to do a rookies' school and then I went to cypher school and I joined Z Force.

Z Force was at *Airlie* on the corner of Domain Road, [Melbourne] and I was just told to report there, and I knocked on the door and I was taken in and the officer said to me: 'Now you've sworn an oath already about security, but this is a bigger one that you are to swear now and if you break anything to anybody about what you do here,

Patricia Penrose, Z Special Unit, in camp in Melbourne, en route to the ablutions block. Note the butterfly clips in her hair, pom-pom slippers and real dressing-gown; most made do with their shoes and greatcoats.

then you can be shot under national security regulations'. And I was never even allowed to say where I worked.

Z Special Unit was formed to carry out missions and drop people into different places like Borneo, New Guinea, the Solomons, Timor, and to search and destroy, perhaps get people on side, get guerrillas together to work for you. Our work was to encipher and decipher signals they sent in. I only knew them as parties and every party was called a different name—for example it could be Party Lizard [which operated in Timor], or some other animal. So that we never saw the whole pattern of what was going on, it was only our commanding officer who did that. But we did know it was very, very dangerous.

People didn't realise that within the outer war there was a secret war going on and that was going on from Australia, continuing on through the islands—they had no idea about this. The people who started the Z Special Unit just selected people from various services, people that would fit into what they wanted to do, and of course the security had to be great too, and they had to be very brave men.
Patricia Penrose, Z Special Unit, Melbourne

4 Produce more food

I was called up in my age group and I was quite prepared to go into the army, but the fellow behind the desk just said, 'Look, you're no good to us, you go back home and look after your farm; it's more important that you go back home and produce'.

I suppose there was some disappointment, a bit of anger, that after you'd sort of worked yourself up to the fact that you were going into the Army, you were just told to go home. But then I said, 'Oh well, if that's what you want me to do'.

'We were very conscious of the need to produce more food': Bill Graham and wife Norma preparing land for wheat-growing in 1944 in Gulgong, New South Wales.

You were very conscious of the fact that you had to produce food. We were told this in the screeds that were sent out from time to time—produce more food, produce more food. And so we tried to do that: you worked longer hours and you tried to satisfy that demand, and in that way you felt you were helping the soldiers that were in the Army anyway, and you certainly worked a lot harder to achieve that.
Bill Graham, wheat farmer, Gulgong, New South Wales

Australia was only seven-and-a-half million at that time so in a city like Brisbane, for example, with about 300 000 people, you can imagine the influx of say 70 000 troops moving in and being billeted and fed. It taxed the availability of foodstuffs and it made it hard for the civilians, all the foods that were being given not only to the American Army but to the Australian Army. It meant that civilians just had to put up with less and less.

A lot of the stuff of course was imported military rations, but all the fresh foodstuffs and things like that were provided by Australia, grown here to be issued to the American and Australian troops.
Bill Bentson, staff sergeant, US Army

When I was thirteen, my father took sick and we couldn't get labour and I left school to come home and help mother look after our dairy farm. We also planted a lot of potatoes for the war effort—they went to the Army, and they were all done by hand, with horses, and so was our harvest. Petrol rationing didn't worry us because in those days it was all horse-drawn, but labour and materials were all hard to get—for example you couldn't get fencing materials.

Our job was to produce food and that's what we had to do. But of course the women were helping the men on the farms, we'd have been shot if it hadn't been for the women.

Charles Janeway, farmers' son, Mt Gambier, South Australia

There were very few young men left in the district, so I left school and I came home to work on the farm. But we had a reasonably large property and my father heard that there were prisoners of war that you could get for farm work so he applied and got two. They were two extremely nice people, and they worked very well—Vic and Joe we called them.

They couldn't talk English and we couldn't talk Italian but my mother got an Italian book and she picked out a few phrases and the same phrases would do for a lot of things, and with a lot of arm-waving we could communicate quite well. All the prisoners of war had maroon uniforms, probably ex-army ones, dyed, so they showed up. But if you asked them did they want to run away, they simple said, '*scapare dove*'.—where would we run? There wasn't anywhere to run. They liked being there I think, because it was better than being in a compound with a lot of men and walking round stirring up the dust.

A canteen used to come, about fortnightly, and it brought them things such as cigarettes, chocolates and cool drink, and with it came an officer and he asked them, as far as I could gather, how they were getting on and did they have any complaints, and that was their check-up by the Army. I remember once they brought them a newspaper that they could read, in Italian, and that was a great joy to them because they probably felt like our early settlers, rather cut off from everything—I mean unless we told them what was happening in the war, they didn't know.

Beryl Haley, farmers' daughter, Gulgong, New South Wales

From the camps then they started to despatch some people to farms, but only if you wanted to go. So I put my name down and they sent me to *Wongombara*, Sutton Forrest [NSW], to work for Mr and Mrs Badgery and I stayed eighteen months and I really enjoyed it. After that I always dreamt one day to come back and buy land round there and do something and that's all I used to think about. The Badgerys treated me like a son, from the word go, because I really used to work, they had to stop me working rather than push me to work.

Ric Pisaturo, Italian POW

The Manpower people said they needed girls on the land because the boys were going overseas, and they had these crops—cattle, sheep, pigs, everything had to be tended—and they needed girls and I thought, 'Well that's for me, I'll get into this'. So I joined the Land Army.

*Beryl (Fortescue) Haley having a smoko at work on the family property;
Italian POW 'Vince' is second from left.*

The films that were shown to me were of girls posing behind the
orange blossom and it looked glamorous, so that attracted me. I'd
never been out of Sydney and I went to Leeton and the
Murrumbidgee Irrigation Area, full of importance—I was going to
conquer all of this, I was going to be the best little Land Girl there
was.

I'd signed my own papers because my father was in the Army, and
he was very angry because I sort of forged his signature and he said,
'My girl, you will never last, you will never be able to do that work'.
He was so right—five minutes into that first day I decided I couldn't
do that work, and only that my father had said that, I'd have been
home, because at first you weren't forced to stay on. But when it was
too late to pull out, I knew that I liked it and I was going to stick
it—I didn't want to get out then.

Peggy Williams, Land Army

Probably 85 per cent of the girls who went into the Land Army were
city. The country girls were much too wise, they knew how hard the
work was, they all went and joined the WAAAFs and the AWAS where
they got all the nice perks.

I saw the Land Army office and I walked in there and I said, 'Do
you send girls away?'. They said, 'Yes'. And I signed the paper and
that was how I became a Land Girl really, without a thought of what
I'd be doing. I think I believed I'd be walking through the orchards
with a basket over my arm picking the fruit in a dainty little manner
and so forth. I didn't realise that I'd be carting a twelve-foot ladder up

and down hills and through blackberry bushes, so my first day in the orchard was pretty scary. I really thought I'd done the worst thing.

I'd never been away from home on my own before, although I was nineteen, and I was very spoilt too because I'd never even washed out my own clothes and I used to have my breakfast brought to me on a tray while I was getting dressed of a morning, so it was a shock when I got to Batlow and found that 30 girls were going to use the same bathroom as I was and nearly all of them in there at the same time too.

Being so homesick I really thought I wouldn't be able to take it and I sent a telegram telling my parents that I was coming home. But in the meantime I got a letter from them saying how proud they were of what I was doing and that really shamed me into thinking well, I'd stay a little while longer. And I stayed and stayed and stayed—until the end of the war actually, so I had almost four years in the Land Army.

Jean Scott, Land Army

One day I was sent out to work for this farmer and when I arrived I found he was an Italian. And that was a shock, to think that I was going to work for an Italian while our boys were fighting the Italians overseas. I thought well that's not right, I'm not going to do this, and I said to him, 'Look, I can't work for you, I'm not very well'. So I sat under a tree all day and he kept popping down to see if I was all right and in the afternoon he came down and he sat and spoke to me. And he had a son who was fighting with my brother, and I was so upset to think I had done this to this man. So that weekend I went out and worked with him in my own time—he and I took grapes off

'The best little Land Girl there was': Peggy (Feast) Williams, who joined the Land Army in 1941.

A group of Land Army workers in Leeton in 1943. Peggy Williams is second from right.

by the caseload, and 'til that man died, he sent me cases of fruit after the war to thank me, even came to see me, and thank God his son came home safe and my brother came home safe too.
Peggy Williams

Six thousand is I think the overall number of Land Army throughout the country, and it really isn't very many when you think it was mainly through our efforts that we were helping to keep not only the population fed but also the service people and when the Americans came of course it meant that they were wanting canned fruit juice and things like that.

In most cases we were fairly well looked after. After they realised that we were doing our worth of work, the country people really took us to their hearts. But one farmer I worked for, he had grapevines to be pruned, and he was just so unhappy at getting girls. He said, 'I used to pay my men a bonus if they got the job done in five weeks'. We got the job done in five weeks but he got such a shock I think, he forgot to pay us the bonus.
Jean Scott

Most of the Land girls did many things, went all over the place. We got paid 30 shillings a week and our keep, but that was enough because there was nowhere to go. It was a good time, a wonderful time. It was very hard work, I've never worked so hard in all my life but the times that we had, and the stories we told—oh it was fun.
Peggy Williams

*'Front-page Hurley': Adelie
Hurley in the darkroom of the
Sydney* Sun, *her employers
during the war.*

5 Living two lives

I started working on newspapers because a lot of the photographers
were sent away to war and there was a vacancy. I started off pretty
much as an amateur but it was great fun and I photographed what the
women were doing for the war effort, the Red Cross, the Army girls,
the Land Army, the munitions factories, all that sort of thing.

I started getting front pages and I finally earned the nickname of
'Front Page Hurley'. But the sabotage!—oh dear. I remember once I
was sent to photograph a very big social event, fundraising, and
somebody switched the flash setting on my camera so that when I got
back to develop the negatives there was hardly anything on them. So
of course panic-stricken I raced straight back and took more pictures,
but the press were only allowed a certain time at these social
functions, and it had passed, so I had to sneak behind bushes and
bob up and take whatever I could. They were pretty awful pictures
and the next day I was on the carpet. Frank Packer called me in and I
was blasted up one side and down the other, but I didn't tell him
what had happened.

They resented me—the very fact that I was a woman, and that I was
doing very well, and really worked hard at it.
Adelie Hurley, newspaper photographer, Sydney

Edith Cavell was my ideal and when the war began I thought, 'I'm
getting into this'. But I hadn't finished my training and they wouldn't
take you under 25, so I had to wait, but finally I went with a friend
down to the barracks and we both enlisted and I finally got posted to
Concord Hospital as a theatre sister.

Then they called for volunteers to go north and knowing the

Japanese were attacking Darwin I thought I might as well get as far as Darwin if not overseas. There was such a spirit of patriotism then, it was rife, and I think that the further north you went, the more you felt you were going to do, actually helping in the field itself. I wasn't afraid, I don't think any of us who were prepared to go into the battle scenes were afraid at that stage.

But as it happened we moved up to Tamworth, NSW, that was supposed to be the most strategically placed hospital. The boys were flown in directly with acute injuries and we had spinal wounds, from bullets in the spine, and malaria and various tropical diseases. And the boys that I nursed were glad to be back but a lot of them wanted to get back again into action, so they were being patched up for that.
Lesley Daniels, Army nurse

I was mostly in North Queensland, and I had several trips down and back from North Queensland, eight to nine days on the train. You'd get into a big troop train down at Spencer Street in Melbourne and nobody was supposed to know, it was dead secret, and nobody was allowed on the platform. But all the other platforms were full of civilians and as the train began to pull out, this long train with sailors, airmen, soldiers and us VADs and nursing sisters—we were all separated, great demarcation in the army, and we were the lowest of the low—the civilians would sing 'Wish Me Luck As You Wave Me Goodbye'.

At the beginning we did mostly inoculations for fellows going away, then we had men coming back from the islands and they of course had malaria to a man, and always had the worm, so we were nursing them.

The men from the Middle East came back after the great fuss—'we need them back here in Australia'—they came back and we patched them up so they could go up into New Guinea and do battle. I remember we had a matron who'd been in the Middle East, and one day she just lost her cool. I was out at the steriliser and she came out and I suppose she knew I was young and stupid so it was all right to lose her temper, and she said, 'All we do is patch them up so they can get out there and get shot again'. And it was the first time I realised, really what we were doing and it seemed just slightly immoral.

In the end we were getting fellows almost directly from the battlefield in New Guinea, just with big field dressings stuck on them, they were getting flown in; and it was interesting listening to these fellows, because they'd talk—they hadn't had time to talk 'til then.
Patsy Adam-Smith

Of course having the training that we had in our day there was a lot of discipline attached to it, and I think when you have to face up to these things you're very very glad of that training because you had to learn to control your feelings—I can tell you we had many a weep in

'Lots of the men at that time thought "Oh, women in the army, how are they going to cope!" ': Thelma Long, instructing a cadet at the Women's Army Service Officers' School, Victoria, where she was on the teaching staff in 1944.

our tent at night but while you were on duty in front of the boys, we didn't ever give way to tears. But they were there, as you can imagine.
Meg Ewart, army nurse, Darwin and New Guinea

I was one of the first three women drivers to set foot in the Royal Military College, Duntroon, and we had a most horrific time because anything that went wrong with the trucks or the cars or tanks, we had to fix ourselves. The big job they sent us to, which we weren't supposed to do, was to the railway siding at Queanbeyan to unload barrels of beer for the officers' mess at Duntroon and we used to struggle off the train onto the truck with these big barrels of beer. And we had to get blocks of ice—because there were no refrigerators in those days—and take them into the officers' houses. And the wives used to stand there and say, 'In there driver, put it straight'. And I thought, 'If only my father could see me now'. We used to laugh when we got outside but it wasn't funny sometimes.
Joy Boehm, AWAS

Lots of the men at that time thought, 'Oh women in the Army, how are *they* going to cope!'—this was their attitude. And there'd be occasions where for example a sergeant might be waiting for a new group of members to the coastal artillery or Ack Ack battery, and a truck would drive up and out of the truck would come not men but a whole group of women. And the sergeant's face would absolutely drop. And sometimes the sergeant or someone in charge would say to one of the female members, 'Oh, go on, get along, move those cases over there—you joined up to do a man's job, so do it'.
Thelma Long, AWAS

In one place I worked there were some men who were obviously conscripted because I would be doing the work and I'd say, 'There's a lot of messages there'. And they'd say, 'Oh well, you were silly enough to join up, we didn't'. So when the day came that they were moved out of cypher, it was one of the happiest days of my life. They were given rifles and told to get going, and we got the office full of women. We only needed half as many women as there were men. And the most amazing thing is that in three-and-a-half years, among those women nobody ever had an argument because we were all so desperate to get on and win the war.

Patricia Penrose

I was called in by Colonel Sybil Irving and she said, 'We want you to accept a posting to Innisfail and Proserpine and you'll be officer-in-charge of the AWAS. They'll be experimenting in chemical warfare'. She said, 'There'll be professors from all over the Commonwealth but you'll be the only female officer there'. 'And', she said, 'it will be a very lonely position, you mustn't leave the camp on any account and it will be strictly top secret'.

She gave me five minutes to think about it but I said, 'I accept madam, thank you very much I think it's a great honour', so that was it. But I couldn't tell the family and I felt very embarrassed about that, being very close to my father. Anyway, they came to the station to see me off and the guard came for my ticket and I handed it to him and he said, 'You damn women, why can't you put "woman" on the thing, I've got you in a sleeping car with a man, now I've got to change it all'. He wasn't very amused but we were. And so we went up to Innisfail.

The reason for it all was that we had heard that the Japanese were

Elva (Balkie) Batt, Sydney, who became a nursing VAD, later part of AAMWS.

'You were always with your mate': Patsy Adam-Smith with two other VADs in Sydney in 1944 on their way home on leave.

experimenting in this sort of thing, and the Germans, and the whole idea was that we might be able to find something that could cope with it, to stop the dreadful effect that the gas had on the body, because it infected your whole system.

I was there for about two-and-a-half years. We were in the jungle with the officers and the men, and they used to fly over and drop mustard gas. Then we'd go through and rescue the boys that had volunteered to go in without protective clothing, and bring them back to camp, and sometimes that was horrific because they were so badly burnt. I cried the first one I saw, it was really dreadful and some of them were burnt so badly they were scarred for life, but they all still smiled, they were absolutely wonderful—I'll always admire them.

They also had a special chamber and the men had to run around in this gas chamber, in their ordinary army gear, or shorts, until they were out of breath and couldn't take any more, and then they came out. And I remember I said to one of the young boys, 'Why do you do it?'. And he said, 'Because it might be helping a fellow Australian'.

My fiancé was a prisoner of the Japanese and I used to lie in bed and think 'Where is Alan, is he in Singapore? is he alive?'—because we hadn't heard. And when I saw the first effects of these gases I thought 'Oh my God, what if they use it there, and he gets burnt like this'. And it was lonely because you couldn't talk to anyone about it.
Joy Boehm

Next to my office in the AMP Building was the combined Intelligence room for the Allied air forces, and the people doing the nitty-gritty work were Australian women. Translating and interpreting captured

Japanese documents, scraps of paper from the fallen Japs on the Kokoda Trail, maps, notes, these women turned out to be superlatively good at this. It was so good an intelligence centre that MacArthur did not want to change it. But when he moved his headquarters to New Guinea the Australian Government decided that no Australian women would be allowed out of Australia into the war zone. We sent three deputations no less from Head-quarters to Canberra to try to persuade them to let this particular cadre of women go with the Intelligence section to Moresby. We didn't pull it off. The Section Officer, in command of these women, came into me and she said 'I just have my new posting, I'm going to be mess officer at Toowoomba'. I think this is one of the most shocking things that I experienced in regard to women during the war.
Beryl Daly, Australian serving in MacArthur's headquarters, Brisbane

I'd always been in love with the sea and read books about it, and I'd had a sailor boyfriend and as soon as I left school the only thing I wanted to do was join the Navy. Friends said the best way to get in was as a wireless operator, so I went to Mrs McKenzie's wireless school in Sydney and learnt Morse code there, no good applying unless you learn that. And it was very exciting because to join the Navy was like a dream really. I'd always said that if I'd been a boy I would've been in the Navy, so there I was having an opportunity as well, because there hadn't been women in the Navy before. This was something new, and we were not an auxiliary force like the Air Force and the Army were, we were actually members of the Royal Australian Navy and subject to King's Regulations and Admiralty Instructions.

I think we all thought that we would be sent off to the war on a ship, or sent to some islands way out in the Pacific to fight against the Japanese, but I'm afraid not, we were in Canberra from beginning to end. We were sent to HMAS *Harman* where there were 400 girls and twenty sailors living in this old, already established communications centre which was the centre for the whole of navy operations in the South Pacific. All messages to and from ships in the entire area, be they American, British or Australian ships, all came directly to Canberra, all in code of course, and then were transmitted to other places in Australia.

We always saw ourselves as helpers because we would talk to the men with our Morse sets, men in the islands in the Pacific and it was almost I suppose as though they were calling home, and they'd make jokes with us and they made us feel good—I think they appreciated what we did.

We had a visiting British Admiral once and he was expostulating with the CO about all these girls here—'Can they row?' he said and the CO said 'No' so he said 'Get them on to the Molonglo River, can't have chaps in the Navy who can't row, you know'. But rowing on the Molonglo was the closest we ever got to sea.

Shirley Fenton-Huie, WRANS, who was stationed in Canberra: 'Rowing on the Molongolo was the closest we ever got to the sea'.

But it was a funny life there because we'd nearly all come directly from school and it was a very strict sort of place, HMAS *Harman*, with a Commanding Officer who regarded us as his girls and was very protective about us. We were told not to fraternise with the Army or the Air Force. I can only once remember that we were allowed to have a dance there and boys from the Air Force and some of the other camps were invited to dance with us and the CO was jumping up and down about this because he really worried about his little chickens and he saw some of the girls holding hands with some of the boys and he got so horrified that he said, 'There'll be no more dancing, where there's dancing there's sinning!'.
Shirley Fenton-Huie

A lot of the women I photographed thought the work they were doing was pretty boring but they realised it was necessary to do. And lots of them thoroughly enjoyed it—they were out of the house, out of the kitchens and they were living an entirely different life. They were living two lives actually, they were working outside and they were working at home as well and trying to keep families together. Most of their men had gone off, a lot of them were at the war. And they were driving ambulances, they were driving trucks, they were working on the land and they were loving every bit of it—I think they thoroughly enjoyed being out in the world doing things and of course it was for the war effort.
Adelie Hurley

6 Why aren't you in uniform?

The big stigma was not being in uniform. There were people in reserved occupations, there were essential services, the non-Australians who weren't allowed, the medically unfit—they suffered the worst, I think they got a badge or something in the end. So just not having a uniform on was a stigma. You would get certain people who would abuse you, the 'Why aren't you in uniform?' approach.

Ted Hartley, conscientious objector, Sydney

Those fellows that were reluctant to join up and didn't join up and who were physically fit, I wasn't too happy about and I don't think that any one of them should have been left behind. I think that it's total when there's a war on, everybody's got to be in it, and I feel that everybody should be in uniform. I don't think there should be any civilian clothes or anything. If there's a dance or something like that, a special occasion, they can wear their civvies or the ladies get into a nice dress but for general use why should they do it better than the fellow that's laying his life on the line and living like a pig half the time?

Alan Low, 6th Division

My stand was that conscription was illegal: it was an illegal extension of the state's powers, and that I couldn't comply with any of the conditions. When I was called before the court then, I read my statement and I was rejected straightaway—that was the situation. I didn't give them any option really.

I came out of court and it was the first time I'd met any pacifists other than in the Scouts. I'd heard ministers who were pacifist ministers but I hadn't really been in touch. And this girl put her hand on my shoulder and said, 'Oh tough luck, laddy', and I nearly cried. I had a month before I had to appear in court, I was called up for sentencing for not taking the oath. You get a summons, just like any other criminal, to appear in court. And finally I went to jail for six months.

I didn't mind roughing it and the rest of it and I didn't feel any shame. But it was seen as a terrible disgrace. Although my parents boasted, 'Oh, we're not going to bring pressure, there's no question of white feathers', when the pressure came on them it was seen as a terrible disgrace. And there was also the fact that 'Gosh, here's you with your career finished'—letters from my uncle, 'You'll never get a job here'. Yes, there was a stigma attached to it.

Ted Hartley

There was no resentment—not that I experienced, anyway. When the Manpower Act came in, everyone was really conscripted in some way or other. It was assumed that if you didn't end up in the services, there must have been a very good reason.

You had a secure job and you worked long hours but you got paid for it. I would think all factories worked 24 hours a day, seven days a week, certainly the ones I worked in did. We had two shifts, twelve hours each. But though the hours were long, others were getting it worse. The soldiers were battling on the Kokoda Trail, why should we complain? It was really no hardship.

I can remember when Montgomery and his troops gained the upper hand over Rommel in North Africa. Someone came in waving a newspaper and said 'They're knocking them back like steam in North Africa'. And someone else shouted out 'Back on the dole by Christmas'. That really summed up the cynicism of a lot of those men who had been unemployed for years: they carried the scars, they never forgot. They were thankful to have these jobs, and a lot of them, including myself, had jobs that were infinitely better than anything they'd ever done before.
Bob Bahnsen, machinist, Sydney

Most of the people that lived in the area where I was living at the time worked at Holdens and were in reserved industry. There were quite a few men who worked at Holdens who did volunteer to join up but as soon as the authorities found out where they worked, and what they were skilled at doing, that was the end of that, they just couldn't be replaced and so they weren't allowed to go. They were vital to making the tools that made the munitions and guns and so on. And to indicate this to the general public they were given a badge to wear which said that they were in a reserved occupation, they were vital to the war effort, so that explains why they're not in the services.
John Drennan, schoolboy, Adelaide

I'd wanted to join up from day one but until I got of age there was nothing much I could do about it, and when I *was* old enough, I was then in the clutch of the Manpower controls, and because I was working for a protected industry, the Pool Petroleum Group, there was no way in the world they were going to release me, and I was transferred to Townsville, as a civilian, in the section that was supplying the armed forces with fuels and lubricants.

Pool Petroleum was virtually the nationalisation of the liquid fuel supply of Australia. There were companies like Shell and Caltex, Vacuum Oil, Plume, they were all brought together—under an Act of Parliament I suppose—and all petrol and all lubricants were handled by the one organisation, Pool Petroleum, and 90 per cent of the customers were the Army or Navy.
Robert Squires, clerk, reserved occupation, Townsville, Queensland

The dockyards were very important and every union, not only painters and dockers, but ironworkers, shipwrights, joiners, carpenters, they had a big influx during the war years because they classed it as protected industry, none of them was ever sent out of the docks to go

to war, or called up for war service. I wouldn't say that they joined it to get out of going away but they either had to get into what they called protected industry or they'd be put in the Allied Works Council or the Civil Construction Corps.
Alan McMillan, dockworker, Sydney

When war broke out, there was a shortage of waterside workers, and they opened their books and a great many criminals became waterside workers because it was a protected industry and there was no way they would be called up for Army service or to go away to Darwin and places like that to work with the Allied Works Council. They became waterside workers in Sydney, Melbourne, Brisbane and of course they couldn't break away from their old habits so they became involved in black-marketing—stealing from trucks, stealing from ships.
Ray Blissett, policeman, Sydney

You looked down on people we called Army dodgers. A lot of them were young fellows. Their excuse was that they were in a protected industry. But my brother was in a protected industry, and the man I married. They were in protected industries but they joined up because they were fighting for their country, that was their reason, not that they liked the Army life, they detested it, but they were fighting for their country.

But some men that weren't in the Army used to call men who were in the Army 'five bob a day bludgers'.
Edna Macdonald

Blokes would get in a pub and say 'I went away and fought for you' and all this caper, that went on; blokes would say that with grog aboard, more or less to be spiteful. Of course they don't know the circumstances of the bloke they were talking about, he might have had a team of kids and they could get a general in the Army cheaper than what it would cost to send him over there.
Alan McMillan

People had a strange feeling about men who didn't go away because unless they wore the Returned badge or something, they didn't know if they'd come back sick or something like that and they wondered why they weren't over there doing something when everybody else was fighting.

I was going out with a gentleman when war broke out and he was an engineer which meant that he couldn't join any of the services. Now the minute I got involved with all these Service situations I wasn't interested in him any more. I couldn't think of anything but winning the war and getting into camp and doing that. So I couldn't ally myself with someone who was staying here doing engineering work, even though he couldn't help it.
Patricia Penrose

I worked at AWA [Amalgamated Wireless of Australasia] and I don't really know what the men did but they were chemists about the factory and they had white coats on and they'd all come trotting in and feel very superior because they were at home and all the girls were there and all the boys were away at the war. And we used to give them a terrible time, we gave them hell actually—'You cowards, you conscientious objectors, you only became a chemist to get out of going to the war'. We used to drive them absolutely mad, they'd be screaming at us—'We're not, we're essential, we can't be sent to the war because they need us'. Dear, we gave them a dreadful time.

But you resented anyone who stayed at home. The boys were called up at eighteen, and a lot of boys would hide and not register, and everybody had that feeling, 'Why aren't you at the war? My husband or my brother is at the war, why aren't you?'. It wasn't your business, maybe he had a reason but you didn't know why he wasn't there, you couldn't get past that, and you'd talk to your friends and you'd say 'Did you know so-and-so didn't even try to go to the war?'. It was terrible I suppose, but when it's dead serious like that you expect everybody to get out and do their bit.

Anne Pellew, staff canteen worker, Sydney

8

Cuckoos in the Nest

I have had considerable experience in dealing with conditions that exist here in Australia and although I have to gnash my teeth on many occasions, I cannot help but realise that I myself cannot change things. We constantly have to deal with our Allies. Their system, their methods and their line of thought are different from ours . . . Great patience is necessary. It behooves all of us to know when to give in and when to be firm.

Brigadier-General S. J. Chamberlin, Chief of Operations HQ South-West Pacific Area, writing on 26 September 1942 to the American commander of a joint training unit.

The arrival of thousands of American servicemen in Australia during the Second World War had a profound effect on the nation. Australia was a largely insular society. Most people had not travelled overseas, and they had no concept of conditions in other countries. They still considered themselves to be 'British', and many spoke of Britain as 'home', even though they had never been there. Although the Americans spoke English and had similar cultural values, it was soon discovered that they were different.

Inevitably, friction developed between Australians and Americans, and this was found at many levels. At the highest level, relations between the Prime Minister, John Curtin, and the Commander-in-Chief South-West Pacific Area, General Douglas MacArthur, remained excellent throughout the war. Curtin trusted MacArthur's judgement on military matters, and in November 1943 ended a radio broadcast with these words: 'I am indebted to General MacArthur for the high statesmanship and breadth of world vision he has contributed to the discussion. The complete integration of our concepts which has been a source of such strength in the past, will continue to the end'. Astonishingly, these last two sentences had been written by MacArthur himself. He had requested Curtin to add them to the statement. Some would say that the harmony at this top level of government was purchased at the price of Australia's compliance with MacArthur's wishes.

There was less harmony at other governmental levels. For example, in January 1944 the Australian Minister for External Affairs, Dr Evatt, arranged an agreement between Australia and New Zealand in which the countries undertook to act together in matters of common concern, but it upset the American government. And there were constant wrangles about the Lend–Lease agreement between Australia and the US, by which Australia received military equipment and provided food and other supplies and services to the

US forces. At the end of the war, Australia became one of the few Allied countries not to have incurred a financial debt to the US.

Curtin's acceptance of MacArthur's advice soon led to disquiet among Australia's senior military commanders. In Chapter 6 it was related that at MacArthur's urging, Curtin had sent General Blamey to New Guinea in September 1942 to take personal command of the Australian and later American troops fighting there. After the campaign, MacArthur set up an American army so that in future operations American troops would not fight under Blamey's command. Gradually Blamey's position as Commander, Allied Land Forces became redundant, but when he eventually complained to Curtin, the Prime Minister chose not to press the matter with MacArthur.

Similarly, Curtin bowed to MacArthur's judgement over the command of the RAAF. The Air Force's operational forces came under MacArthur while administrative responsibility rested with the Australian Chief of the Air Staff. Despite the debilitating effect on the RAAF, MacArthur was happy for this divided command to continue and Curtin would not force the issue with him.

Military relations were not helped by MacArthur's comments about Australian troops when they were withdrawing along the Kokoda Track and fighting at Milne Bay in August and September 1942. Several months later, after the Americans had fought badly at Buna, General Blamey told MacArthur that he would rather used tired Australians than fresh American as at least he knew that they would fight.

Military relations tended to improve once troops began to fight alongside each other. The critical comments by MacArthur and others about the Australians in late 1942 were made before the Americans got into action. It is significant that the most well-known violent incident between troops of the two nations took place at about this time. On the night of 26 November 1942, Australian troops and American Military Police clashed outside an American Post Exchange (canteen) in Brisbane; the Military Police used fire-arms and nine Australians were wounded, one fatally. There were other violent incidents in the early months of 1943. Mounted police had to be used to break up a brawl in Melbourne in February 1943, and in the same month a brawl involving 1500 men at Bondi Beach narrowly avoided becoming a 'serious riot'.

There were also violent incidents between Americans and Australian civilians. The best-known case concerned Private Edward Leonski who murdered three women in Melbourne during May 1942. He was convicted by a US court martial in July and was hanged at Pentridge Prison in November 1942. At times the Americans were the victims of criminal assault.

These violent outbreaks should not be overplayed. While many Australians and Americans have recollections of such incidents, an equally large number never saw any fights and enjoyed friendly relations. But at the same time, few would deny that there was friction at a cultural and social level. Contrary to the views of some observers, public sentiment did not change overnight. Within a few weeks friction had developed in some quarters. Elsewhere Australians and Americans remained friendly throughout the war.

The disputes usually revolved around two related issues—women and money. Naturally the US servicemen sought female companionship, and many Australian men were away from home on active service. The Americans were a curiosity—their uniforms were attractive, often they had charming manners, and even more importantly, they had more money than Australian servicemen and had access to scarce items such as cigarettes and nylon stockings.

The interviews in this chapter often refer to the disparity in wealth between the Australians and the Americans. Taking into account his allowances, a US soldier had about twice the spending power of his Australian equivalent. For example, a US private first class received about £17 a month while an Australian private received about £9 15s a month. A US sergeant received £32, an Australian sergeant £17 5s; a US lieutenant £63, an Australian, £29 15s; a US captain £74, an Australian £36 15s; a US major £106, an Australian £44 15s; a US lieutenant-colonel £141, an Australian £51.

Within a short while of arriving in Australia, some US servicemen were seeking to marry Australian girls. Perhaps the first marriage took place on 13 February 1942, the US soldier involved having arrived in Melbourne on 1 February. The marriage was successful, but many similar ones were not. At the end of the war the Australian brides set sail for the USA on ships chartered by the US government. It is not known how many of these marriages survived. Some of those interviewed put the failure rate as high as 70 per cent. On October 1947, the Australian Consul-General in San Francisco estimated that 85 per cent of Australian–American marriages had survived.

It is difficult to determine how many Americans visited Australia during the Second World War, although the often quoted figure of 1 million seems rather generous, even counting those who were in port for only one day. In Chapter 5 it was stated that there were 200 000 Americans in Australia and New Guinea in June 1943. Perhaps 120 000 of these were in Australia. The number reached a peak in September 1943 and thereafter dropped rapidly. By June 1944, there were over 500 000 Americans in the South-West Pacific Area, but only 55 000 were in Australia. General MacArthur left Australia permanently in October 1944 and soon established his headquarters in the Philippines.

The rapid reduction in numbers of Americans in Australia corresponded with the shift in balance in the fighting in the South-West Pacific Area. By early 1944, the Americans had taken over the major combat role in New Guinea. Soon US reinforcements and supplies went straight to the combat zone, bypassing Australia, which was no longer the main base for MacArthur's advancing forces.

The US 'invasion' of Australia had lasted for less than three years. It had a major impact on Australia, dragging it out of its insularity. The US armed forces in the Pacific in the Second World War set the pattern for American domination of the region for the next 40 years. For millions of Australians, the reality of that power was brought home by the presence of thousands of American servicemen in their midst during the Second World War.

1 We quickly became ungrateful

During the clear summer nights we got very clear reception from
Tokyo Rose and she would pass down all these messages to various
segments of the Australian Army about the American soldiers down there
taking our girls and wives out, and trying to make them feel unhappy
and disrupt them. It was all aimed to break down your morale.
Tip Carty, North Australia Observer Unit

I would say that within six months, when it became apparent that we
weren't going to be overrun after all, public sentiment changed and
the attitude to the Americans changed quite a lot. I can remember
being on the Manly ferry one evening and I could hear two girls and
their Australian boyfriends singing an anti-American song—and that
was only six months. So from being saviours and heroes, they very
quickly wore out their welcome.

I think it was inevitable. They really cut a swathe through the
female population, there is no doubt about that, and this was
resented, it would have been resented by parents, and by the brothers
of the girls who were got into trouble, as they used to call it. It is
inevitable I think if you have a large army. Once the threat was gone,
once we didn't feel that we needed them anymore, we very quickly
became ungrateful.
Bob Bahnsen, machinist, Sydney

When the Yanks began to flood in, and they did flood in, people
became less happy, particularly the men because the girls were all
going for the Americans and that thing that they're 'overpaid and
oversexed and over here' began very early. It was around quite soon.
John Hinde, ABC war correspondent, Sydney

But you never hear people tell you the Yanks' retort—'the trouble
with Australians is they're underpaid, undersexed and under
MacArthur'.
Ted Hartley, conscientious objector, Sydney

Australia was invaded by the Americans and we acquiesced in it. The
Americans needed Australia for a base for their war with Japan, and
we were dragged into it willy-nilly and as a result we were flooded
with American soldiers. Most of them were nice fellows, but there was
a lot of hostility towards them. They tended to tell everybody that
they'd come to save Australia, which didn't go down all that well.
**Niall Brennan, Department of War Organisation of Industry,
Melbourne**

The Australian soldiers coming back from the Middle East and going
to New Guinea didn't like the idea of being told by the Americans
'Actually, we're here to save you'—they really didn't like that much.
Ren deGaris, Wireless intelligence, RAAF, Darwin

'Australia was invaded by the Americans and we acquiesced in it': Niall Brennan, pacifist.

The Yanks came out here at about the stage where the 6th and 7th Division were coming back from the Middle East and these boys had been fighting for three or so years by that stage and there was a little bit of a feeling that some people had come in a bit late, and there were a few jibes one way and another—'Hey mister, I've been with your sister', and so there was quite a bit of animosity.
Peter Huskins, North Australia Observer Unit

We went into this hotel in the city, Sydney, and there wasn't one Australian in the place, all Yanks, and we went to the bar and they didn't serve us, and I demanded a drink and it was, 'We don't need your type in here, only Americans'. And I thought 'This is not on' so we went out and we got a few of the 6th Divvy boys and we took about 30 back to the pub. We didn't want to put a blue on with the Yanks, all we wanted was to make sure we got service. Well we got our service OK. From what I understand though, once the 6th Divvy moved up north, they went back to only serving Yanks.
Alan Low, 6th Division

I always thought they were a gun-happy lot of cowboys. I remember saying to one bloke, 'What were you before you came here in the Army?'. And he said 'Ah hed a hawg ranch in Arkansas'. And there were hundreds of them, they'd never had a life like it—they had plenty of money to buy black-market liquor and all that type of thing, they had a carefree sort of attitude. We weren't allowed to use police cars, they were parked outside the station to save petrol, but you went down around the wharves and the Yanks were washing their clothes with petrol, they didn't give a damn about anything.
Ray Blissett, policeman, Sydney

There was a widespread feeling that the Americans weren't very good at war—and they weren't, in the sense that the Australians were, the sense of improvising and giving it a go and being very individualistic about things. They did terribly silly things very often, and they weren't good in the field, they weren't good at pitching a camp, and they had a tendency to expect things to be done by somebody else. They were terrific soldiers with what they had, because they had a terrific amount of armaments and it was all the best stuff. But they never bothered to repair anything, whereas of course to the Australians at that time, everything was repairable, so that annoyed people.
John Hinde

These Americans I saw in Rockhampton were so young and inexperienced, they'd just been sent out here to be trained and to help defend Australia, and they were more or less waiting for someone to put something in their hands.

I was quite horrified one day when I looked up and there was this huge transport plane and this tiny little pilot seemed to leap from the cabin and I said to him 'How long have you been in the services?'. And he said 'Oh four or five months ago I was in the entertainment industry, I was a song and dance man'. And I said 'Good heavens!' and he said 'We're being trained so quickly that some of the fellows are not able to negotiate the sea flight, so some don't even make it'. And I thought 'Well, we really are in a bad state'.
Thelma Long, AWAS

But the Yanks were all done up in very resplendent uniforms whereas we had almost the same as what our father had in the First War, I think, and we were on six bob [60 cents] a day as a private and ten bob a day as a corporal—whereas the Yankee privates were on about three dollars a day.
Peter Huskins

And the Americans had an awful lot of privileges, their PXs were stuffed with goods that we couldn't get at all and that Australian soldiers couldn't get either, including nylons which were a mad article of commerce with the girls, and chocolates and liquor, terribly cheap liquor. And they became unpopular with the civilians in general because of this.
John Hinde

They knew that MacArthur was going to take them back to the Philippines, and therefore they were in for a lot of battles when they left here. So they were making sure they had a good time. They liked to go to Menzies [a Melbourne hotel] and all the eating places, and they'd tip five pounds to get a seat at the table. If you were lucky enough to have one of your friends come back on leave, that chap mightn't get a table, and he couldn't get a taxi, because the American would get one first. And that was a bit hard to take.
Patricia Penrose, Z Special Unit, Melbourne

The Americans had number one priority on taxis and quite a few nights I walked several miles from work to where I was living at the time. Taxis would drive by with just one Yank in, and that was one of the disheartening parts of the war years, because after all you weren't wanting a lift for nothing, you were paying your way but you were only paying the normal taxi rate so of course the Yank bought the taxi as the saying is, and you just walked.

Athol Meers, aircraft construction supervisor, Sydney

2 Where's my mother?

My wife and I went to the show on Sunday and it was *Bambi*—Walt Disney's *Bambi*—and it got real sad in one place where Bambi was lost and Bambi was saying 'Mother, Mother, I want my mother, where's my mother?'. And there came this great big Australian accent—'SHE'S OUT WITH A BLOODY YANK!' and everybody just roared.

Bill Bentson, staff sergeant, US Army

Lots of girls of course fell madly in love with the Americans and they used to sit in the women's common room and show photographs of these glamorous looking officers and some of them of course were married already and promised all sorts of things about how they'd come back after the war, but were never seen again.

Dorothy Hewett, university student, Perth

Well, some people were so stupid. There'd be women, their husbands away and they might have five or six kids, and the Americans would say they were going to marry them and they really believed it, and a lot of marriages broke up because of it.

Dulcie Cunningham, housewife and mother, Beaudesert, Queensland

My dear old dad was a very funny man. I was going back to camp one day and when he took me to the train there were some Yanks and he said to these Yanks, 'Now you keep your hands off my daughter' and I was terribly embarrassed.

Peggy Williams, Land Army

I was coming home this evening and there was an American soldier standing there and he said 'Good evening'. And I said 'Good evening soldier'.

So he said 'Would you like to stop and have a little tickle up?'. So I looked him up and down, and gave him my answer, but I realised then what our girls were up against.

Nell Stronach, AWAS welfare worker

I remember dancing with this American and he wanted to take me

home and I said, no I wasn't going home with him, so right in the middle of the dance floor he said 'No loving, no dancing' and he just left me in the middle of the floor and walked off—I never forgot that, I felt so embarrassed. An Australian boy would never have said that, and got away with it, but they seemed to be able to say anything. 'Could you tell us who plays?' they said, 'we haven't got time to mess around or court'—as if I was going to tell them. I said, 'There's no way I'm going to put you in touch with anybody!'.
Dulcie Cunningham

I got tailed by six Americans, following me back to the hotel, and I said 'This is not safe'. Well then a decree came out that women were not allowed to go out unescorted unless they had somebody with a revolver escorting them, that's how bad it was—there were cases of rape up there then.
Toni Mooy Hurley, Army records office, Darwin

After the Americans had arrived the city became very crowded of course, and there was a lot of activity, night shows and what have you, in the city. So there were a lot of people around, but quite suddenly in the papers we started to read about these murders, and there were three girls murdered.
Glenys Kirk, office worker, Melbourne

Everyone was petrified, it went on for about two months. Anyway they caught him, and he was a Russian American, Leonski, an enormous fellow and he was quite mental. He had something about voices, and that's why he strangled.
Edna Macdonald, munitions worker, Melbourne

There was a big ruckus politically, the Australian police wanted to prosecute him for murder in the civil court, but MacArthur said 'No, he's going to be tried by court martial', and MacArthur finally won out and he was court-martialled by the US Army and he was hung in Pentridge Prison in Melbourne.
Bill Bentson

But he'd built a lot of fear into the girls—I know I never came home by myself ever again.
Glenys Kirk

There were always these stories going around—you had to be careful of the Americans because they had drugs and they'd feed you Spanish Fly and you'd find yourself raped in the bottom of an air-raid shelter or dead or whatever—it might have been better to have been dead than raped, who knows, that was more or less the impression you got, and naked of course.

And there was one story that hit the headlines about a group of Perth socialites. There'd been a party and they'd had a fountain made

of champagne—that sounds very exotic, specially for Perth—and all these girls had sat around naked dipping their breasts into the champagne and then the Americans would suck the champagne off their nipples and one of the Americans got carried away and bit one society lady's nipple off and she had to be rushed to Royal Perth Hospital. Now whether it was true or not I don't know but it was certainly told and delighted in, in Perth.
Dorothy Hewett

People were very judgemental about the girls who fraternised with the Americans. Lots and lots of girls on principle wouldn't have a bar of going out with an American.
Bob Bahnsen

There were very mixed feelings about it. There was a general disapproval but I think it was OK if they were officers—if they were just ordinary ratings, that was fairly frowned upon. But it really wasn't much use disapproving because virtually everyone did it of course. But after the war it was very interesting because lots of girls who'd been quite notorious for their affairs with Americans seemed to become super-respectable and pretend that such a thing had never happened in their lives. I always found this most amusing and you would think that the American invasion amongst the respectable young Perth matrons had never happened.
Dorothy Hewett

I would never go out with an American, like a lot of other women, because we felt we were being disloyal to our men who were

'I always remember "VD and a rabbit-skin coat" ': Dorothy Hewett saw another side of the American 'invasion' when she worked as a court reporter in Perth after leaving university. This photo was taken at the outbreak of war, when she was 16. (Photo: Betty Picken)

fighting. We just thought they were out there fighting and we shouldn't be home here having a good time.
Patricia Penrose

I didn't go out much with Americans, I went out with a submarine rating a couple of times but I didn't find him very interesting—he wanted to give me his class pin but I wouldn't take it. I preferred Australians. I think the American habit of showering gifts on their girlfriends embarrassed me more than anything else. I was fundamentally suspicious of the motives of people who did this sort of thing and I was, I guess, an Australian patriot and I went out with Australian servicemen who didn't give you anything except a fuck. This was what I was used to and I felt at home with this sort of situation.
Dorothy Hewett

My boss, who I was working for at De Havilland Aircraft at the time, he had given me a lift into town when I met Fred for a date and of course he saw Fred in his American uniform and we were never friends after that. He completely ignored me. I didn't know the reason at the time but one of the other workers told me—'He saw you going out with that Yank'—and so that was the finish of the friendship with him.
Margaret Blair, office worker, Sydney

It just didn't do to go out with Americans, you were suspect. They were said to be fast—we always used the word 'fast'. Two of our girls went out with Americans when we were in Queensland—one went on a hayride. We'd never heard of these hayrides and when we learnt what they were, oh yes, she was really sent to Coventry. It was being disloyal to your own menfolk to go out with them. And the Yanks, they were like any boys in a foreign country—when you get away from home all the barriers are down.
Patsy Adam-Smith, VAD nurse

There was one corner that wasn't quite desirable at the Trocadero, and when I say undesirable, there'd be quite a few young ladies that we didn't wish to know, they were not such nice types, and they dressed rather tarty we thought. And quite often the Vice Squad would come in and take a few girls off with them, which astounded us because we didn't quite know what was going on, at the time.
Nora Symonds, textile worker, Sydney

One of the social concerns at that time was what was called promiscuity. All these girls had come to the cities offering their favours to these blokes in uniform who were probably going off on final leave and what have you. The prostitutes were very outspoken about it, they called them 'charity roots'. And the beats seemed to be around all the parks and the beaches and around the harbour wharves, to round up these girls. The blokes got off free and the girls

seemed to be put through a very humiliating routine, I think they were locked up and the next day they were put through a humiliating medical examination.
Ted Hartley

I know there were a lot of girls that were very promiscuous with the Americans. One thing they used to laugh about, though, a lot of them didn't want to go to Sydney because they said that anyone that goes to Sydney always came back with the Sydney cough, they called it—which was VD.
Dulcie Cunningham

They found suddenly that the Americans who had arrived here, healthy and certainly without any sign of VD, when they got hold of some of the amateur Australian girls (not the prostitutes), they had, with the first contact, probably got themselves a venereal disease. Amateurs were all the nice little girls who swarmed around them like flies. Many of them were kids, particularly from the country, who were drawn into the city and they had no idea of city life and they saw these nice boys, with strange accents, who were very friendly and by far more sophisticated than the Australian soldier. And it was unfortunate, because the prostitutes looked after themselves, they knew that it's part of their earning capacity to stay healthy.
Alfred Ruskin, Army medical corps

The Vice Squad was very active and they would roam the parks and the back seats of the cinemas and pick girls up; particularly anyone who was under 21, with an American, could be picked up. It was an appalling time in many ways. When I was a reporter one of the things that I used to see in the Children's Court was very young girls, some of them no older than twelve. They would have gone off with some American—because unfortunately the Americans seemed to have a passion for very immature girls—and these girls would be absolutely entranced by chocolates and clothes and money and nightclubs and the whole bit, and they would disappear from home, and the American would find them a room, usually in Fremantle because that's where the ships would be docked.

Then the girl would be discovered either by parents or police or Vice Squad or somebody, the American would have gone, and she'd be left absolutely destitute and often these girls would come into court and I always remember 'VD and a rabbit-skin coat'—that was what many Americans left these young girls with, and they'd go off to reform school, and God knows what happened to them. So there were tragedies like this which were very widespread. Because in a very old-fashioned and conservative society which Western Australia certainly was, and an overgrown country town, which Perth was, the influx of a whole lot of young men from a completely different culture, with a lot of money to spend, and much more sophisticated, and with no sense of responsibility—because soldiers don't have,

they're transients and anyway, a week, a month, they'll be dead perhaps—this absolutely rent apart the fabric of that society in a most extraordinary way.
Dorothy Hewett, court reporter, Perth

My sister had become attached to an American and he got me a job in the chaplains' office with the American Navy in the Grace Building in Sydney. And some of the girls would come in trying to find the chaps who had 'done them wrong'. Now there was one lass came in and she was about to give birth and the chaplain and I got her in a taxi and rushed her off to the nearest hospital; and she was looking for the man that did her wrong. There was an awful lot of pregnant girls that kept coming and going but in between there were girls who were quite nice types and you can't blame the girls really, the Americans were sort of rather overpowering, you either did or else I don't see you again.
Toni Mooy Hurley

The saddest part as far as I was concerned was that there were so many neglected children. Blokes would be away at the war getting five or six shillings a day and they would leave their wives behind and they'd have two or three children and if the children were of school age, their mothers would perhaps go down and have a beer if they could find a pub open with some beer, and they'd meet up with a Yank and become enamoured with him and he'd become enamoured with them of course, and they neglected their children, you've got no idea. I, with my mates at the Glebe over the years, we took numerous children away and charged them—had them taken to the Children's Court as being neglected and hauled their mothers before the court and charged them under the Child Welfare Act with neglecting them. And I thought that was one of the sad things about the war, that women were so prone to neglect their children and run around with Yanks who had plenty of money in their pockets—didn't give a damn what became of the kids.
Ray Blissett

The Americans naturally went out quite a lot with women who were already married to servicemen who maybe hadn't seen their husbands for years, and it was a delight to them I imagine to have male company and to have somebody making a fuss of them and to have a sexual experience with somebody. And of course some of these women had children and they also got from their husbands their allotment, and therefore there was a sort of very strong moral frowning upon all this kind of thing and often neighbours who for some reason or other didn't like the woman or were very narrow-minded or whatever, would put these women in to the authorities. And their allotment would be stopped; the husband— wherever he was—would be told what was going on; and they would be dragged into court, sometimes a Children's Court, where there

would be a hearing. And I saw children dragged away from their mothers physically, bodily, in court, with the mother screaming and crying and the children, little children, screaming, because she was considered no longer a fit mother. These scenes I've never forgotten, they were appalling, and in many cases it was simply because the woman had an American boyfriend and that was her sole crime.
Dorothy Hewett

3 Our buddies were not our buddies

MacArthur was pretty unpopular really because he was seen as a 'big I Am' Yank which indeed he was, and it was felt that he had taken over the war and that the Australians had no say in it anymore, all we were doing was providing soldiers for gun fodder and that all the decisions were being made by the Americans. This was I think a very bitter feeling amongst all Australians, not just the troops themselves—I know it was very strong amongst them—but amongst the people at home as well, their wives and girlfriends and people who talked about the war. So MacArthur was not seen as the liberator or the great military hero—he was seen as a blustering takeover merchant largely, by most of the people I knew anyway.
Dorothy Hewett

He was a man who understood the uses of the press, and of drama. He was a very fascinating character, and a dangerous character in a way—he certainly suppressed the achievements of other generals and other armies. He didn't make the most of them to say the least.

The GHQ communiqués were very much related to American troops and made very little real mention, certainly no fulsome mention, of Australian troops and there was nothing much we could do about that. Their communiqués were sacrosanct and what we could add was all subject to censorship. And I'm quite sure that the Australian exploits at Buna and on the Owen Stanley Track, for instance, could have been better told at the time than they were. It caused worry, and resentment too, but there wasn't much you could do about it.
John Hinde

We pushed the Japanese back down the Kokoda Trail—the Australians did that, but General MacArthur put out his bulletin, the American and Allied troops took Buna and Gona or whatever, and that got me very mad, it really did and I altered all his communiqués, always, to say Australian and American troops. Oh God, it just got me so mad I hated his guts and so did all my boys, they were all the same way because they were in the cutting rooms. We were very anti-MacArthur and I'm still anti-MacArthur because he was a poseur.

He never missed an opportunity to put the American troops in front and not even mention the Australians so that when you went to America later on they didn't even know we were in the war up there.

This was absolutely vicious, quite an untenable attitude, but he did it and that's why I have no great respect for him.
Ken G. Hall, managing editor, *Cinesound Review*, Sydney

It would start off all right while they were drinking together, a lot of them were good blokes, and them Yankee dollars, they'd buy all the time. And then someone would say something and it'd erupt from there, finish up in a blue—there was a fair bit of that went on.
Alan McMillan, dockworker, Sydney

It developed into a standing riot one day when the whole of Collins Street was turned into a battlefield and it finished up with one American soldier who'd been arrested and he was being questioned as to how it had all started and the poor boy said 'That Australian—he had questioned the honour of my mother'. Well of course it was obvious the Australian had just said 'You bloody Yankee bastard' or something—but they were still at it four hours later.
Niall Brennan

There was a huge fight in Perth in one of the pubs. The New Zealanders were there with some Maoris, and there were southern Americans who of course were very racist and they refused to drink with the Maoris, and there was one hell of a fight. And there were some stabbings went on—Americans stabbing Australian soldiers. In fact there was one park in Perth which was known as a very notorious park and you didn't go near there after dark because there were often murders and attacks and various other things between warring servicemen.
Dorothy Hewett

We were camped up in Townsville and four of us had gone into town and we were going across the main bridge in Townsville, and we came upon these Yanks walking from the opposite direction and they wouldn't get out of the road. Next minute a fight broke out, which wasn't hard, and we were punching up and one of the Yanks pulled a knife and stabbed one of our fellows and of course this was really infuriating, we always reckoned it was Queensberry Rules, more or less, and so we tossed a couple of the Yanks off the bridge and the others ran away. And our mate was a pretty sick boy, he was boarded out medically unfit after that.
Alan Low

If a troop train got stranded in Mackay, as it often did in the wet season, the Australian troops were kept on the train, fed there, then allowed to march down town as a unit, but they were never allowed to wander around individually, and you wouldn't see a Yank in town when they were in. So we never had any problems in Mackay, not like they did in Rockhampton and Brisbane.
Roger Jones, schoolboy, Mackay, Queensland

If the American fleet was in you wouldn't find the Australian fleet or
the Royal Navy, because they'd alternate their leaves. They just didn't
want them to clash too much I suppose, because some of them used
to be a bit jealous of each other, that's how I understood it.
Joy Boucher, aircraft construction worker, Sydney

I think it was played down an enormous amount, that hostility
between Australian servicemen and the Americans, but it was very
very noticeable in Perth. And of course in Brisbane there was a sort of
mini-war on the streets.
Dorothy Hewett

Our canteen [in Brisbane] was pretty basic, whereas in the American
canteen they had all the top food, ice-cream and sauces and chicken
and everything else, and the Australians weren't allowed in the
American canteen. And a fellow in our company called Ted Matthews
had palled up with a couple of Americans and they'd said, 'Come on
Aussie, we'll take you to our canteen'. So when they went to go in,
the two American guards on the door said, 'Sorry buddy you can't go
in there'. And Ted said 'Look I'm with my American friends, we've
been to the Australian canteen, now we're coming to yours', and so
on—'Sorry buddy, you're not allowed'. Well that upset Ted a bit and
he'd had a bit to drink anyway—so he dropped the guards.

That didn't go over too well, and from there it started into quite a
battle and it was a case of hit a head if you saw it and it was well
and truly on. There would have been several hundred, probably a
thousand or more people involved in it.
Peter Huskins

And it eventually ended up up half a block down the street and more
Australians gathered and no-one knew what was going on, but
anytime there's a big crowd the rest of the guys want to come down
and see, and I don't think half of them knew what was going on that
evening. But this animosity had been building up.
Bill Bentson

It's interesting to really see a riot from above. It's terribly ineffective,
people just push each other around and give each other a thump now
and again. If you don't fall down it's really just like being at the races.
But it was pretty savage, they were very angry.

For the next night or so there were American patrols, mostly
Marines, marching in platoon strength and vigour through the streets
of Brisbane. And I remember crossing the street and there was a
crowd of Marines marching down towards me and there was one
terribly nervous Marine who, presumably accidentally, pressed the
trigger of his machine gun and started spraying blasts of fire around. I
actually heard a bullet whizz past me and I went and hid behind an
electricity switchbox on the edge of the road. But a girl in a

'I actually heard a bullet whizz past me': John Hinde was there as a war correspondent during the 'battle of Brisbane' when US and Australian troops fought each other in the streets of the city.

moviehouse ticket office, she picked up a bullet—I don't think she was killed. It was really remarkably tense.

John Hinde

There was every reason for conflict you could imagine. There was a cultural clash of gargantuan proportions. They tried various ways of solving the problem, but it was an insoluble problem, it just didn't work—our buddies were not our buddies.

Niall Brennan

9
All Normal Life Suspended

I do not think the enemy can now invade this country. We have proved that, with the resources we have had, together with the command of the seas established by the gallant United States Navy by decisive victories at Midway Island and the Solomon Islands. We are not yet immune from marauding raids which may cause much damage and loss. I believe, however, that we can hold Australia as a base from which to launch both limited and major offensives against Japan. This conception must be the pattern to govern the nature and extent of Australia's war effort . . .

The Prime Minister, John Curtin, in a press statement released on 10 June 1943.

The threat of Japanese invasion in 1942 had a remarkable effect on Australian social, political and economic life. There was a complete reorganisation of the military with General Blamey appointed Commander-in-Chief of the Army. Over a dozen army divisions were raised, and by August 1942 656 000 Australians were in uniform. The largest number in the services at any one time was 732 000 in August 1943, from a population of a little over 7 million.

In the emergency the government handed over strategic direction of the war to General MacArthur, and in return US ships and planes helped defend Australia. The government used the threat of invasion to seek additional men and military equipment from the United States and, assisted by MacArthur, was partly successful in obtaining additional Allied support.

A range of domestic measures was introduced, designed to make the best use of available manpower and to raise the output of war *matériel* and primary produce. The latter was to supply food not only to the Allied forces in the South-West Pacific but also Britain. As discussed in the introduction to Chapter 7, manpower was controlled, austerity measures were introduced, and regulations controlled strikes, information and interstate travel.

By the early months of 1943, it was clear that the nation could not sustain this war effort and that cutbacks would have to be instituted either in production or in the armed forces. But MacArthur was anxious that there be no reduction either in the supplies provided to his forces, or in the number of Australian divisions available to him. Using the threat of invasion, Curtin could maintain the war effort at a high level, but eventually it would become obvious to the public that this threat no longer existed. Finally, on 10 June 1943, after advice from MacArthur, Curtin announced that Australia was no longer likely to be invaded and that the focus would now be on offensives against the Japanese.

It took some time for the government to undertake the difficult task of reallocating manpower, but on 1 October 1943 War Cabinet agreed that 20 000 men were to be released from the services and 10 000 from the munitions and aircraft industries by June 1944. The monthly intake into the services was to be fixed at 5000 men and women, and the RAAF was to be limited to 48 squadrons. The War Cabinet wanted Australia to continue a military commitment which would guarantee Australia 'an effective voice in the peace settlement'. But before implementing this plan the government wanted it to be approved by MacArthur and by the British and US governments.

In the meantime, the strategic situation improved considerably. Following the defeat of the Japanese on the north coast of Papua in January 1943, a Japanese troop-carrying convoy was sunk by Allied aircraft in the Bismarck Sea, and from January to September 1943 the Japanese were driven back from Wau to Salamaua. Then in September, three Australian divisions conducted a major sea, air and land assault on Lae. The Japanese were defeated and withdrew from Salamaua and Lae. Following up quickly, Australian units landed by sea at Finschhafen and advanced up the Markham and into the Ramu Valleys, heading towards the rugged Finisterre Ranges. Sattelberg and Shaggy Ridge were taken, and by April 1944 Madang had been captured. For almost two years the Australians had carried the brunt of the fighting in New Guinea, and in early 1944 the main combat role was taken over by the Americans.

The principal Australian combat divisions spent the next nine to twelve months retraining in Australia before undertaking the final campaigns of the war. By the end of 1944, Australian divisions were in action on the islands of Bougainville and New Britain, and in the Aitape–Wewak area of New Guinea. But General MacArthur seemed reluctant to use the remaining two AIF divisions in his campaign in the Philippines, preferring to use American forces to liberate the islands to which he had vowed to 'return'. These AIF divisions were not committed to operations in Borneo until mid-1945, and by this time it was only a matter of time before Japan was defeated.

In April and May 1944, Curtin visited London and Washington and secured Allied agreement to the proposed reductions in the Australian war effort, but when he returned to Australia there were further arguments about the extent of reductions to be applied in the Army and Air Force. Against strong resistance from Blamey, in August 1944 Curtin directed that the Army was to release 30 000 men and the RAAF 15 000 men over the next nine months.

Despite these reductions, Australia maintained its war effort at a high level. During 1943 and 1944, Australian aircrews took part in bombing offensives over Germany and suffered cruel casualties for what, in retrospect, was doubtful strategic gain. The surrender of Germany in May 1945 had little direct impact in Australia. At that time the RAAF had about 16 000 men in Europe; 12 300 of these were aircrew. Australia was the only nation whose war effort increased after the defeat of Germany. In July 1945 Australia had six divisions in combat—more that at any time in the war.

The task of maintaining this war effort had been borne by the Labor Government headed by John Curtin. At times his government was criticised for the apparent pettiness of its austerity measures, and the nation was governed by a mass of regulations. The Commonwealth Public Service more than doubled in number from 47 000 permanent and temporary employees in June 1939 to almost 100 000 in 1944. Commonwealth government departments expanded from twelve in 1938 to 25 in 1944, including the important Departments of War Organisation of Industry and Post-War Reconstruction.

Despite the increasing regulation of society, the public generally approved of the government's handing of the war effort, and this was shown by its re-election with a large majority in August 1943. It was a tribute to the leadership of John Curtin; as the journalist Keith Murdoch wrote at the time, he 'lifted his own side to a dignified level and tried hard to move it to the middle of the road with promises of moderation that must make the Sydney Trades Hall shiver'. But the effort badly affected his health, and after several bouts in hospital with a 'strained heart', he died on 5 July 1945. The Deputy Prime Minister, Frank Forde, assumed the leadership, and after a party vote the Treasurer, J. B. Chifley, became Prime Minister on 13 July. With the end of the war in sight, he would face a different set of challenges to those tackled during the previous three years.

For the last two-and-a-half years of the war, the public was buoyed by the news of a succession of victories, both in Europe and closer to home in the Pacific. After the threat of invasion in 1942, they knew that there could be no let-up until Japan was defeated, and generally they accepted that normal life had to be suspended. The daily life of average Australians during this time became markedly different from anything experienced before or after.

1 An exciting time

I felt like I grew up and we were at war all the time I was growing up—all my school years. But for me as a child, and not understanding how serious all this was, they were great years. I thought it was an exciting time for a child.
Lillian Harding, schoolgirl, Adelaide

Trenches were dug at school, and I was only in the Infants School and if an air-raid siren went off, I had the distinct impression I was to sit at the corner of the trench and look up into the air, and if a bomb came, I was to shift all the children out of my trench into another. And I went home and told my parents and they said, 'They wouldn't ask a seven-year-old to do that'—but I was convinced that that was my job to do.
Helen McAnulty, schoolgirl, Canberra

Children carried identity discs which the government issued, probably after the Japanese entered the war, and we had to wear them all the time. They were on a string around our necks, and you were supposed to leave them on while you were in the shower or

swimming, and there was a number on it I think. And a lot of us carried a whistle as well, so that if you were pinned under a fallen post during a bombing raid, you could whistle for help.
Maurie Jones, schoolboy, Perth

All children had to carry air-raid bags, with a cork to put in your mouth, between your teeth so that when the explosion came your teeth wouldn't break, with cottonwool to put in your ears, and barley sugar to chew and you weren't to touch that. And of course over the years that you carried this bag, the barley sugar got worse and worse and worse, you can imagine. And a comic to read while the bombs were falling.
Helen McAnulty

And two bandages, one a triangular one in case of a broken arm. And we had to hang this bag over our neck and go down to wherever we had to go for air-raid practice. And the first practice we had I remember we went to an area where there were bull ants and most of the children got bitten.
Margaret Burton, schoolgirl, Adelaide

I was a Zero aeroplane one day and a Wellington bomber the next. We had our heroes, a lot of British heroes and I always liked being Guy Gibson because he got a Victoria Cross. That was up 'til he was killed then I picked on somebody else. But I can remember spreading my arms and running round the backyard and making frightful noises like machine guns and all the kids did it and one minute you were a German and then an Aussie and the next minute you were an American. You always came back to being an Aussie though, that was the main thing.
Ken Haylings, schoolboy, Sydney

We felt that it was a serious time and that things were really bad but we still played our games, and they were war games—there were Japanese and there were Germans and there was us. I had three brothers and I always had to be the enemy. We had things made up to look like swords and things fashioned out of pieces of wood to look like guns, and I always had to play dead and hide amongst the foxholes and rabbit holes.
Rosemary McCourt, schoolgirl, South Australia

We were all so into the fact that the Germans and the Japanese were baddies. And we were always on the lookout. There was a poor bus conductor called Gus and I don't know why but we thought Gus was a German. I think it might have been because he didn't stand up for 'God Save The King' at the pictures one afternoon. And we gave him a terrible time—children can be so cruel. We didn't have Japanese of course, but Chinese were regarded with some suspicion and I was living in Canberra which was much more racially mixed than other

towns of course. So we did come into contact with other races to be suspicious of. We were all very insular I think.
Helen McAnulty

Our street was quite near the South Parklands [in Adelaide] so that was our playground and the Army took over the Parklands during the daytime for the soldiers for drill or whatever, and all the kids in the street used to hang around and watch them and we never thought a great deal of it, we were rather cheeky. Someone would come charging at a sandbag with a bayonet and they'd miss and the kids would say, 'Naa naa na naa naa, you missed'.
Lillian Harding

A lot of the children had fathers away at the war—two of the boys in my class had fathers as prisoners of war. But some fathers were away, *not* at the war but the family put out that they were. That sort of stunt covered a lot of things that weren't talked about in those days—when fathers left families.
Margaret Maxwell, schoolgirl, Swan Hill, Victoria

I was seven when the war started and I lived in Woodville [Adelaide] and we were surrounded by all sorts of munitions factories and army camps. The classrooms that I occupied in grade six and seven at primary school faced the Port Road and quite often there'd be a column of troops marching, there'd be trucks going by with all sorts of war munitions and every now and again the teachers would say in the middle of the class, 'Right, we'll have a quiz. How many men in that platoon, what do the badges mean, what sort of rifles are they carrying, are they Australians or Americans?'.
John Drennan

I loved all the war movies, I quite believed everything in them, they were great propaganda for kids like us. I just never had any fear that we were going to lose the war, I mean they told us in the movies—the goodies always win, the baddies always lose.
   I saw as many as I could—not that our mother could afford to give us money to go, but I had another way of getting money to go to the pictures. We used to have these cards with little squares on them, for fundraising, and you had to collect a penny and put a prick into each square with a pin, that was your way of receipting the money you were getting. But I was a bit crafty, I wanted a bit of money of my own to go and see all these pictures, so I would pretend to prick the card and as soon as that person had gone away, I'd put the money in my pocket. And that's how I came to be a movie buff of all the 1940s movies—which wasn't very honest.
Lillian Harding

There was a war bonds rally at one stage and they had a Messerschmitt that had been shot down during the Battle of Britain

and brought back to Australia. They charged 6d a sit and you could climb in and sit in the pilot's seat and smell all this oil—I'll never forget that oil!
Margaret Maxwell

I went to Petersham Primary School and a plane—I think it was a Mosquito bomber-type plane—exploded over Petersham for no apparent reason and of course the bodies were strewn all over the place and one landed in the playground at Petersham School. It crashed through a tree, and I don't want to be gory about this but there was quite a dent where the body landed.
Ken Haylings

2 Getting the news

During the war we wouldn't miss a news broadcast, not for anything—you'd go along the street, you'd pass a radio shop and as soon as you knew the news was on you'd stop and listen. Everyone would, there'd be crowds around the door of the radio store because the radios would be there with the news and some of the broadcasts were very bad for a long long time—everyone was waiting for something good to happen with the news.
Joy Boucher, aircraft construction worker, Sydney

We weren't allowed to breathe when the 'British Grenadiers' came on, the music that always preceded the news of the war, and we sat there in silence the whole time the news was on.
Roma Wallis, store assistant, Gulgong, New South Wales

At home we had a huge map of the world on the kitchen wall and the wireless was in the room and when the shortwave radio or the news came over the BBC we had to sit in silence so that every word could be heard and then my father used to pinpoint on the map just what was happening overseas in Germany and in Europe and the Pacific.
Rosemary McCourt

We had the wireless on all the time because, in those pre-television days and especially in families like ours that didn't have much money for regular movie-going, the wireless was the great thing, all the serials and so on, 'Dad and Dave'; patriotic serials as well—there were a lot of those and then of course the news. We listened to the news regularly, seven o'clock in the morning, two o'clock in the afternoon, five o'clock and then seven o'clock. And it did play a big part in everybody's life because it was your quickest way of getting whatever was the latest news. Probably people listened to the radio more during the war years than they did before or have done since.
Maurie Jones

You lived by the wireless, it was a great source of news, but I can remember vividly too the concerts they put on for the troops and they were always very very popular, with singing and telling jokes and all this carry-on and I can remember listening to the AWA bakelite radio sitting up on the mantelpiece—we all crammed around that every night after the evening meal—we'd done our homework, we were allowed to listen.

And then you went to the local picture house on a Saturday night because the newsreels were on. You always looked forward to the newsreels because they emphasised the war. You'd see great masses of marching troops and the Brits would go through and they'd get a cheer and the Yanks would go through and they'd get a sort of subdued cheer and the Germans or the Japanese would come on, of course they got booed, but when the Australians came on, that's when the feet'd start to thump on the floor and the clapping of hands and the cheers and everything. That was really morale boosting, it was a really good show.

Ken Haylings

My brother fought overseas, in Greece and Crete and then in New Guinea. Mum and Dad and my sister Peg, we used to follow the news and just pray that he wasn't in whatever bad part, and at the movies you'd watch every newsreel, just hoping you'd see him—I mean what were the chances, but still, you did that.

Nola Bridger, schoolgirl, Sydney

As daily homework, we had to read the papers and pick out newscuts on what was going on and we'd then have to paste them into school books and write a short story perhaps about the progress of the war as a kind of geography lesson. We kept a war diary, almost, and that was part of our normal daily school work.

John Drennan

Letters were my father's lifeline. We wrote every Friday night, the three of us, and my sister always did crosses and scribbles until she learned to write and we used to hold her hand and she'd write a few things. And we had to be very careful what we wrote because our letters were censored as well as his. So all we could do was just write little things that happened from day to day. Another thing, my mother never said we were sick because she felt that that would upset Dad.

Margaret Burton

In the early part of the war, it was lucky if we got a letter which was less than two months old. I wrote regularly to my mother, once a week when I could, I numbered all my letters and she numbered hers to me. Many more of hers went missing than mine did. She kept all mine, and I've still got them.

Roy Hall, Admiralty Yachtsman Scheme, ordinary seaman, RANVR

We used to make the grey blankets for the army. And my friends and I decided we would put little notes inside with our names and addresses, tuck them into the blankets, hopeful that we'd get a letter back from a soldier. So we waited and waited for some time, and then eventually our manager told us that they'd all gone to the Fuzzy Wuzzys [sic] in New Guinea. So we didn't receive any letters.
Nora Symonds, textile worker, Sydney

Some of the girls were wonderful, they never stopped writing. They were waiting to be called to a customer and they had a shoebox with the paper inside still scribbling away, writing—writing all the time to the boys.
Florence Paterson, department store clerk, Sydney

When we were living in Burwood it was a great thing to go down to the Burwood Road and the railway station went across the top of it, and we'd stand there and the troop trains would go through, and just like snow you'd be showered with letters and I've no idea how many penny-ha'penny stamps we bought and put on them. They'd written them, put them in an envelope but no stamp, and put the address on the front, and we'd send them off to whoever they belonged to. We used to go down and collect them off the road—hold the traffic up and collect all these letters before they ran over them—from their sons to say, 'We're leaving now Mum, we're on our way', 'cause it was the only way they could tell their parents where they were. That always went on when the troops were going out, always.
Anne Pellew, staff canteen worker, Sydney

When I met Eric, who became my husband, I was sixteen; and I didn't see him again for two-and-a-half years, he was in the Mediterranean. Then I saw him for one night in Sydney and he was up in the Islands for another eighteen months. So we used to write, and we'd number the letters. Sometimes when I got home at two o'clock in the morning I'd start writing a letter then, because I'd find there were two letters there numbered, and I hadn't answered them. And I had to answer every one, because that's all they lived for—their letters.
Joy Boucher

We had one letter that arrived which you could barely read, because in those days they wrote in pen and ink. And it was all run where it had been sunk, but apparently that was fairly common. The supply ships that went to Tobruk from Palestine, some of them were sunk and what they did was they sent out navy divers and brought up the mail, it was so important to them.
Margaret Burton

During the war you didn't wait to go and get your mail—you were waiting for the postman to come, everybody would be out the front

waiting and he used to say, before he'd get to the house—'Yes, you can smile today'—he was very very personal to everyone. Like, everyone would have a boy away.
Nola Bridger

3 Not for love nor money

Everything was tight, you couldn't get this, you couldn't get that, everything was going up overseas to the troops and they were getting the best of everything, what was left behind was getting the crumbs off the table.
Alan McMillan, dockworker, Sydney

In the beginning we all complained, but after a while, we got so used to doing without.
Beattie Crawford, store manager, Melbourne

Everyone was behind the war effort and I think a lot of the civilians were far worse off than we who were in the services, because they had to put up with all sorts of rationing, which we didn't have to, we were always fed and clothed and our transport looked after, our health and whatever, so I think it was often a harder war for those who were left.
Elva Batt, AAMWS amenities officer

When it was rumoured that there were going to be shortages, people did go mad and tried to stock up and build up supplies of all sorts of merchandise. Most people managed their food rations fairly well, but I think clothing and petrol were very hard.
Beattie Crawford

And I'm sorry to say that a lot of people rushed to the shops and hoarded in a most ridiculous way. I know for a fact that one woman bought 30 pairs of shoes and I hope they all got mouldy, myself.
Mary Holmes, schoolteacher, Sydney

There was a big clamp-down on luxury activities and luxury goods, and many goods were controlled in that you had to have a permit even to buy them. This was designed to slow down commerce generally so that people could think more about the war. Luxury goods were silk pyjamas, perfumes, things like that. There was a big argument over lipstick and the things that ladies need. Were ladies entitled to some sort of preferential treatment in some matters? Could they have silk underwear and not the gents?

All of these things were very seriously debated over big conference tables. On the day of the invasion of Normandy there was a high-level conference which was seriously debating the permissible size of babies' commodes; so some of the stuff that the department did was probably quite relevant and quite useful, but an awful lot of it was terribly bizarre—ripe for Gilbert and Sullivan.

On the other hand we dealt with a lot of individual things. A lady wrote to us once and said she badly needed some clothespegs. The clothespeg industry had dried up completely but we found one guy who was still making them so I remember I actually arranged for a dozen clothespegs to be posted down to her. I felt I was doing a patriotic duty.

Niall Brennan, Department of War Organisation of Industry, Melbourne

We got a delivery once a week from our warehouse and I allocated the goods to be sold so much a day, and I put it on sale at a different time every day and different times every week, so customers never got a pattern for it. And in that way, I was trying to give everybody a fair go.

Beattie Crawford

You couldn't sell out everything in one day, so the quota system was evolved. Each department had a certain amount of stock that they could sell each day, and then the girls got onto the knitting, not a minute was wasted; they started knitting and making camouflage nets, that's how David Jones used their staff's time.

Florence Paterson

But we were very short of staff. A lot of the girls went into the Land Army or nursing and then they employed a lot of very old ladies, well into their seventies some of them. I don't know where they came from—they must have advertised and in they came. It was better than nothing, I suppose.

Lesley O'Donnell, shop assistant, Sydney

Quite often if you were going through a shop you'd see people queuing up, so you'd join in too, just to see what they were queuing for. Of course, it might be something that you really wanted.

Barbara Doig, housewife and mother, Perth

The way rationing worked, you could only buy what the coupons would buy. So you would have, say nine coupons for a pair of shoes, twenty coupons for a nightgown, I've just forgotten for the moment how much for a lamb chop but we handed over the page and the coupon was taken off and that went through with the docket so that it obviously had to be taken before the product was handed over to you.

Florence Paterson

I had a job in the *Daily News* as a reporter and I got the sack for lining everybody up in queues to exchange their ration books when it

was the wrong time and they didn't have to do this at all, so they sacked me—they had all these irate housewives ringing up.
Dorothy Hewett, Perth

I remember my mother used to send us to the shop with the coupons with a warning, 'Don't lose the coupons!'—I think she would rather have lost one of us than the coupons, I mean the coupons were *food*.
Lillian Harding

I did quite a lot of work in the black market field, looking for the fellows who were printing coupons, it was a pretty thriving industry, this forging of clothing coupons and food coupons.
Ray Blissett, policeman, Sydney

There were incredible shortages in almost all paper goods—lunch wraps, and toilet rolls and paper bags and writing pads and all those stationery items, elastic, and you couldn't get thermos flasks for love nor money.
Beattie Crawford

I started school using a slate. When I got into the third grade we had an exercise book which we had to be very careful of so we didn't write a lot in it, only the important things. We had very few books to learn from—I only had one reading book for each grade in those first years, and if we wanted to read anything else, if anyone had anything at home they would bring it in.
Rosemary McCourt.

You only had a certain number of clothing coupons to use per year, so you really could only have one outfit a year. And materials were very scarce—there was very little about if you made your own clothing. So we just had to make do with what we could. But we got through all right, we still got our stockings from Coles for two-and-six a pair, and our make-up too. Starlite, from Woolworths or Coles, that's the one we used to buy.
Nora Symonds

It was a time of make-overs—gorgeous slacks made out of men's trousers and jackets that had been a man's. The only material you could get without coupons was unbleached calico so that was precious and we must have sold miles of it, not only for the thousands of cakes that were sent overseas, but girls made shirts out of it, and dresses.
Florence Paterson

Some of the best and finest of the factories went over to making military boots; so that we didn't actually have army boots, but fashion went out the window.
Florence Paterson

'No cuffs, and no double-breasted suits': Nora (Element) Symonds caught by a street photographer in George St, Sydney. The string bag was indispensable for wartime shopping.

It was very difficult to get lots of things, specially personal things—perfumes and that, but I can remember one day my husband was going over east and I knew you could get a lot of things over there that you couldn't get in the west and he said, 'Well, what can I get you?' and I said 'All I need is a bra'. And he said 'But how? What size?' and I told him he'd just have to judge it by the girl that served him, whether she was bigger or smaller. Anyhow, he brought them back and they fitted very well. I think at the shop he just put his hands up and said, 'About that big'.
Barbara Doig

There was no knicker elastic and we had buttons on our knickers and they were dreadful, I hated them, because the buttons would come undone and you'd be losing your knickers—not very nice!
Margaret Maxwell

Parachute silk was readily available, I suppose from parachutes which had been made and rejected as not being up to standard. It was always in odd-shaped pieces—like the panels of a parachute—and they were in great demand, particularly for women's underclothes and babies' dresses and things like that.
Maurie Jones

You mostly just wore recycled clothes, and lots of people made overcoats from blankets and they used to dye hessian for curtains. And you set your hair with bobby pins. Well, they were obsolete, you couldn't buy bobby pins, and if anyone stole your bobby pins there'd be a great old row.
Edna Macdonald, munitions worker, Melbourne

Everybody wore their suits for so long that they were quite shiny on the bottoms and the backs and I remember one chap saying, 'You should be run in for shining a light in the blackout'—the suit was so shiny.
Ken Muggleston, schoolboy, Katoomba, New South Wales

We did have a lot of balls and dances for fundraising and we always wanted a new evening dress, so we bought mosquito net which didn't take coupons and we dyed it and we put it over our ordinary evening dresses to brighten them up or we dyed our evening dresses a different colour. Sometimes we even swapped dresses just so we could say we had a new frock.
Roma Wallis, store assistant, Gulgong, New South Wales

Lots of girls didn't get married in bridal. Lots of wedding groups were just in a nice suit or frock and the husband in uniform. They evidently couldn't get the frocks. My wedding dress was very much in demand, it went the rounds because nobody had material and everything was on coupons, it was used at least five times and I was only too happy to lend it.
Mary Comer, soldier's wife, Gulgong, New South Wales

And even to make your own, you couldn't get silks or satins, and laces were just unheard of. Wedding presents—well, it was a very very meagre range then because there were no imports coming into the country.
Nora Symonds

You couldn't have a hot-water jug unless you had a doctor's

'My wedding dress was very much in demand': Mary (Adams) Comer, Gulgong, New South Wales whose dress was used by at least five brides during the war.

certificate, and I don't think I was able to even get the old traditional toaster. It was all baking dishes and money for presents.
Florence Paterson

You couldn't get stockings and that was when leg make-up came in and we'd spend hours with an eyebrow pencil trying to draw a straight seam up the back of our legs to simulate stockings and when it rained or you got very hot the stockings would run, with disastrous results.
Dorothy Hewett

And we'd get into terrible trouble from our parents because you can imagine the sheets. In those days you were lucky if you had two baths a week, that was normal, you had your weekly bath—sounds a bit strange now, but that's the truth.
Edna Macdonald

Rubber was a commodity that they needed in the war, so corsets and foundation garments were no longer made, so the slogan was 'Bulge for Britain'.
Roma Wallis

I rode a bike when I went to high school and we had to fill in numerous forms to get new tyres and tubes, because there was no rubber.
Margaret Maxwell

The petrol rationing, as I can recall from my father's experience, was two gallons a month for a small car, and four gallons a month for a larger car. For special situations you could get an extra allowance by going to the post office with a declaration.

   Gas producers came in, and most of them were on trailers, towed behind cars, although there were a few smaller models mounted on the back of cars. Its biggest failing was that it was very dirty as far as the engine operation went, and also it only produced about 75 per cent of the power that petrol would. But it was one way of covering distance if you had to cover distance.
Robert Squires, schoolboy, Warwick, Queensland

But annual holidays became a thing of the past. Travel was difficult.
Maurie Jones

I used to go to Gundaroo [southern NSW], where my uncle and aunt owned the general store. And I'd be this skinny little kid coming up from war-torn Sydney, and my aunty used to grab me, first up, soon as I arrived I'd be taken into the produce section to be put on the scales. They weighed me in. And about four weeks later when I was going home, I'd be weighed out to see how much weight they'd put on this skinny kid.
Brian Loughry, schoolboy, Sydney

There was some food you just couldn't get—like rice and sago. As it happened, I got yellow jaundice and one of the few things that you can keep down is rice. So the doctor prescribed rice and I was one of the few people in Adelaide who actually had a rice ration.
John Drennan

They banned coloured icing on cakes, the cochineal or the colouring all had to go into the war effort—what they did with it I don't know, probably used it for camouflage.
Ken Haylings

If I went to my friend's place for lunch or dinner at night, I would take my butter and sugar. And I remember one time when I was only about six or seven, my girlfriend and I decided we would surprise my mother by making a cake and we used all the butter and sugar ration. And she came home and she was anything but pleased of course.
Helen McAnulty

I remember going into the kitchen one day and I said, 'Oh what are you making Christmas cakes for Mum, now?'. And she said, 'This is for your uncle overseas'. And the last sugar and the last raisins and the last practically everything went into the Christmas cake, and we didn't have any Christmas cake. I hope my uncle got some.
Ken Muggleston

And the stringbag had come—people quite forget that until the war, things were delivered, women didn't have to carry them. Then suddenly Manpower restrictions meant that women had to carry things—and they didn't have things to carry in. I can remember my Aunt Anastasia saying that she took a pillowslip to bring things home in because she had a big family, she tried a suitcase, that looked a bit silly. So then, they were making camouflage nets all over the place and somebody realised that a camouflage net could just as well be made into a bag and that's how stringbags came about.

Well of course the first story that came out of them was a woman in Sydney swinging her stringbag around getting on a tram and it hooked in a bloke's fly buttons. I think that's apocryphal but it was the story that went round everywhere.
Patsy Adam-Smith, VAD nurse

There was a great shortage of grog, even beer—the pubs would open for half an hour and they'd drink all the beer, all that wasn't being sold on the black market to the Americans that is, and then they'd close.
Laurie Aarons, factory worker and Communist Party member, Sydney

Dedman was Minister for War Organisation of Industry and they treated him mercilessly; but it was largely his own fault because poor

old Dedman was a humourless Scot and who can be more humourless than that. He was a doctrinaire socialist, stuffed full of half-baked economic ideas, so he was able to introduce into his department a lot of absolutely bizarre schemes like the Austerity Suit, he forbade things like cuffs on suits, cuffs on trousers, and at one stage they accused him of banning Father Christmas because he tried to control Christmas spending. He was a terrible fool like that, who couldn't see that he was laying himself open to lampooning by the press. I think he deserved it actually.
Niall Brennan

Of course we always had a Santa Claus, so that was it. Whether he was banned or not. But there weren't many toys around for the children, you just had to make things. There were elderly gentlemen around the place that would make wooden toys. But the children never got very much in their stockings.
Barbara Doig

I did have a doll. But I must have been a pretty dumb kid because the doll used to disappear, around about November every year, then turn up Christmas morning with something lovely crocheted or knitted on it, something new. And of course it was the same doll. Mum used to take it to the Dolls' Hospital, and she'd have its cheeks painted and its lipstick on and everything, and that was it. She was a beautiful doll.
Dorothy Loughry, schoolgirl, Sydney

They were very trying years, you had to do a lot of things that you wouldn't ordinarily have done, you had to make do with clothes and you never threw away anything, like buttons, because you couldn't buy buttons, pearl buttons or anything like that. You had to be very careful—I still am, my family complains that I'm still miserly with things, but it was the years that I had to do it to get by.
Barbara Doig

It was irritating but people put up with it, I think they realised, or thought, it was necessary. I'm sure that for people who had to run a household, which I didn't have to, it was much more difficult. And of course there was the black market and that was flourishing, and people got together lots of tinned goods and things like that, but this was frowned upon, this was not patriotic—to do this sort of thing—and stories were told about people who did this and they were a bit outside the pale.
Dorothy Hewett

4 But most people had their little lurk

There was an enormous black market. Grog was hard to get in a lot of places, and standard items like butter were hard to get but you

could buy a pound of butter and a bottle of beer for a fiver on the black market. I don't know how the black marketeers got it.
Jack Pollard, cadet journalist, Sydney

Now and again my sister used to bring up some of the American officers and they'd come around and go to the dance and party on nearly all night at our place and they had a trailer full of grog which you couldn't get during the war, but they could always get it.
Dulcie Cunningham, housewife and mother, Beaudesert, Queensland

Most people had their little lurk, including my mother, and she had an arrangement by which every two weeks on a Saturday afternoon a stranger would turn up on a bicycle and hand over a parcel. Mum had four bob ready for it. And it was a piece of freshly slaughtered pork. Somebody kept pigs in the bush, out beyond the vineyards, and my uncle worked for them and so he was a sort of go-between.
Maurie Jones

Well it was going on everywhere. Someone would get the mail about someone up the pub selling cheap butter, well you'd race up and get a few extra pound, all this was going on. Thieving, there was a bit there.

There was tobacco going and all that caper. Everything was short, you couldn't get tobacco, they were bringing out all these cheap brands, some of them would kill you if you were smoking them, and so if you got on to a bit of good tobacco, you'd go get it. Well, it was all black market, we knew that; but you asked no questions, you got told no lies sort of thing; everybody knew it was going on.

If you could get a bottle of whisky, which was very scarce, those that had it were selling it to the Yanks because that's their national drink but they wasn't paying money, they was giving them cartons of cigarettes, Pall Mall, Phillip Morris, they'd give you five or six cartons of them for one bottle of whisky, now you could sell them for five quid a carton. Well a lot was doing it and they made good money out of it because they had access to where to get it.
Alan McMillan

A lot of damaged ships came to Sydney and one of the things that was always missing was their manifest, and no one, from the skipper down, knew what that ship had amongst its cargo, and the wharfies just had an open go and they really made hay while the sun shone.
Ray Blissett

I remember the wharfies always carried these Gladstone bags and it got to a point where there was a lot of pilfering going on at the wharves. There was a lot of different food items went, and shoes, boots, and wristwatches. And the Americans said, 'Well, we're going to search all these Gladstone bags that are going out after work'. And

then there was a big uproar about that and politically they didn't want
to get involved so they had to overlook it.
Bill Bentson, staff sergeant, US Army

You'd get on a ship and you'd be working there and you'd say to the
Chief Steward—he was in charge of all the foodstuffs—'We haven't
tasted a tin of salmon for a long while and haven't had a decent
fowl', and all this. 'Oh, get a couple in your bag, get a couple and
take them home'. And that went on—wasn't what you'd say stolen, it
was given to you.
Alan McMillan

I remember my sister Jess came over to have a look at some flats in
Manly and we were given lots of keys to go and look at places. And
one place we went into, one of the rooms was completely filled with
French perfume, stockings, whisky. It was black market, someone had
just moved all the black market in there, and then left, because that
was the time people abandoned their houses when the Japs were near.
Dorothy Loughry

There was one particular hotel in Glebe known as 2UW—it was never
off the air, and it traded 24 hours a day every day and it always had a
plentiful supply of not so much the ordinary bottled beer, but quarts.
     Kate Lee was a black marketeer, she and a publican named Ada
Sutton. As far as bottled beer was concerned, they probably had the
biggest black market in Sydney and old Ada Sutton she had a hotel
up William Street near the Cross and another one at Ultimo, and
between her and Kate, they made a lot of money buying these quarts
and selling them to the Yanks. See the taxi drivers knew where to
take the Yanks to get the beer. And the black marketeers sold their
bottled beer in what we called CSR suitcases—a CSR suitcase was a
sugar bag. If you packed a dozen of beer properly in a hessian sugar
bag, it packed in perfectly and it wouldn't break or anything unless
you dropped it of course, and there was a huge black market in this.
Ray Blissett

There was a black market at the factory—some person had Swami
[shiny clinging material like fine jersey] underwear and oh, it used to
sell like hot cakes. He'd have somebody that supplied him, and he'd
be working there and he'd bring it in and everyone used to rush
them, scanties and slips and things like that. I was a very good
customer of the Swami underwear; I think we all were when we
could get it. It helped a lot.
Edna Macdonald

And the stealing of tyres—if you parked your car on the street, it was
nothing for people to get up next morning and find it jacked up on a
few house bricks and all four wheels gone: the tyres to sell to taxi

drivers, they were the main buyers of tyres, they would pay an excellent price for them.
Ray Blissett

I also knew of a fellow, he used to deliver meat from the abattoirs, and he used to have these sides of beef under the bonnet of his truck, and he'd have to get past the guards, they'd never think of looking there, and I believe he built a beautiful home after the war with the proceeds of the black market.
Edna Macdonald

One of the things about War Organisation of Industry was that you controlled industry, you controlled output, and a number of industries were banned, prohibited or severely restricted. So the big tycoons who were responsible for those industries got themselves jobs as assistant directors of something, in the Department, and they proceeded to rectify the whole thing. And by gee, I learned about patriotism as the last refuge of a scoundrel. I've altered that old saying of Sam Johnson's, to patriotism as the *first* refuge of a scoundrel, because of the number of magnates and tycoons and big business boys who got themselves jobs in the government in which they feathered their nests shamelessly for the war years. It really was a terrible scandal, the whole thing, how people exploited the war situation.

There was one particular case for example, bathing costumes were regarded as non-essential. Now this hit the bathing costume industry so a very big-time bathing costume manufacturer got himself a job as assistant director of clothing or something in WOI and proceeded to alter the law so that bathing costumes came back on the market.

There were all sorts of ways you could do this you see, particularly when the Americans started invading the country, with their own particular appetites. It was probably not difficult for the American army to say that bathing trunks were absolutely essential for their boys, because that's what they did with ice-cream. We substantially banned the manufacture of ice-cream during the war until the Americans came, when the ice-cream industry had to be revived because ice-cream was an essential frontline food for American troops. You can imagine how the Australian troops on bully beef and biscuits felt about this.

But you could juggle things in all directions if you were in the money game somewhere. And the big business boys of course got richer and richer. So war had that other ugly side and I saw a lot of that and I have vivid memories of it, and I'm always a little bit ashamed of some of my patriotic fellow Australians.
Niall Brennan

5 Give 'til it hurts

We used to go out on trucks on Saturdays to collect paper and scrap iron and so forth. Just go and knock on doors and scrounge what you could, any old iron, that sort of thing. Aluminium and brass were the things that were mainly sought after. Books for pulping up into paper and cardboard, magazines, newspapers. There was an enormous amount of newspaper collected. And if you went to the pictures and you put an aluminium saucepan in a bin, you got a penny or threepence off the price of entry to the pictures.
John Drennan

We had to collect old bones, and they'd be piled up at the school, and I can remember one time dragging a horse's head all the way to school and it wasn't very decomposed I'm afraid.
Rosemary McCourt

Everybody had to contribute something. An uncle of mine who was in a wheelchair, polio victim, his part of the war effort was to knit a camouflage net a week. He had arthritic hands and he still managed to do it, tie it to the fence and put the strings through. Granma put a bonnet on and won the prettiest girl competition and she was 80 years old. My other uncle raised hundreds of pounds in the Ugly Man competition. He used to stop his car by the side of the road and get everybody to vote for him, a penny a vote. So the whole community even out west was sending comforts to the soldiers.
Ken Muggleston

There was always something going on. At one stage I grew lettuces and sold them for 3d a pop and I raised a pound—for which I got a certificate. We had all sorts of fundraising ventures, there were street stalls and raffles, all that sort of thing, concerts and dances, mind you I wasn't too involved in the dancing bit because I was too young, unfortunately. We used to have all sorts of church functions, too, to raise funds. It was a very tight, close-knit community, a country town, different to living in the city.
Margaret Maxwell

We were always raising money for the Red Cross. And this was a great thing, it gave me a wonderful opportunity. An as eight year old, I was writing scripts and forcing my friends to act in my dreadful little plays and charging people money to come. And people of course felt obliged to come because these were children raising money for the war effort.
Helen McAnulty

There were a lot of fund raising efforts in country towns. Right through, there were baby contests, there were garden parties, there was buckjumping shows, parades in the street—all to raise money for

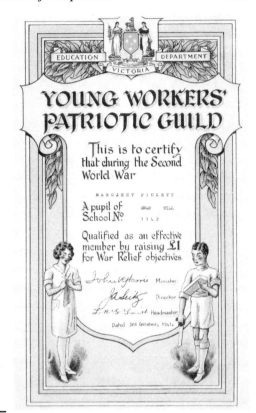

EDUCATION DEPARTMENT
VICTORIA

YOUNG WORKERS' PATRIOTIC GUILD

This is to certify
that during the Second
World War

MARGARET PICKETT

A pupil of SWAN HILL
School No. 1142

Qualified as an effective
member by raising £1
for War Relief objectives

John K Harris Minister

Director

Smith Headmaster

Dated 3rd October, 1941.

The certificate received by Margaret Maxwell of Swan Hill, Victoria, when she raised £1 for the war effort by growing lettuces.

the war effort. The main fundraising group in my local town was an organisation called 'Be Happy Keep Fit Win the War'. My father was the main director of the whole idea and they used to run a weekly show in which everyone would come and pay their entry fees and get credited on their card and after they'd been sixteen times they got a War Savings Certificate. I think from memory it was the biggest single war savings group in South Australia.
Ren deGaris, Millicent, South Australia

A lot of people worked very hard at it. My mother and other women, hundreds of them, used to go and do all the cooking and serving in a canteen which handed out free meals at lunchtime and in the evening to any Allied servicemen and women who came in. If they came in uniform, they were given a free meal. Mum and a lady who lived next door used to go in there three or four nights a week.
Maurie Jones

I would've liked to have joined the WRANS, but because it was wartime production where I was involved, we weren't allowed to be released so I did other voluntary work, and I worked as a hostess at the Dugout which was a canteen run by Myer Emporium during the

A fund-raising concert troupe that toured the south-eastern area of South Australia. (Photo: Alan Smith, courtesy Ren deGaris)

war. It was a place open to all servicemen where they could come down and write letters, perhaps sit and chat, have something to eat or else dance, especially the evenings—there was an orchestra and they danced all evening. A lot of the boys became regulars at the Dugout—they'd be on leave, perhaps they were interstate boys and had nowhere else to go and they went to the Dugout I think because they weren't under any pressure—they could just sit and talk to the girls or they could dance.
Glenys Kirk, office worker, Melbourne

I worked in the prisoners-of-war restaurant doing odd jobs. I'd be called up to come and wash the dishes or something like that, which we all did very voluntarily, and worked hard. Of course the funds from the restaurants all went to the prisoners-of-war parcels. The prisoners-of-war group sent parcels but whether they ever got to them, we never really knew.
Vi McLauchlan, housewife and mother, Melbourne

When I went home full of the patriotic spirit to get some money for the War Savings Certificate, my father said you won't put a razoo into it. He had been to the First World War, he was only seventeen and he put his age up to go. He was blown up and gassed, and he had a hatred of war, it had left a scar on him for sure. He was actually a TPI, totally and permanently incapacitated from the First World War.
Bob Taylor, Adelaide

I came back to Sydney on leave in May and the matron-in-chief called me up and sent me out to join the staff for the Austerity Campaign, encouraging people to invest in the War Loans. I said to her 'I can't do that, I've never been very fond of acting or debating'. She said 'You're in the Army now, you do as you're told'. So off I went and it was quite an experience, I didn't know we had so many factories around Sydney, and I did that for three months.

I had to speak of my experiences in Darwin, though that was rather difficult because the censorship on Darwin was very very strict at that time, they had not given the correct figures of casualties. But we went to about five factories a day, each service person speaking for about five minutes, to encourage people. The boys called me the tearjerker because I used to make the old men cry.
Meg Ewart, Army nurse, Darwin

'Give 'til it hurts' was the phrase that every patriotic organisation used—'Give 'til it hurts'. Which I think people did.
Maurie Jones

6 Living for the moment

Wartime always produces a measure of hysteria and pleasure-seeking. I remember in Melbourne a great deal of very blasé enjoyment, almost, of the hysteria and the permissive atmosphere generated particularly by patriotism.
Niall Brennan

In the city, going from one street to another after work, half-past four in the day, everyone was on leave in town and you had to more or less run the gauntlet from one street to the other to get your tram home. They'd stop you and ask you if they could take you out, take you to the dance or take you to the pictures. There were a couple of Red Cross canteens and other places where they could go, but a lot of them just used to roam around. Sydney streets were full of troops in uniform, you've never seen anything like it, ever.
Joy Boucher

There was this sense that it was important that you lived for the moment because there mightn't be any other one, mightn't be many more moments or perhaps none, and therefore a tremendous amount of licence and liberation came into people's lives which would never have happened—perhaps at all, particularly in a place like Perth.
Dorothy Hewett

We used to go to the Trocadero, which was a magnificent ballroom [in Sydney], just huge inside, and there were two beautiful big dance bands. The men's orchestra was the jazz section and they'd play all the big band numbers, the quicksteps, the jiving numbers. Then the big stage would revolve around and the women's orchestra would

come into view, violinist and saxophone and organist, and they'd play the lovely slow foxtrot and slow waltzes.
Joy Boucher

And of course when the jitterbugging came in, it was that as well. It was just fabulous. When the Americans were in town, the Trocadero was absolutely packed out. And I could honestly say no girl ever was a wallflower while they were in town, you wouldn't miss one dance.
Nora Symonds

The last long dress I wore, though, was at a Red Cross Ball in Adelaide Town Hall in 1942. After that, we didn't wear long dresses because we didn't feel it was right to dress up with a war on. But we used to wear these jiving skirts, they used to swing out like a ballerina's skirt when you danced, and wedgies—little wedgies to jive in.
Joy Boucher

With men very scarce, even a twelve-year-old in short pants was an acceptable partner at a dance, and so since most of the dances used to raise Comforts Funds and things for the soldiers, I thought I was contributing my six penn'orth as they say, and I'd go along and I'd be a dance partner to quite grown-up women. I remember every time you danced with the over-sixties you could feel the corsets, tightly laced, as you did the progressive barn dance, and I can hear it now in the little hall at Katoomba. . . 'She's my lady love . . .'—'Lily of Laguna'.
Ken Muggleston

Canberra is very cold in winter and we used to wear overalls to walk from our houses up to the radio station on nightwatch. When we washed the overalls and put them out to dry, quite often in the morning if we were lucky they were frozen solid so we used to bring them in and stand them around and they used to be our boyfriends—we'd say this one's mine, this one's yours, tall ones and short ones.
Shirley Fenton-Huie, WRANS, Canberra

At that time I was on the CWA [Country Women's Association] and the Comforts Fund Committee in Beaudesert, and we used to run the dances for the different troops. The moment they arrived in town on R and R we'd hold the dances because one lot came, they were there for a certain length of time and then they would go and another lot would come, so we were always kept busy socialising.
Dulcie Cunningham

There were thousands of men in the Territory and only a couple of hundred girls. We went out to lots of dances and dinners, you'd never dance for very long with the one man because you'd be grasped by someone else and danced away, but I remember going out thirteen nights in a row, and the fourteenth night I was supposed to go out and I thought this is it, I just can't go out one more night. But there were so few of us, which was quite a change from when we were down south in Sydney and Melbourne—men were very scarce because they'd all gone up north, and it was just a marvellous feeling to think oh, you're just so popular.

Elva Batt, AAMWS amenities officer

There were no contraceptives available—I never heard about them. It wasn't only that I was young, they were not there. There was never any mention of such a thing, never, and I don't know that there was in the other services. This was pre-pill time, people always forget that there's a great dividing line, the pre and *après* pill—and here we were, young girls, young men thrown together and girls got pregnant.

The most awful thing that happened to girls in the services I think were those who got pregnant. Now there wasn't all that much chance because you often went out in groups, you only got one night a week out, to one minute before midnight and there were certain hotels that were out of bounds, all sorts of things, but girls got pregnant and the dreadful thing was they then disappeared—we never heard of them again, they were discharged, and they'd walk away from all of us girls who'd had such fun. I think that might be one of the blackest periods for women in the services, it's haunted me ever since. Because a woman would have to be a fool if she didn't say, there but for the grace of God go I.

Patsy Adam-Smith

We had so many restrictions, we had to have three girls in the party before we could go out, and if we went on a moonlight picnic, we had to have ten girls. We didn't like it at first but we soon realised it had to be, because there were thousands of men up in the Territory and only 200 AWAS and we realised the dangers if we didn't have a lot of discipline.

Phyl Proctor, AWAS, Northern Territory

If a man made a proposal, you didn't take him seriously because there was the hot tropical night and the moonlight and you realised he hasn't seen another woman for so many months, and if you said 'Yes' you might get back home and find he's changed his mind—and a few did just that.

Elva Barrett

It was very difficult. Fellows wouldn't put the hard word on you, but worse than that, from inside them, right from their heart, they wanted a woman and we used to have a lot of cuddling go on. And there was this American song:

'In my arms, in my arms,
Ain't I ever gonna get a girl in my arms

In my heart I've got a funny notion
If I've got to cross an ocean
I need a girl in my arms tonight'.
And he'd be dancing and singing in her ear, and you know it'd be a
hard girl who could resist, I think it'd be a hard girl.
Patsy Adam-Smith

We used to meet a crowd at the Trocadero, dance with them and go
off home again. But sometimes you'd meet someone you might go out
with for a little while, and you had to be careful—the chaps were
going to war and if they met someone they liked, they'd get very
serious so you had to be careful not to hurt them or go out with them
too much because it would mean you were becoming too involved
and you didn't want to hurt their feelings. So it was a very sad time
sometimes.
Joy Boucher

When fellows were going to go overseas they always knew, they told
you what day the ship would sail even, though it was never in the
paper or anything else, and the cuddling and the kisses and the tears,
lots and lots of tears, lots. And you formed a quick friendship, you
had to be quick, because they weren't there for long but you didn't
mean it was going to be for life. But of course when men are away in
battle I suppose they hang on to that—that that girl is there.
Patsy Adam-Smith

7 So hard to part

I met my husband, a very handsome young man, at Bankstown where
I was based. This was in December 1941. He and his group were due
to go overseas with the Empire Air Training Scheme but the Japs came
into the war and they were taken off the boat in Sydney Harbour.
    We went out together for a while, and at first he had the idea that
you shouldn't get involved at all, and then he thought you could fall
in love, you could get engaged, but that was as far as it went. You
didn't get married because if you were sent overseas something might
happen to you. So we became engaged in June 1942. Then very early
on the morning of 12 October he came to see me and he said, 'We've
got to get married, I've been posted overseas'.
    We started at half-past eight and by six o'clock that night everything
was organised and we were married. The girls from my shift came
and my mother, who was a wonderful woman, she'd organised a little
reception at home—and that was our wedding day. A few days later
we said goodbye at Lindfield Station and he went overseas on the
Monday.
    He wrote wonderful letters and I wrote to him and it wasn't easy
when they were away like that. At times you didn't know where they
were and whilst you did your work you just had it in the back of

June Stone with her first husband, Paul Clancy, on the day they bought their engagement ring. He was killed in the Middle East soon after their marriage.

your mind all the time, and prayed that they would come home. But there was always a possibility that they wouldn't, and on 21st July 1943 I got a telegram to say that he had been killed in Iraq.

A number of us in the service received news like that over a period of time, and we just kept doing what we had to do. It was a difficult time but it was a lovely time too, because even though you did lose somebody, a very dear somebody, that was an experience you had had; and also you'd given that person a great deal of pleasure, you'd given him something to hold on to while he was overseas and I think made life worthwhile for a lot of them.
June Stone, WAAAF, Sydney

There were lots of weddings through the war. It would have been wiser to wait until they came back but when you are young you don't think of those things. I married at nineteen; and a lot of women followed their husbands around the camps, several women from here did, but my husband didn't want that, he said he'd prefer to know that I was here with family and friends.

It was so hard to part with someone you love and don't know if they're coming back, and every time he came home on leave I hoped that I would get pregnant and have a child while he was away, that was something belonging to him, but it just didn't happen.
Mary Comer

I finally came home on leave from Darwin and we were married within a few days of my arrival. We didn't regret marrying, there was never any doubt that we would do it, but then I went up to New Guinea, and from the time that we were married in April 1943, I only saw Betty once more before I came home at the end of the war.
George Telfer

It was lonely, it was devastating I suppose I could say—as it was for

all the others in my situation. Nobody thought anything of it because it was happening to so many people. I would see other people coming home on leave and would feel really really lonely. But you knew there were lots whose husbands were unable to come home, some of them even in prisoner-of-war camps.
Betty Telfer, radio station typist and programmer, Adelaide

8 Waiting and hoping

The *Sydney Morning Herald* had a 'Killed in Action, Wounded in Action, or Missing' column on the front page every day and my mother used to go down it and look and there'd be some person in the country that she knew, or name thereof. So that was a daily reminder that the war was on our shores.
Ken Muggleston

I was quite concerned about Dad, how it was going over there, whether he would come back or not and I used to keep track of where it all went on in the war, as much as you could from the news and there was always that feeling that you might not see him again because there were people being blown to bits and the rest of it. Being the eldest I guess it might have gone through my mind—'Gee, I'll have to look after the family', and how I was going to do that. I was ten or eleven when Dad went away.
Kevin Shepherd, schoolboy, Adelaide

We had strict instructions that we were not to talk to anyone about our father, what regiment he was in, where he was or anything, and we felt very conscious of this because it could have meant his life. We took it very seriously. So we felt a bit isolated from the rest of the children.
Margaret Burton

The loss—learning to live without your loved ones around was maybe the hardest. Everyone you'd meet in the street, that had sons or a husband or loved ones away—it was always your first conversation: 'Have you heard?, where is he? and how is he?' and things like that.
Nola Bridger

You dreaded the thought that one day a message might come to you as it was coming to other people in the district—something tragic had happened, people had been killed, badly injured or wounded. It was a very unhappy experience. After all you'd grown up with these people, worked with them, played with them and then suddenly found they were killed. So that thought was always in your mind.
Bill Graham, wheat farmer, Gulgong, New South Wales

When I was in England my Uncle Arthur, who was in Gallipoli in

'Blouse off, straps down, arms folded, and this is the result. I remember it like yesterday': Joy Boucher, Adelaide/Sydney in a pin-up photo taken in 1941 to send to her boyfriend Eric Pix, serving with the navy in the Mediterranean.

World War I and in France, happened to say to my mother, 'Where's the young bloke, where's Gerry?'. And she said 'He's in England, he's a fighter pilot'. And he said, 'Oh I'd give him about three hours'. That was the accustomed period that a fighter pilot in World War I would last, you see, so of course every time the postman came up the street, she thought the worst.
Gerry Judd, Empire Air Training Scheme pilot, UK

Dad was in Tobruk when I was ten and his father was in the Somme or somewhere when he was ten and his father was killed. And I never said anything to anyone, but I always had this terrible fear that the same thing might happen again. So that I'll always remember my eleventh birthday, because I was eleven and Dad was still alive.
Margaret Burton

The last card we received from Cliff, it looked like a little secondhand card because you couldn't buy them in England, and it was snowing down, and Cliff had written 'Hello Robbie'. He said 'Santa Claus will be here soon. I hope Santa will always be able to bring you whatever you want, Robert, 'til Daddy comes home, which will be soon'. But Daddy didn't come, and in the log you read about the flight and then you just read—'Failed to return', and that is finis. That's life.
Margaret Hopgood, airman's widow, Brisbane

Gulgong had always been a town that pulled together and the war was a special time—everybody had somebody away or about to go away and so their own family and friends would all be helping. But Gulgong was a desolate sort of town, there was an emptiness about the place.
Kathleen Loneregan, store proprietor, Gulgong, New South Wales

'There were probably other teenage cowards in Australia but we didn't know of each other's existence': Maurie Jones, pictured in Perth as he neared conscription age in 1945.

People asked me what I felt like when I had a boy at the war. I said 'What would you think about it, how would you get on?'. I said 'He's only a kid, he's gone with all the other kids, they hardly know they're born yet—how would you like it?'. I prayed every night for him to come home.

Louisa Hughes, soldier's mother, Gulgong, New South Wales

As the war proceeded and I got nearer and nearer to conscription age, eighteen, I was dead scared, I really was. There were probably other teenage cowards in Australia but we didn't know of each other's existence because it was something you didn't admit to. You would have disgraced your family, been a traitor to your country, invited the white-feather brigade to shower you with their attentions. But that was how I felt.

Maurie Jones

You always had that terrible feeling, you couldn't get rid of that. I used to get down in the dumps, I got to a stage that all I could do was sit down and cry. But you just had to go on, you couldn't do anything else. We were poor people and had to work, no conveniences or anything, and the boys being away made it harder. I had four other children and I had to think of them. But oh heavens you looked forward to the letters and if they didn't turn up—'Oh my hat' you'd think, 'They're gone'.

Auntie Dot Kent, farmer, mother of four soldiers, Millicent, South Australia

I was on tenterhooks for a while, frightened. Every time you heard of anyone missing or if you didn't get a letter on time when you was expecting it you'd think 'Oh gee, I wonder if anything has happened', and I was wondering what I'd say to the kids if anything did happen to their father. Sometimes I wouldn't get a letter for two perhaps three months, it would be held up—and you'd think the worst.

Queenie Shepherd, woodyard proprietor and mother, Adelaide

My brother Steve was killed in New Guinea. He was wounded first and he should have left the battlefield, but he wouldn't leave his men and he stayed and he was killed.

I was at the picture show, Saturday afternoon matinée, and I met my father running up the street to send a telegram to my mother, who was away, and I remember Dad saying 'Steve has been killed' and that was just the end of the world. I remember I ran like a mad goat all the way home crying my eyes out and people kept on stopping me and saying 'What's wrong?'. And I said 'My brother has been killed in the war'.

We kept on getting letters back that we had sent to him, that came back with the red hand on it and 'Return to sender'. And we kept on getting letters from Steve to us—for weeks and weeks after he was killed, we were still receiving letters from him. Every letter from him was a thrill because it was another contact with him, but to get your own letters back was sad because you thought—'Oh I wish he'd heard that' or 'I wish he'd seen that', you know, different news that you were telling him, that he never received, and thought, 'Oh, I wish he'd known that before he died'.

Nola Bridger

I used to get upset and talk to my father about him going back the second time, to the Islands. He said 'Look, if my name's on the bullet, I'll be dead and if my name's not on the bullet I won't be, and that's the way you've got to look at it'. And I think that's actually the way our family did look at it.

Margaret Burton

I think that women that stayed behind during the war, even though they weren't in the fighting front, they suffered just as much as the men and I think given their rights they would have preferred to be fighting alongside their husbands because I knew a lot of them whose husbands were away and the stress, the anxiety they went through—every time a telegram came they didn't know whether it was to say their husband was killed or wounded; and they were left home to care for the children, and I know that they went through hell.

Dulcie Cunningham

I didn't believe he could be killed—although I had thought of it of course—because I have a fairly strong faith and I think that was what kept me from believing that such a thing would happen. That didn't stop me from getting a bit depressed about it at times. What kept me going was the thought of the future, the letters kept coming and we

'At the movies you'd watch every newsreel, just hoping you'd see him': Nola (Jackson) Bridger, who was a schoolgirl in Sydney and, right, Nola's brother Steve Philps, killed in New Guinea. His letters kept on coming for months after he died.

made so many plans for the future. I did think of joining one of the services but I rejected the idea because I thought, 'Well, how do I know I will be able to get leave when George comes home?'.
Betty Telfer

Even though my husband was dodging all those doodlebugs in England, I did know where he was, but a lot of my friends didn't even know where their husbands were prisoners, and that must have been terribly painful. The husbands of a lot of my friends were POWs and they heard nothing for five years, some of them. Others would get one little card from the Prisoners of War Association or the Red Cross and that was very sad because they wouldn't be able to say anything on the card, only that they were alive, and lots of sadness came out of those cards.
Vi McLauchlan

Australians more than most people, especially in those days, depended on letters, we were a nation of letter-writers because we were so remote. But suddenly we're in no position to write to them and they're in no position to write to us. They did indeed through the Red Cross, but we didn't get them.

I did get one card from my sister—I got it in 1944—and it said, 'Mum's puddings are as lumpy as ever, love and kisses Pat'. And that was all I needed to know—my mother was a dreadful cook and the

Margaret Holmes, Sydney, with her children in a photo taken to send to her husband serving as a doctor in New Guinea; this was his first sight of the twins, born in his absence in 1943. A pacifist, Margaret Holmes had three children during the war because she felt that she 'wanted to do something constructive and positive, to make a tiny contribution on the other side from the awful massive destruction and desolation going on elsewhere'.

fact that she hadn't changed because of the war was rather heartwarming and encouraging. But she received nothing from me, like the parents of many men who were in the 8th Division, no word at all, and had to await our return with no more than maternal faith.
Russell Braddon, POW, Changi and Burma Railway

There was a pall of grief spread over the community like today's pollution is spread over our cities. And everywhere you went there was a family bereaved: parents, and girls who'd lost their boyfriends, and women who'd lost their husbands—and it was all-pervading if you scratched the surface. And it was dreadful, it really was.
Bob Bahnsen, machinist, Sydney

9 A lot of disillusioned men

When I was in Perth the war had finished in the Middle East and had gone to New Guinea and there were men there from the Armoured Division who were out in the bush of Western Australia and they called themselves 'Curtin's Koalas'—they were not allowed to be shot at and they were not allowed to be exported. They were anxious to get into the fight and just felt as though they were in a backwater.
Elva Batt

The big men were drafted into artillery units, and we were sent up to the God-forsaken Torres Strait where they had a couple of guns, they were looking at Booby Island. What we were doing there was covering the entrance into the Reef which was through Booby Island

and we were also covering the main air force base which was Horn Island.

The troops would have done anything to get off the island after a couple of years there—or well before that—because you could feel that you were in a hopeless situation, that you had a couple of six-inch artillery guns there and you knew that if the Japanese ever bothered to run across you with a few bombs that they'd knock you out, but they never did bother.
Merv Lilley, artilleryman, Torres Strait

I was working at Edenhope in Victoria on a sheep farm when I heard the call, and I rode my push-bike for miles in the rain with a case on the back, to volunteer. We had to do our training for three months at Tanunda [SA] and from there we went over to Western Australia, thinking we've got to go and save the West.

But one morning on the Nullarbor the train stopped and we all hopped out and we finished up in six camps guarding prisoners of war in the Nullarbor. In the summer it would be over 120 degrees, every day, and we used to get dust storms so bad you couldn't see where you were going. The prisoners of war lived in a compound with concertina wire around it, about 50 of them and eighteen or twenty guards to a camp. They were putting new sleepers in the railway line—with the war there were a lot of troop trains and goods trains going through. They were Italians, and they were very fine blokes—they were no trouble at all because they weren't soldiers, they were just like us.

We didn't do much guarding. Often we used to go out on the track with them and we'd take our shirts off and we'd put the rifle under the tarpaulin and we'd work with them. And the Italians had a gramophone given by the Red Cross where we had nothing, no wireless, no fridge, nothing. So at night we used to go up in the compound and dance with them. We'd have been shot if we'd been found out, but it's true: dancing on the ground out in the moon.

It was essential work I suppose, somebody had to be out on the Nullarbor. But it wasn't what I joined up for. My ambition was to go overseas and do my part.
Arthur Bridgman, infantryman, Militia/gunner, 2nd AIF

There were a lot of very disillusioned men about but this is all a part of war and although you're not in the front line or anything you're under a great deal of stress and there were men who shot themselves or who shot their foot off or did something like that to get out of the Army. You wonder if you'll ever go into action and you wish you would, and you're never going to go into action because the whole war and everything else has passed you by.

You were there if the country was attacked and you'd do your best, but army or war under those circumstances has little or no meaning to it.
Merv Lilley

The worst time perhaps, for most of us, when the real boredom of it set in, was when we realised that we were just forgotten and the war had passed us by; and things became very very bad. The married men of 35, 40 years old were probably the worst—the poison pen letters that came in and said that your wife is playing up with the Americans, things like that, and that really pulled them apart.

And if you can understand what it's like: we were living in an area the size of a football field, barbed-wired in, with 128 men, in top of the range temperatures, 90, 95 degrees all the time. With prickly heat, scorpions, flies, Singapore Ear and a very bad diet, and plenty of time and nothing to do.

Roy leRougetel, anti-aircraft gunner, Darwin

As the threat retreated, desertions increased most markedly—soldiers deserted and took off and got jobs on farms, and farmers were desperate for men so they kept quiet about it.

Bob Bahnsen

I went to coastwatch up in Arnhem Land, where for several months there were just three of us, living in a post right on the shore where you couldn't have lights at night-time, waiting once a month for a vessel to come round from Darwin with supplies, and one of the chaps really got upset by this.

One night we were all in bed except one of us was at the little lookout watching out over the sea, and I was in bed, and this other chap used to sleep with his rifle and he cocked his rifle and I thought good heavens that's somebody cocking his rifle and then bang! and a bullet whisked from this rifle though the soldier's feet and it whisked through my tent and matter of fact nearly took off one of my toes, and then outside. And this chap had woken up and he said he saw a Japanese head down near his toes and he got him and I said, 'You didn't get him, you nearly got my toes'. But he broke down completely and the next day we radiocd in to Winelli which was the wireless headquarters and they sent a bloke round to take him off.

Amory Vane, North Australia Observer Unit

There was one chap went home from leave, he was an old bloke—an ordinary fellow, a kind of bushman—and he never come back, and they told us that he'd wrapped himself in barbed wire and thrown himself in the waterhole when it was time to come back. So he wasn't too keen on getting back there, was he.

Merv Lilley

I was posted to Darwin in 1943 and it was a very boring time to be in the Northern Territory. You felt isolated, there were no civilians there, no shops within hundreds of miles and the war had passed by, it had gone to New Guinea and I think the general feeling was that there was no point in being there. Browned off was the expression in those days. The men felt that it dragged on and they couldn't see any point

in still going on with army exercises when there was just no more war to fight so it was just the tedium and monotony and day after day of doing the same thing. People grasped any opportunity of doing something different.
Elva Batt

In the Northern Territory the army staged some of the most colourful race meetings that had ever been—they got these old neddies from farmers and graziers, wherever they could lay their hands on an old horse they grabbed it, and they built their own stands and their own boxes where you could put the money, and they'd bet a month's pay on these old things that couldn't run at all. But you'd get 70 000 spectators at a meeting, and in the war you put your last pounds on a horse and didn't care if it lost. There was a certain recklessness in the war years about punters.
Jack Pollard

You're at that age when if you were in civilian life, you'd be making your way in the world—you're totally cut off and you're growing older and your brain's not working much any more. And you know that when you get back, that everything will have changed, that nothing will ever be the same as it was, and you don't know what it will be like.
Merv Lilley

'People grasped any opportunity of doing something different': 'Song of the Danube', Darwin, March 1945. Elva Batt is the dancer on the left. As an AAMWS amenities officer she organised and performed in many revues and concerts for the troops stationed in the north.

10 Weary of it all

It was that feeling of what future have we got. You couldn't plan for tomorrow. Our boys went away and you never thought of when they're coming home, you just hoped one day they would.
Anne Pellew

It was a long period of uncertainty, you didn't know whether to get married or you didn't know whether to have children or not if you were married. You were afraid of what the future might hold. It was a very traumatic experience. You were worried about the Australian soldiers that were being killed and taken prisoner and of course by that time you had the knowledge that some of them had been so horribly mistreated and you were very sore about that, very savage about that, so the war years were a long, hard period for most people.
Bill Graham

People were very weary of it all. You could see it in their faces: they were weary of the restrictions, they were weary of the strain, they were weary of the fact that they never knew whether their friends, husbands, brothers, lovers, were coming home or not or whether they'd be killed. They were weary of the strain of brining up families alone, weary of the struggle to get basic foodstuffs at times, weary of the struggle to clothe and buy footwear for children—that was one of the most difficult things, to get shoes for children. All those things. People looked drained, particularly people who were older than I was, who were already mothers with families to support.
Dorothy Hewett

On the home front there were no heroes, only heroines, and there were many many heroines. All those girls whose boyfriends were in danger of being killed, maimed, missing—thousands missing. The mothers whose sons were gone, you couldn't help feeling for them. I guess they never had a decent night's sleep from beginning to end. They, I imagine, would have lain awake wondering and worrying and the next day they'd get on with their lives as best they could, and that night again . . .

And they were working, as well. Other women were trying to bring up their children alone and living in rotten accommodation, two or three young children in one room. And this went on for five years in some cases.
Bob Bahnsen

Who was there to dance with? Most of the men were away. Anyway, you were too tired to be wanting to go out very much. There was nowhere to go really. Pictures, you'd go to the pictures. And of course with food rationing there wouldn't be much entertainment like inviting people for dinner. You'd have barely enough to keep you going.
Edna Macdonald

The work I was doing, it was a very responsible job for young women to be doing. A lot of these things never got into the newspapers and when you can't talk to anybody, even the people you work with, about anything, you are constantly worrying. Also we had the worry of our menfolk. All the men that I knew had gone, some of them ended up locked up in Changi, and there was the constant worry of this.

Patricia Penrose, Z Special Unit, Melbourne

We didn't anticipate it would go on for such a long time. We thought that when the Americans came in that that would accentuate the end of it. Actually it dragged on for a long long time and we were beginning to count the cost of it very much in the last two years of the war—everybody was looking at the cost, not only the cost of what was being destroyed or lost in bombing raids but the cost of lives that were being lost. It was coming home to us then I think how futile war can be.

Bill Graham

Even during the times of excitement when dramatic things happened, there was a terrible tedium. I think the tedium looking back on it, was 'Isn't it ever going to end? Isn't life ever going to be normal again?'. And that was in addition to the sense of loss that you felt when people who you knew were killed. It was just a feeling that life isn't meant to be like this. It's meant to be better. And there was this terrible, I won't say boredom, but a *tedium*—which is different. It was anything but boring at times, but the tedium remained there. And it went on and on, and I suppose people just put up with it.

Maurie Jones

That was the thing about the war, you really didn't know if it was going to end, or if it was just going to go on, and that was a scary feeling. And I used to love that song, 'When The Lights Go On Again All Over The World'—because we missed our neon signs and we missed our streetlights and we missed the excitement of being able to play in the streets as a kid in Redfern at seven and eight o'clock at night.

Pansy Hickey, textile worker, Sydney

10

The Long War

Fellow citizens, the war is over.

The Japanese government has accepted the terms of surrender imposed by the Allied Nations and hostilities will now cease . . . At this moment, let us offer thanks to God. Let us remember those whose lives were given that we may enjoy this glorious moment and may look forward to a peace which they have won for us. Let us remember those whose thoughts, with proud sorrow, turn towards gallant, loved ones who will not come back . . .

The Prime Minister, Ben Chifley, speaking on radio on 15 August 1945.

For about three weeks before Mr Chifley's fateful announcement it had seemed possible that the Japanese might shortly surrender. On 26 July 1945, the Allied leaders meeting at Potsdam in Germany had published terms of surrender. After Japan rejected the terms, on 6 August an American B-29 dropped an atomic bomb on the Japanese southern city of Hiroshima, killing some 60 000 people. Three days later a second atomic bomb was dropped on Nagasaki, and the next day the Japanese government announced conditional acceptance of the terms. On 14 August the Japanese Emperor accepted all the terms, and the surrender was announced on 15 August.

The Japanese surrender presented a number of pressing military tasks. The Japanese forces fighting throughout the South-West Pacific Area had to be informed and ceasefire arrangements had to be made. On 2 September, General Douglas MacArthur formally accepted the Japanese surrender on the battleship *Missouri* in Tokyo Bay. General Blamey signed for Australia. Then Australian senior military officers in Borneo, Morotai, New Guinea, New Britain and Bougainville accepted the surrender of local Japanese forces in their areas of responsibility.

Japanese troops had to be taken into prisoner-of-war camps and, in due course, repatriated to Japan. Meanwhile, thousands of Australian servicemen had to be sent home for demobilisation. An urgent task was to deliver aid to the 14 340 Australian prisoners who were in the hands of the Japanese, and bring them home to families who in many cases had not heard from them for over three years. These former prisoners were the survivors of about 22 400 who had been captured at Singapore and elsewhere in the islands, and had suffered cruelly at the hands of their captors.

Australian troops were required to restore civil government in areas formerly occupied by the Japanese. In Australian territories, such as New

Guinea, this was relatively straightforward. In British Borneo, it was a little more confused, and in the former Dutch territories in Borneo—the Celebes, Ambon and Timor—it was complicated by the aspirations of Indonesian nationalists. The Army was also required to raise an infantry brigade of volunteers for service in the British Commonwealth Occupation Force in Japan. It became the nucleus for the Australian Regular Army established a few years later.

Back in Australia, the government had to restore the economy to a peacetime footing, and slowly rationing, quotas and other restrictions were dropped. Thousands of young men were demobilised and they sought to pick up careers, marry, start families and carve out for themselves lives that they could only have dreamt about for six years.

Fewer Australians were killed in the Second World War than in the First—about 27 000 compared to almost 60 000 in the earlier war. But many more Australians were directly affected by the war. It had continued two years longer; it was closer to home, with the enemy actually attacking Australian soil; much greater demands were made upon the economy; and thousands of American servicemen were based in Australia.

Undoubtedly the Australia that we know today was shaped largely by our experiences of the Second World War. There is merit in the comment of one of those interviewed that it is a myth that Australia came of age at Gallipoli, and that the national turning point was the Second World War. As a result of the war, the Australian government realised that it would have to establish a capacity for making its own assessments of international affairs. It could no longer rely solely on Britain, but would seek security within a wider framework of alliances, including the British Commonwealth and the United States. At the same time, the nation would have to look more to its own defences, establishing a Regular Army and expanding the peacetime Navy and Air Force.

It was believed that the population was too small to provide for adequate defence or to support a worthwhile industrial base, and an extensive immigration program was begun which was to enrich the nation's cultural and social life as well as provide workers to develop the country. Adding to these numbers was the post-war baby boom, which continued through to the mid 1960s.

During the war Australia had been forced to establish tool-making factories and other industries, such as vehicle, ship and aircraft construction that had never previously been possible. These wartime industries became a base for Australia's industrial development. In 1949, for example, large-scale production of the Holden motor car began.

Australian government was changed by the war. The Commonwealth government gained in power and influence. The collection of income tax was taken over by the central government and was never restored to the States. The Commonwealth Public Service expanded rapidly. The long tenure and relative success of the Curtin and Chifley Labor governments forced the conservative political forces to re-evaluate their philosophy, and out of the United Australia Party's defeats of 1943 and 1946 came an invigorated Liberal Party that was to rule for a record-breaking term from 1949 to 1972.

During the war, Curtin, who lived in Perth, chose to run the government from Canberra rather than Melbourne where most government departments, including the key defence departments, were located. The war accelerated the move of these departments to Canberra. It also accelerated the establishment of national institutions such as the Australian National University.

In retrospect then, modern Australia was born out of the experience of the Second World War. But the biggest legacy was in the minds of the millions of Australians who had worked together, suffered under austerity campaigns, shared the sorrows of death, endured the absence of family members, and made a thousand small and large sacrifices for the common good. It is their shared experiences which built the Australia of today.

1 It's over

Throughout the war, I and millions of other people in this country, and in others, shared a sort of wish that our side would develop a secret weapon which would end the whole thing very quickly. We usually thought, in our ignorant way, of a Buck Rogers/Flash Gordon type death-ray which would just mow our enemies down. Little did we know that over there in the deserts of the western United States they were preparing the bombs, as it turned out.
Maurie Jones, schoolboy, Perth

They told us there was a bomb that had wiped out an entire city—oh we were thrilled to bits! It was just Japanese. That was the attitude, we didn't realise that it was such a horrendous thing.
Margaret Maxwell, schoolgirl, Swan Hill, Victoria

Instead of everyone throwing their arms in the air with joy, they just sat down and cried. We sat around in circles and we just cried that day, we were so relieved that it was all over.
Pansy Hickey, textile worker, Sydney

We didn't do no work that day because everyone was that excited, everyone was running—'The war's over, the war's over'—and then we'd stop and have a little gas here and a little gas there and a little gas somewhere else. We got some flags, the little paper flags you could buy, and they were waving them down round the port. All the kids had one, they let the kids come home from school.
Queenie Shepherd, woodyard proprietor and mother, Adelaide

An assembly was called and we were all standing there all jumping around with the excitement, the euphoria, it was just such a relief. It was all over.
Margaret Maxwell

Oh it was wonderful, I can remember kids in the street standing up on the roofs of the houses and the aircraft flying over and that was

just so exciting. I think everyone went into the city and there was singing and dancing and it was just so exciting, I'll never ever forget it.
Lillian Harding, schoolgirl, Adelaide

I always promised myself that when the war ended I would ring the bell that was placed at the fire station as an invasion bell. And I grabbed a flag, I don't know where I got the flag from, I wrapped it round myself and I ran up to the fire station and rang and rang the bell.
Roma Wallis, store assistant, Gulgong, New South Wales

I went to Adelaide and the jubilation was unbelievable. I can remember seeing the policemen being kissed and that was a very unusual thing. Policemen were generally held at arm's length. But their horses were being written on with lipstick and the jubilation was really quite remarkable.
Bob Taylor, Post Office worker, Adelaide

The factory closed for the rest of the day and the streets were packed with people cheering, hugging each other, running crocodiles a quarter of a mile long or so. They were delirious really, the relief was colossal.
Bob Bahnsen, machinist, Sydney

Kings Cross was totally packed and you couldn't move through it at all, with people cheering and wild celebrations. I always remember one lady had a cake tin in her hand and as she passed she banged us all on the head with the cake tin.
Beryl Haley, trainee nurse, Sydney

My brother was home on leave and we and my sisters went into town where the biggest crowd ever seen in Perth, 100 000 people—almost half the population—had gathered, and everybody was doing the conga. And when we came to the National Service Office, there were these junior clerks throwing all the call-up papers out the windows. I'd turned eighteen about a month before and I had been served my conscription papers, which you filled in and sent in to the National Service Office. So of course I looked for mine. I didn't find it, but people were just tearing them up, especially if they had a son of military age. And in fact young fellows who turned eighteen after I did were called up, and spent a couple of months doing nothing, but I never heard another word from them.
Maurie Jones

I was in Concord Hospital with malaria and they said anyone who can walk can get up and go on leave and I staggered out with the nurses down the street to the pubs. It was a wonderful day, definitely the best day of the war. Dancing and cooeeing and shouting and waving bottles of beer about, and flags—all night I think it went. I passed

out—they took me in an ambulance back to Concord about eleven
o'clock; I was buggered, but it was a terrific day.
Hilary Hughes, returned soldier, Sydney

I came to town on the bike and the thing to do seemed to be to go
into the pubs—and remember, I'm not supposed to be in the pubs at
that age, but never mind. We got in the pubs and I'm sorry to say I
spent a fair amount of that evening under a bench in the park and
that was my memory of the end of the war.
Charles Janeway, farmers' son, Mt Gambier, South Australia

There was this terrific celebration in Martin Place but I didn't want to
go to that. I just stayed at home. I felt it was great to have that war
finished, but I didn't want to celebrate it; it wasn't a celebratory thing
somehow. I just felt it had been a mad affair all through.
John Hinde, ABC war correspondent, Sydney

I had always said, 'We'll have a party when the war ends'. But when
it came, I didn't have the heart for it. I just felt we'd all been through
so much. A lot of the boys were dead, and some were still away,
including my husband. So it wasn't quite the celebration we'd planned.
Kathleen Loneregan, store proprietor, Gulgong, New South Wales

There was such happiness, you could feel it everywhere. Ticker-tape
paper, kissing everybody in the street—black, white or brindle, they
were all your buddies, you kissed anybody. I can remember taking my
mother into Hyde Park, I can even remember what I wore: I wore a
grey edge-to-edge coat and a grey hat, I don't know what happened
to the hat. My mother was being almost mutilated with all the pushing
and shoving and the hugging but my heart was sore. So many of the
people's husbands coming back, it was hard—but a wonderful thank
you that it was all over. Because it's a long time to have a war.
Lillian Malcolm, airman's widow, Sydney

2 Homecoming

We left Singapore harbour on this terrible old tub but it seemed like
the *Queen Elizabeth* to us, and we were fed bully beef and we got
fat—I put on three-and-a-half stone on the way home, and all the
sores healed up and everything else. Bliss—sailing through one of the
most magically beautiful seas, towards Darwin, our first sight of
Australian territory after the war.
    And there are a whole mob of Australian soldiers down there on the
wharf all sort of waving sardonically as Australians do, and we
shouted out 'What's the beer like?' and they shouted back 'No beer in
Darwin, only lolly-water'. And we looked around at this terrible town
in this terrible-looking swamp, with the prospect of nothing to drink

but lolly-water, and a cry broke out from the entire convoy—'Send us back to Changi!'.

We came back to the same kind of return as we'd experienced on our departure, people waving flags, and instead of saying 'Good luck' they said 'Welcome home', and then we were driven through the city and kissed—it was enormously heartwarming and touching.

And some sons like myself came home and said 'Hello Mum' to a mother who stared quite blankly and refused to acknowledge me. I was standing on top of a staircase at Greenslopes Hospital in Brisbane, the lawn in front covered in waiting parents, and my parents at the foot of the stairs, ten feet away, and I stood there looking very pretty—I'd done my hair and cleaned my teeth and I looked fine and so I said to the girl who'd announced my name, 'Do it again'. So she said 'Gunner Braddon NX6190 Russell Braddon'. And I looked down at my mother and I smiled and she looked up at me and she nodded as if someone had made a silly mistake, she was quite courteous about it, so finally I rushed down the stairs and I said 'Come off it!' and we all burst into tears then.

But it didn't end then because each of us had a job to see those whose families we had known and go and tell them that their boy wasn't coming home. That was not a happy duty, and it was made none the happier by the fact that one perceived it as one's responsibility to lie about the way in which the boy had died. Nevertheless it was done, and then life could start again, one could go home and be with the family.
Russell Braddon, 8th Division POW, Changi and Burma Railway

3 But some will never come home

I had so little time with Reg. I only had three-and-a-half years living with him as his wife and I just remember a lovely person. And my daughter—his daughter too—she resembles him even to the joints of her fingers. Sometimes when she smiles I see in the corner of her eyes—'Oh goodness me, you look like Reg'—and even her walk. As I said to her, 'While ever you're alive, your father will never be dead'.

She often says to me 'I wish I'd known my father'. They miss out on a lot, the children.
Lillian Malcolm

At this little village in France where Cliff's plane came down the Germans said that the bodies weren't to be buried decently but the village people decided there would be a burial and they came from far and wide, made them crude coffins of wood, and there were thousands there. I always said 'One day I'm going back to thank the people of France', and I did eventually—I went to the little village. It was such a poor little village, and they declared a public holiday and it was beautiful. I met the mayor, the doctor, the ladies who'd helped

'Some sons like myself came home and said "hello Mum" to a mother who stared quite blankly': Russell Braddon with his mother in a photo taken before he left for overseas. Although she did not hear from him for three and a half years, she refused to believe he was dead. Right *'They miss out on a lot, the children': Lillian Malcolm with daughter Wendy White.*

move the bodies, and the police that buried them, and we laid a wreath and we were all crying. And I thanked them and I said it'd be a little part of France that would ever remain Australia.

It was a wonderful, wonderful day and I thought, 'Well at least I know where Cliff's sleeping'. I'd wondered about that and I often thought—he was so young, they were all so young, going into these bombers, it'd often pass through my mind—Were they frightened? Was he frightened doing it?
Margaret Hopgood, airman's widow, Brisbane

We felt very bitter about Steve because we felt he'd done his share in Europe, why did he have to go to New Guinea? Especially after he was killed, we thought, 'Why did they have to send him when he'd done his part in those three years?'. It was such a long time out of his life to be away, and he was home for such a short time.
Nola Bridger, schoolgirl, Sydney

My mother never really coped again after my father was killed. The neighbours would sometimes hear her not coping with me as a child and they'd come in and they'd take me for a couple of days until Molly got over it. But I was the reason for her living, the only thing of Brian that she had left and I was never allowed to do dangerous things, I was very protected. I used to feel as though it wasn't me that my mother loved, so much as that it was what she had left of Brian that she loved.

'I said it'd be a little part of France that would ever remain Australia': Margaret Hopgood addresses the French villagers who buried her husband more than thirty years before.

From my earliest memories my father was the person that I always looked up to, I was brought up with him on a pedestal—he was somebody that seemed to be without fault, everyone seemed to speak of him as a wonderful person. It was hard to live up to what he had been, but I wanted to be like him and sometimes it was too hard an act to follow. It shaped my life, all my father's traits I've tried to emulate which I don't think you do if you've got a normal situation.

I would often when I was a little child hide behind the couch and just look through the photo albums of him, and I resolved that one day I would go to see where he was buried at El Alamein. So I did go eventually—and it was strange. There were those photos of him and there was the documentation, but I'd always felt they were spinning me stories, that in actual fact he was still alive. But after seeing his grave, it made me realise he was dead. I felt very sad and emotional but very pleased, and a sort of calmness came over me when I placed the flowers there. I just thought, 'It is true, I know that he is there'.

But there were so many graves, there were about 2000, and I realised there must be so many children like me, whose fathers were buried there.

Christina Mowbray, war baby, Millicent, South Australia

I know that in our street, my brother and five other boys never arrived back. And my poor brother, he must have suffered very badly because he was a prisoner of war.

Edna Macdonald, munitions worker, Melbourne

'I used to feel as though it wasn't me that my mother loved, so much as that it was what she had left of her husband': war baby Christina Mowbray with her mother Molly Hemmings, and, right, *her father's grave at El Alamein: 'I realised there must be so many children like me, whose fathers were buried there'.*

My father died in a prisoner-of-war camp. He was beaten rather badly while there and he wasn't a young man—he was about 44 or 45—and I think if anybody lost a loved one in circumstances like that, you remember that for the rest of your life. There are a lot of people who will never ever forget.

Gerry Judd, pilot, Empire Air Training Scheme, UK

My brother was a Lancaster pilot and he was killed over Germany in March 1945. He was a bit unlucky really because he only had a few weeks to go before the end of the war. The death of my brother did have a great effect on the family, probably more than with me, though when I came back I was in hospital for two years with tuberculosis and that also was a fairly heavy burden for them.

The business—stock and station agent—was in the family for almost eighty years but after the close of World War II all the sons of the four brothers who ran the business, our losses were fairly heavy, and they decided it was no longer suitable to carry on to the next generation, so the business was sold.

Actually the number who were killed from Millicent from the Second World War was nowhere as the First World War of course. Nevertheless there is a gap in the community when you look at the names of people who you know would be important in the structure of the town. There's no doubt that if you take out both world wars, the loss of their adult people must have had an impact on small communities.
Ren deGaris, wireless intelligence, RAAF

4 Life could start again

People come out of a war always, of course, with feelings about the future—that this is a new day and a new age.
John Hinde

And we felt this very strongly and hopefully, that after the war was over, life would be very very different.
Joyce Batterham, Communist Party worker, Sydney

I think after any big upheaval like a war, the youth of that period—who feel that they've made the great sacrifices—feel that they expect to get something out of this. In the First World War there was the idea that this was the war to end war and they fought it and it turned out not to be true. Although I think there was more cynicism about these Utopian concepts—and they were Utopian—after the Second World War, they were still present, I think very strongly; and that we thought that our generation would change in some way the world we lived in, that we would make it a better world. All the journals postulated the idea that after the war there would be a better society.
Dorothy Hewett, Perth

The magazines, I remember, used to make predictions of what life is going to be like after the war—everything from the design of houses to the design of cars to what clothes were going to look like and so on. And economists would write about rebuilding the world's economies and industries. So we did expect a fair bit, perhaps all over the world: a world fit for heroes.
Maurie Jones

When I was getting out I went to the Sydney Showground. I was down in the dog pound there for about a fortnight waiting to be discharged, went and seen this refugee doctor and I got me ration

coupons for tobacco and clothes. Me deferred pay was about 300 quid and that was it, on your way. The only thing good they did, they called you 'Mister'. They called you 'Mister' the day you handed your bloody paybook in, that was the only thing that was worth anything.
Hilary Hughes, returned soldier

The first feeling is just a feeling of—you're lost, you're free like a bird out of a cage I suppose, you can go where you want to go, please yourself what you do—but you miss the routine army life.
Roy leRougetel, returned soldier

It was very hard for a while to readjust, it was a lost sort of feeling. I mean after five years in the Army you get set in your ways and you miss that. They never gave us anything to help, they just gave you a little book, 'Rehabilitation' or something they called it—what to do, what you didn't do.
Hilary Hughes

I had a lot of problems. I got wounded and I picked up a rare disease and I finished up having three years in hospital. I had half my chest chopped away and a few other things, but still you just plod along—that's life, one of our legacies of what happens to you.
Sandy Rayward, returned soldier

To settle back into civilian life was very tough for all of us. Blokes that'd done six years away from civilian life, been in situations where you was told what to do, when to do it, why to do it, how to do it—to come back and to get freedom again, you were inclined to go a big berserk and overindulge in things like grog.
Alan Low, returned soldier

Many people had a rather uncertain identity before they went into the Army. They'd been unemployed for a long time, or their families were perhaps a little turbulent, and they found themselves members of a cohesive structure with a worthwhile task and all sorts of psychological supports. And when the war was over it all went away; but this in one sense had been a highlight in their life and many people of course longed for that again, because there was security, purpose, status, all you want. It's gone, and what do you replace it with? Perhaps hard work and getting on with life, but not everyone has the good fortune to do that, so the past is attractive and you meet your old mates and they're all having a few drinks and you have a few more drinks and so it goes on.
John Ellard, returned soldier and Army psychologist

Down on the beach I used to see quite a lot of the blokes who were at a loose end. The war was finished and they didn't know what to do with themselves, they couldn't fit in, they were too long in the war—three-and-a-half years was too much for them, being told what

Betty Telfer reunited with her husband after George's discharge in December 1945: 'We could hardly believe it—he was back again and he wasn't going away anymore and all we had to do was pick up the pieces and the whole future was ahead of us'.

to do and being with their mates and their mates looking after them and getting them out of scrapes. When they were suddenly on their own, they couldn't handle it and they just drank their deferred pay.
Sandy Rayward

I think most soldiers after the war went through a drinking phase, but as time went by I think they found that there was definitely comradeship among the soldiers whom they knew, even among soldiers who hadn't known each other in the war, there definitely is a comradeship with them and even World War II veterans can talk to World War I.
Amory Vane, returned soldier

We didn't understand them and they didn't understand us and this, as happened with every man who came back from the war, drove us frequently out of the comfort of hearth and home, into the company of those who did understand, which was back at the pub or the club or on the golf course or on the beaches or whatever. It did make us difficult to understand—we were changed.
Russell Braddon

I think we feel that outsiders don't understand what we're talking about. Anzac Day you might get some of the mates, you might talk

about it then, but not normally outside because there's some terrible bloody things happened, things that aren't in the history books, and you never forget it, never. I still wake up at nights dreaming, it's still in your mind, the things that happened.
Hilary Hughes

You don't have to come out of the war with an arm missing or a leg missing or a bullet wound. You come out with a mind that's been churned up. I was fortunate, I come back out of it pretty well except for nerves when I first came back. I was a bit of a wreck as far as they were concerned.
Alan Low

I nursed at Kenmore which was the mental hospital in Goulburn, the Army took over the wards. There were all sorts of soldiers—from the boys who'd been guerrillas in the islands in the north to just ordinary soldiers who couldn't take it, young men who had become depressed over the episodes that had occurred in New Guinea and various places. You had all those people who were not meant to be soldiers.
Lesley Daniels, Army nurse

He did change, my husband. When he come back, you couldn't scratch, you couldn't do nothing as would make a noise, he used to be that irritable. We had an open fireplace and Rex, my son, was sitting there one night eating his tea and the old man came in, in a frightful mood, and Rex said something and he went over and give him a boot, kicked him in the fire, all his tea and all went, he got his hands burned. Another night he picked up a knife and threw it at him—things he never done before he went away. He couldn't work, and eventually he finished up getting a TPI pension. But he was that irritable you couldn't bear him home, he'd have to go back into a hospital or a home, whatever'd take him.
Queenie Shepherd

Ted, my brother, was on the Burma railway, at death's door at one stage—he weighed about six stone. But fully recovered, he looked very fit, a typical Aussie digger. He came home outwardly very little different from when he went away, but it scarred his life and also scarred his health. His life was traumatised, it caught up with him in the end and he suffered from war neurosis, this brave man—it was very sad.
Bob Bahnsen

Quite a lot took their lives. There was one that got in a car and put a pipe in it and gassed himself, one of my best friends. Another one hung himself out in Frenchs Forest [Sydney], he was a lieutenant-commander, and another chap drank a bottle of Lysol down in Manly on the waterfront, just drank a bottle of Lysol. Another one went under a house and cut his throat—things like that, they had seen too

much and just didn't want to go on. These were just young blokes my
own age, we came out of the war at 22, 23.
Sandy Rayward

It's nevertheless one's duty as a returned soldier to adapt as quickly as
possible. Most did, and settled in, but I was one of those weaker
characters who didn't adapt—I waited for society to adapt to me. And
it wouldn't, so in 1949 I took a massive overdose, was caught out,
and woke up in an extreme psychiatric ward. And in 1949 when I did
that, that ward was full of men from the 8th Division. The psychiatrist
found it strange that there should have been this four-year interlude,
but four years is a long time, perhaps long enough, to wait for society
to change to you so that it becomes again what it was when you left.
Russell Braddon

I would say that I owe a lot of my coming back to earth to my wife,
because she really put up with something when I first came back and
we got married. She had to put up with me over-imbibing and having
nightmares and the war catching up with me. And it's thanks to her
that I am what I am today.
Alan Low

5 Use Rinso

After the war was over there was a gradual dismissal from the
factories. The men came back and took the jobs that the women had
obtained and women went back to the usual women's jobs—secretary,
typist, shop assistant, waitress and so on. Some women had been
given responsible jobs in quite managerial roles, and they were
excellent at it, but the men just took over the jobs that the women
were doing so well. The same thing happened to me because as the
war ended our organisers were dismissed and finally there were just
two—a man and myself—and I was pressured: the man had a family
and it was only right that he should continue, and would I resign.
They knew that if I'd stood I would have won it because I'd won
every other. So we were really pressured out of our jobs.
Mary Miller, union representative, munitions factory, Adelaide

When the war was over, I went back to being a clerk in the Bourke
Street store of Coles. I didn't mind because it was made perfectly clear
to us when we were made managers that it was for the duration of
the war only. You've got to remember that women were second-rate
employees and we didn't argue with it. Women just weren't given
these opportunities and we didn't worry about it, it was accepted in
those days.
Beattie Crawford, Melbourne

I think that the general attitude was, 'Well, now the war's over women

can go back into the kitchen and bedroom and forget about anything else'.
Joyce Batterham

Oh yes—'Woman's place is in the home' and 'Use Rinso', and all this sort of thing went on in those years. There was a real campaign to get women back into the homes and that was all right I suppose in some ways, but there was never anything very fulfilling about housework.
Sally Bowen, armaments worker, Wollongong, New South Wales

Although some of them may have enjoyed going back to just looking after a house and children, I'm sure that there must have been others who really resented this, and found it extremely difficult to go back to that rather subservient sort of life, a house-bound life.
Dorothy Hewett

And I guess a lot more of them walked out on unsatisfactory relationships because they discovered they could hold down a job, they could earn a living, they didn't have to put up with any nonsense —whatever it was. I think the world had improved in some ways. It was perhaps one of the good things to come out of the war.
Bob Bahnsen

I had quite a lot to do with organising things for servicewomen and it was amazing how many of their marriages didn't work out. We were always being told in the newspapers to think of the men, they'd been in the desert and they'd been in the jungle and they'd been used to doing this and that, but they didn't think that the same thing applied to the women, because we too had to be rehabilitated. For three-and-a-half years I was told when to get up, when to eat, when to go to sleep, what to wear; I never had to make a decision. A truck will come and get you, you'll go there, do this, do that. And so it was a big thing for us to lose the comradeship and everything after three-and-a-half years.
Patricia Penrose, Z Special Unit, Melbourne

When I left the services I had no idea what it would be like out there. Although I was only there for three years, I'd grown up a lot, but I was still a bit giddy. And to be with 60 girls for all those growing years, that fun, that love, that sharing—when I came out, I never knew such loneliness. I went to Tasmania. I'd met one of the patients and I went down there to him, and it was all right for him, there was the RSL, but nobody took any notice of us girls who'd served, I don't know what they thought we were doing. It was the loneliest time of my life.
Patsy Adam-Smith, VAD nurse

6 A whole social upheaval

Many men had idealised what they would come back to—men who'd
married in a hurry before they went, say, imagined themselves coming
back to a peaceful and sylvan existence. And it wasn't there.
John Ellard

Many marriages broke down because the women just couldn't take
this man coming back and telling them what to do, as he'd always
done in the past. It was a whole social upheaval which lasted a long
time—probably forever.
Dorothy Hewett

I know a lot of people separated when the men came back because
they listened to too many stories which they shouldn't have—'Oh, she
was out with this Yank or she was out with that one'; and possibly
there might be nothing to it at all.

I saw a lot of very nice country girls, their husbands were away
fighting, they didn't know whether they'd ever come back, and a lot
of the girls thought it was a crime to enjoy yourself while the men
were fighting overseas. But after a while, reluctantly, they did come to
the dances, and then they started enjoying themselves. But when you
live in a country town a lot of people do a lot of talking about you,
and if a girl was having a good time and she walked outside with a
soldier or anything—next minute it was all around town, and when
the boys came back from the war I think they listened to a lot of the
gossip. So needless to say, there was a lot of people parted and a lot
of families broke up, which was sad because they had children that
wanted their father and so on.

What I thought was particularly sad about it was they didn't ask
their husbands what they were doing over there. A lot of them were
having good times in between the fighting, but once they heard
anything about their wives, it was the finish. And I saw a lot of very
happy couples—that were, before the war broke out—separated. So a
lot went on during the war that would never have happened if the
war hadn't come. It sort of altered everybody's life.
**Dulcie Cunningham, housewife and mother, Beaudesert,
Queensland**

I met one who was very bitter about it, he came home and his wife
had a boyfriend there, she hadn't come to meet him or anything. He
just walked in the door and he had his rifle and bayonet with him. He
said 'I fixed my bloody bayonet and I said, 'All right you bastard, out'.
And the boyfriend went for his life, and he said 'I picked up my
bloody kids and I walked out the door'.
Bob Bahnsen

The war changed *my* life around because after the war I separated
and a lot had to do with a little bit of mother-in-law trouble: she

didn't approve of me going to dances and things like that. Then my husband listened to a bit of gossip too, and I found it hard to settle down. I still wanted to go out and enjoy life, I wasn't really doing anything bad except I loved to go out and go to the dances. And a few little arguments ensued and my husband said to me, 'You want to be a married woman but have the pleasures of a single person'.

And we parted. But we should never have parted because actually we were quite happy together. If he'd just let things settle down I would have got sick of wanting to go out. For no reason at all we separated, it wasn't anything terrible on either side— but we didn't get back together. So had war not come I would have been a very happily married person to my first husband.

Dulcie Cunningham

I think one of the things that happened during the war was that women became the head of the family. They'd taken over all the responsibility of handling the money, handing the disciplinary problems, handling what would happen to the children, making day-to-day decisions. That was an enormous change. And when the husbands came back the children in many cases had never seen their fathers, they'd never lived in the same house with them, they didn't know who they were. They were strangers, and I think many of those children never related to those fathers again—nor the father to the children.

Dorothy Hewett

My father had problems when he came back because we'd grown up, and we'd grown up without him and in some ways we resented him. We resented being told what to do by a man who we hadn't seen for five years. And another thing I'll always remember—when he came home we met him at the station and afterwards he was a bit cross with me, because his mates had teased him about his daughter and he didn't feel that old I suppose, and he hadn't realised—he couldn't cope with somebody wanting to go out with his daughter. He had known me as a child when he left, and I was a fully grown woman when he came back, and I think that was rather a shock to him. So it took us a while—I think all families had problems with the father coming back into the family.

Margaret Burton, Adelaide

One friend of ours I used to feel sorry for. She was pregnant when her husband Jimmy went away and the little boy was at school when Jimmy came back, and he had to get to know this child that he'd never even seen as a baby, and I'd see Jim holding this little boy's hand and I'd think 'He must feel as though he's adopted'.

Anne Pellew, staff canteen worker, Sydney

I married when I was nineteen a man who was in the Air Force, it was all terribly romantic, and off he went to England and was there

'He had known me as a child when he left . . .': Margaret (Hayden) Burton in 1945, when her father returned; she was then about 15.

for five years. Before he went he was very adamant that no wife of his was going to work for her living, and I wouldn't dream of getting a job, that was the rule. But after I went into munitions, it was different and I became quite confident, and pleased that I had. And he was away five years and met someone else so when he came back he was an absolute stranger.

And this happened over and over again to many women and I suppose that's when lots of divorces took place. And of course a lot of our munitions workers also met Americans during the war, we had whole piles of munitions workers set off for America with the Yanks and a whole lot them later came back too.
Mary Miller

There were war bride ships coming in to Fremantle and there were always great weepings at the dock, the mothers and the fathers would be down there weeping because their daughters were going off to America and when would they see them again, because America was still this glamorous country. Of course the girls all thought they were going off to some heavenly paradise and lots of them got one very rude shock.
Dorothy Hewett

I married an American during the war. I met him in Sydney on a blind date, he was in the American Navy as a navigator. And one of the American admirals I'd met working on newspapers said, 'Of course you'll want to go over to your new family as soon as possible'. So he put me on one of the first ships, the *Lurline*, which was a bride ship. I had to go to Brisbane and when we got to Brisbane we had to have a medical. Now they lined us up just exactly the same I would think as being in the Army and we were stripped to bra and little pants, a great line of war brides behind me and in front of me and there were

Joan Bentson (extreme left), one of the war brides departing in May 1946 from Brisbane on the S.S. Mariposa, *bound for California.*

three medical officers there, doctors, and when I came along they said 'Ah, here's a clean one'. Now I thought that was pretty appalling.
Adelie Hurley

I remember there was one girl I went to university with who could never make up her mind. She'd go down to the ship and she'd sit there and wait for the ship to come in and then she'd be left sitting on her suitcase and there'd always be this picture of her on the front page of the papers—'War Bride Can't Make Up Her Mind'. She did it three times and in the end she left. Whether it ever worked or not I don't know because I never heard of her again.
Dorothy Hewett

My parents of course were there—there had been tears the night before on both sides and I wasn't happy to be leaving them, but I was looking forward to a great adventure, that's how I looked at it. The whole boat was full of war brides and their children—hundreds of them. And it wasn't easy when the ship pulled out, everybody was in tears, there was a band playing 'Auld Lang Syne' somewhere, and I was glad once the ship had got away from the dock and we were out of sight because it was a little hard.
Joan Bentson, war bride, Brisbane

There was like ten thousand war brides or more, waiting to get on ships to go to America. And this girlfriend whose husband was

stationed in New Guinea with Fred, contacted me and said that she had met a chief steward on a cargo vessel from America, and that he thought he could get us on it but she said, 'We have to stow away'. So we organised it—we got on that ship as sailors and the chief steward took our luggage on the night before that that's how I started out to go to America.
Margaret Blair, war bride, Sydney

Well I think they all thought they'd married wealthy Americans. But most Americans weren't wealthy at all, they were very poor a lot of them, and of course out here they had their very nice uniforms and they had lots of money. I think their expectations were far too high because a lot of them went to dreadful places and lived in appalling slum conditions, absolutely horrific, and as a result I think about 70 per cent of the marriages failed—it would be a good 70 per cent.
Adelie Hurley

After the war I was in Hollywood to get equipment and a number of women, Australians, who saw my name in the newspaper, came knocking at the door and said, 'Can you get me back to Australia? I'll do anything'. I couldn't get them back to Australia. But they were all gone off on one of these wild romances, and it didn't work out.
Ken G. Hall, managing editor, *Cinesound Review*, Sydney

Adelie Hurley photographing returning war brides in San Francisco in 1946 where she was the US West Coast correspondent for a Sydney magazine, having married an American herself. Arthur Calwell, Australian Minister for Immigration is on the right. (Photo: Palmer Pictures, San Francisco, courtesy Adelie Hurley)

7 To pick up living again

The saddest time that I remember was when people were being released from the camps. The first family to leave, the second family to leave, and those staying behind that were not being released and were still there. The wondering why, this uncertainty—were you ever going to be released? There were a lot of stories that were going around at one stage, when they said that we would all be put on an old ship, taken out to sea and sunk—these sorts of things did the rounds.

We were finally released from the camp in 1944, but my parents were not allowed to return to Queensland and for six months they had to report to the police every week. So my father said he would only consider coming to Sydney, because my mother had a brother there and he said, 'At least we'll be able to have some family support'. So we went to Sydney, and got ourselves organised and we found a little business at the Cross, a delicatessen.
Francesca Merenda

To pick up living again—because you didn't live in the camp, you just went by your routine—to pick up living again wasn't easy. You didn't know who your friends were, people that you had a lot of time for prior to being put away, you didn't know how they'd take you and I stepped lightly, and many a time at the markets I was told they got nothing for me because I was an internee, I was an alien. It was hard to work your way back into it. A man coming out of jail is coming back to where he started from.
Bob Donato, fruiterer, Sydney

Francesco Merenda with her mother in the King's Cross delicatessen the family operated after release from the internment camp.

The experience affected people in different ways. I know of some people who changed their name completely, or anglicised it. There are people who even today are unable to face up to the fact that they were interned. They talk about it in their family but the next-door neighbour may not be aware of the fact that Joe or Gaetano or Guiseppe or Giovanni had been interned during the war. I myself felt that until recently. It was too deep, it was a hurt that had taken place and affected me so much that I just couldn't talk about it. I felt it was totally unfair—I was an Australian, I was born here, my parents were naturalised in 1928. They were Australians, that's what I had been taught at school.
Francesca Merenda

We had a great life as prisoner of war, I don't think any other prisoner of war was treated as well as we were, in the world. But we had to go back and actually I didn't want to go back, to be honest, I even went to see the Swiss Consulate. They said, 'Look, under the Geneva Convention every prisoner of war must return home'. So I said 'OK, I've got to return home'.
Ric Pisaturo

There was an American liberty ship pulled up in Melbourne and the Germans were informed that they would go on it. And I shot through. I hanged around in Melbourne for about three or four weeks, I'd saved quite a bit of money and I managed to exist. And I went down Little Collins Street and there was an office with a big window on the outside and in gold lettering 'Immigration Office', and there was a door, and I remember all this very well because I was very scared that I would get arrested. I knocked on the door and said 'I'm an ex-prisoner of war'. He said 'Oh no, no, no, they've all gone home to Germany'. And I said, 'Well I'm the only one who hasn't'. And at first he wouldn't believe me but finally he gave me a landing permit via the Immigration Office. And I was home and hosed in Australia.
Gunther Bahnemann

When I got to Italy, I hate the place, I couldn't stand it, I fell in love with Australia. I loved the people, the way of living here, so free, so beautiful, I just had to come back, I was going berserk. I wrote to the Badgerys who I worked for, on the farm, and within two weeks Mr Badgery sent me the landing permit plus my fare to come back.
Ric Pisaturo

It was terribly hard to get a job. People would want you and then you'd have to tell them of your past, then you got the impression that there was no question of it. Eventually I managed to get a job, I think it was about half pay for the work I did, as an accountant and secretary for a battery company.

But I got into setting up a prison reform council, because when I was in gaol, it appalled me, the plight of young kids in gaol. To see

them crushed down with bread and water punishment and solitary confinement, it was no place for young people. So in a sense I found a mission.
Ted Hartley, conscientious objector, Sydney

The hard thing of course during those years was that my parents were not with me, and that not only did I miss them, but that there was a constant very very deep and intense worry and sadness and that of course can't be forgotten or can't be pushed away.

We finally got a letter from my mother in 1945, a very very sad letter, where she told us that our father had died and that she was still in Theresienstadt but was going to Vienna. My father had died four weeks after arriving in Theresienstadt because he was a serious case of diabetes and he didn't get insulin. I don't know if you would call it a natural death. Initially my mother did not even want to come to Melbourne, to my sister and myself, she was so depressed. But she changed her mind and I'll never forget picking up that very very old woman who came off the plane.
Doris Liffman, Austrian refugee, Melbourne

Some people asked me, 'Who would you like to see the war won by?'. And I really didn't want the war won by Hitler—but by Germany, yes—and they were inextricably connected. So when I was asked that I said 'Well, what would you answer to such a question?'. I never answered straight. But it was the most horrible thing, that you had to be

Doris Liffman (standing) with her sister and parents, the last photo taken before the sisters' departure for Australia in 1938. She heard after the war that her father had died in a concentration camp.

ashamed of your country, it is terrible if the country you love behaves
in such an inconceivably horrible way. I never could come to terms
with it.
Irmhild Beinssen, German-born internee, Sydney

8 A part of the world

I think Australia grew up in that period. We'd been living a happy life,
the birds were singing and the koalas were in the trees but we came
so close to war and so close to going down the drain in a war, that
we really matured and became adult.
Ken G. Hall

I think it's a myth that Gallipoli was Australia's maturation or
adulthood. I think the Second World War was the time that Australia
really became a nation and started to break the ties of Empire and all
that rubbish that goes back to the past. So that Australia could not
have become the sort of country it is without the war.
**Laurie Aarons, factory worker and Communist Party member,
Sydney**

The ease with which Singapore fell and the rapidity with which the
Japanese came down to Australia made an immediate rethink
absolutely essential of what the future defence of Australia must be.
And from that time onwards, it's been a basic principle of our defence
as I understand it, and as Curtin established and maintained, that
Australia must no longer look to Britain as the basis of its defence but
must look to the United States of America.
Ralph Doig, Premier's Department, Perth

No matter what people may have thought afterwards about the
American invasion, and there were very mixed feelings about it, there
was a feeling that the Americans saved us from the Japanese, when
the general feeling was that Churchill and the British had been willing
to consider us expendable. So that the whole ethos of Australia then
changed from a British colony to an American colony, in many ways.
Dorothy Hewett

It had been all Britain before, we thought of nothing but Britain, and
the United States had been a distant neighbour. Suddenly we knew
about Americans, we knew that they were there, we knew that we
needed them. And so this was an enormous change; it might have
torn a nation apart, it was so great. But it happened fairly slowly and
we've survived, up to now.
John Hinde

Our leaders have learned I'm sure that we may be on our own one
day, that we can't depend on others to defend us. Maybe they will,

and if they will—good luck. We hadn't learned that lesson in World War II and we almost paid dearly for it.
Bob Bahnsen

It was certainly an experience which you never forgot and it also linked you much more securely to the fate of the rest of the world. Australians no longer felt safe in the old sense that they had felt safe, they now realised that they were vulnerable to what happened in the rest of the world. So that never again could you ever think of yourself as an Australian who had nothing to do with what happened on the rest of the planet.
Dorothy Hewett

9 Changed

I think the first thing one would have to say is that it was a complete waste of everyone's time. You feel you've wasted ten years of your life in that particular field. And yet I wouldn't have not been there for all the tea in China.
Ren deGaris

I suppose I could say, which is the common term, 'I had a good war'. I was a night fighter pilot, and I enjoyed flying, I really did. There is nothing as exciting as chasing another aircraft, you get the thrill, the excitement, everything is there. The war to me was probably the pivotal point of my life—if you weren't there, you can't describe what it was like.
Gerry Judd

I would say that I lived probably ten years in experience and adventure from twenty to twenty-five. I had a feeling later on of deprivation, that probably I'd been deprived of some of the best years of my life, but taking it over all, I wouldn't have missed it.
Roy Hall, Admiralty Yachtsman Scheme, ordinary seaman, RANVR

It had a tremendous influence on my life and I think anybody who was involved, anybody who felt they were doing a worthwhile job, would feel as I do—that it was a terrible time, it was a horrific time, but you wouldn't have missed it for anything because it gave us a different outlook on life, it made us more understanding of a lot of things and it made brothers and sisters of a lot of people who would never have known each other otherwise.
Judy Stone, WAAAF

I think it changed me for the better because I didn't know, the way that we lived at home, how the other half lived—people from poorer circumstances than me—and I think that changed me. I get on now

with people in all walks of life; you understand what they go through and you're able to help in some way and you've got the human understanding which you didn't have before.
Joy Boehm, AWAS

Every day's been a bonus since I got out of the war, every day that I've lived has been a bonus 'cause I've been that near to it.
Alan Low

There are certain things you come in contact with that you'll never find anywhere else. Why is this mateship so deep between people who served in a war zone? I don't know, but it's there—a tremendous mateship that you don't find anywhere else. You find the worst characteristics in war and you find the best too.
Ren deGaris

The certain mystery of danger and of survival and of the fairness of it and the unfairness of it, of the nature of the lottery of life—it's that which you learn at war to accept as part of every day and which other people who weren't there will never know.
Russell Braddon

There's a lot talked about the mateship among soldiers, and they forget women had to have a mate too, for the same reason as men did. You needed someone to cover your back, you needed that companionship and more than that you needed the comfort. I think there's a type of love that we've overlooked when people are put into a pressured situation, and I think that's one of the few beautiful things about war, that women had, and it was the same with men: we had a pure—I mean in the very wide general sense—a pure love that you can't really have in civilian life, other things come between you.
Patsy Adam-Smith

When I went to the war I was charming, I was the most sweet-natured youth who ever drew breath. I was incapable of arguing with anyone, I'd been brought up to believe it was rude to argue. The worst I could say to the silliest statement from an adult was, 'Oh, do you think so?'. And then I felt ashamed of myself. When I got home I would argue with anyone from a field marshal to God Almighty—about anything, if I thought it wrong.
Russell Braddon

When my brother came back and he went to the local hotel to have a drink with all of his Army mates, he wasn't allowed to go in. That's what he talked about most of his life, about the fact that he was not allowed to enter a hotel to drink with his army mates when he returned. He took that up as an issue for equality for Aboriginals and on one occasion he was arrested and locked up for the night and he did that to prove a point, to say to fellow Australians, 'Look, I've been

over there, I've fought for this country, but I really haven't fought for
equality because it's not here, it doesn't exist for me'. And he became
really involved in Aboriginal affairs from then on.
Pansy Hickey

I think it makes you more cynical. And it certainly made me, at any
rate, and lots of others, very very anti-war. I think the Second World
War was inevitable, to stop Hitler. But it does make you think that
war is the last resort.
Maurie Jones

It hardened a lot of my attitudes. I could see how universally
corrupting warfare was. Perhaps that was the most useful experience,
that warfare is not just a matter of dead bodies—although God knows
that's important enough—but it has a corrupting cancerous effect upon
whole communities and there's nothing so revolting as a wartime
patriotic community gone mad. They will do anything, and it must be
a time when the devil is very happy.
**Niall Brennan, Department of War Organisation of Industry,
Melbourne**

I don't think any human being likes war, it's all bloodshed, people get
killed and what's the gain, who gets anything out of it, only the
people what's got the money. Blokes that make the bombs,
aeroplanes, one thing and another, they get the money. Other people
get nothing, only lose their lives.
Alan McMillan, dockworker, Sydney

It's always the youth that pays for a war, that lose their lives. I think
every mother that said goodbye to her son, she might have been
proud of him but the mothers I knew would much rather their sons
had been home. It's all right to join the Army so long as they don't go
to war.
Nola Bridger

It changed my whole life. I went into it very young, and I came out a
woman, a woman much older than I needed to have been, by what I
had experienced. And all those six years had gone, they'd gone in
worrying and responsibilities. So we all say we could have done
without those six years very nicely, thank you very much. But we're
never sorry we served.
Patricia Penrose

I would love to march in that Anzac Day march, that's a terrific sight,
I would love to be eligible to march in that, but apart from that I
reckon I shed more sweat, and I shed a drop of blood too at home
here, and a lot more than a lot of blokes who can march, who went
away. I think they had a better time than I did. The hours I worked,

*'We're never sorry we served':
Patricia (Rattray) Penrose, Z
Special Unit.*

the problems I had. But I think the only time I really regret it is on
Anzac Day.
Ray Blissett, policeman, Sydney

I'd say I matured as a person. I think it is fortunate that I ended up in
a manufacturing job, I think I would have been a very
chicken-hearted soldier. There were thousands of farm labourers, tens
of thousands, who either joined the forces or went into some form of
war manufacturing. Their lives were changed forever, mine was one of
them. They found they had the capacity to do things that they'd never
dreamed they were capable of, and I think that was a plus that came
out of the war. Or you might put it another way, and say that before
the war Australia was wasting its talents.
Bob Bahnsen

I think that working in munitions and at a very young age—after all I
was in my early twenties—becoming a union official, it gave me such
confidence, it changed my life: that never again would I feel
second-class. And this happened to all sorts of women, we suddenly
felt that we were someone, we could do anything, we were capable
people and we were equal to men.
Mary Miller

The war had a tremendous effect on the liberation of women. To be
important, that was the thing: to be absolutely necessary for the
running of the country, that women should work, and this is not a
light thing and it couldn't possibly be forgotten once the war was over.
Dorothy Hewett

They sent us off and they entertained the troops and they wrapped the bandages and they sent the letters that the enemy didn't deliver, they sent food parcels to Britain, they drove huge trucks and collected the garbage, they put up signs on streets—'This street supports a prisoner of war'—they did all the things that women could conceivably do and all that time they anguished because there was a son missing, believed killed, and perversely they believed him still to be alive.

Now whose war was the worst? The war of the women who waited for men to come home or to die, or the war of the men who really in their heart of hearts never believed that they weren't immortal?

Russell Braddon

Names of those interviewed

AARONS, Laurie — factory worker and Communist Party member, Sydney

ADAMS, Ray — farmer, VDC, Gulgong, New South Wales

ADAMS-SMITH, Patsy — VAD nurse

BAHNEMANN, Gunther — German POW

BAHNSEN, Bob — farm labourer, NSW; machinist, Sydney

BATT, Elva — AAMWS amenities officer

BATTERHAM, Joyce — Communist Party worker, Newcastle and Sydney

BEINSSEN, Irmhild — German-born resident and internee, Sydney

BENTSON, Bill — staff sergeant, US Army

BENTSON, Joan — office worker and war bride, Brisbane

BLAIR, Fred — US Air Force

BLAIR, Margaret — office worker and war bride, Sydney

BLISSETT, Ray — policeman, Sydney

BLITNER, Gerry — coastwatcher, Thursday Island

BODDINGTON, Myrtle — housewife and mother, Kalgoorlie, Western Australia

BOEHM, Joy — secretary, AWAS, Sydney

BOUCHER, Joy — café worker, Adelaide; aircraft construction worker, Sydney

BOWEN, Sally — hotel cook, armaments worker, Wollongong, New South Wales

BRADDON, Russell — university student, Sydney; 8th Division POW Changi and Burma Railway

BRENNAN, Niall — university student, pacifist, Department of War Organisation of Industry, Melbourne

BRIDGER, Nola — schoolgirl, Sydney

BRIDGMAN, Arthur — infantryman, Militia/gunner 2nd AIF

BURTON, Margaret — schoolgirl, Adelaide

CANNON, Jim — gunner, Fort Scratchley, Newcastle, New South Wales

CARTY, Tip — North Australia Observer Unit

CHAPMAN, Phil — radio operator, Darwin

COMER, Mary — soldier's wife, Gulgong, New South Wales

COX, Betty — Gulgong, New South Wales

CRAWFORD, Beattie — store manager, Melbourne

CUNNINGHAM, Dulcie — housewife and mother, Beaudesert, Queensland

CUNNINGHAM, Ken — seaman, RAN

DALY, Beryl	Australian serving in MacArthur's headquarters, Brisbane
DANIELS, Leslie	Army nurse
deGARIS, Ren	schoolboy, Millicent, South Australia; wireless intelligence, RAAF
DOIG, Barbara	housewife and mother, Perth
DOIG, Ralph	Premier's Department, Perth
DONATO, Amelia	schoolgirl, Perth
DONATO, Bob	Australian-born Italian fruiterer, Sydney; internee
DRENNAN, John	schoolboy, Adelaide
ELLARD, John	soldier and Army psychologist
EWART, Meg	Army nurse, Darwin
FALL, Connie	matron, 1/2 AGH, 6th Division
FENTON-HUIE, Shirley	schoolgirl, Sydney; WRANS, Canberra
FLETCHER, Murray	Post Office worker, Darwin
FRENCH, Barney	merchant seaman
GRAHAM, Bill	wheat farmer, Gulgong, New South Wales
GRAINGER, Pat	prostitute, Sydney
HALEY, Beryl	schoolgirl, farmers' daughter, Gulgong, New South Wales; trainee nurse, Sydney
HALL, Ken G.	managing editor, *Cinesound Review*, Sydney
HALL, Roy	The Admiralty Yachtsman Scheme, ordinary seaman, RANVR
HARDING, Lillian	schoolgirl, Adelaide
HARTLEY, Ted	pacifist, conscientious objector, Sydney
HAYLINGS, Ken	schoolboy, Sydney
HEWETT, Dorothy	university student, court reporter, Perth
HICKEY, Pansy	textile worker, Sydney
HINDE, John	ABC journalist, war correspondent
HINTON, Christine	textile worker, Sydney
HOLMES, Margaret	pacifist, mother, Sydney
HOLMES, Mary	schoolteacher, Sydney
HOPGOOD, Margaret	mother, airman's widow, Brisbane
HUGHES, Hilary	plant operator, infantryman, Sydney
HUGHES, Louisa	soldier's mother, Gulgong, New South Wales
HURLEY, Adelie	freelance and newspaper photographer, Sydney and Darwin; war bride
HURLEY, Toni Mooy	army records office, Darwin; US chaplains' office, Sydney
HUSKINS, Peter	North Australia Observer Unit
JANEWAY, Charles	schoolboy, farmers' son, Mt Gambier, South Australia
JANEWAY, Melba	schoolgirl, Tantanoola, South Australia
JONES, Maurie	schoolboy, Perth
JONES, Roger	schoolboy, Mackay, Queensland
JUDD, Gerry	schoolboy, Newcastle, New South Wales; pilot, Empire Air training Scheme, UK

KENDALL, George   cinema projectionist, Sydney
KENT, Auntie Dot   mother of four soldiers, farmer, Millicent, South Australia
KIRK, Glenys   office worker, Melbourne
LeROUGETEL, Roy   anti-aircraft gunner, Darwin
LIFFMAN, Doris   Austrian refugee, Melbourne
LILLEY, Merv   rural worker, Queensland; artilleryman, Torres Strait
LONEREGAN, Kathleen   store proprietor, Gulgong, New South Wales
LONG, Thelma   AWAS
LOUGHRY, Brian   schoolboy, Sydney
LOUGHRY, Dorothy   schoolgirl, Sydney
LOW, Alan   6th Division, 2nd AIF
MACDONALD, Edna   munitions worker, Melbourne
MALCOLM, Lillian   airman's widow, housewife and mother, Sydney
MATERA, Pasquale   Italian POW
MAXWELL, Margaret   schoolgirl, Swan Hill, Victoria
McANULTY, Helen   schoolgirl, Canberra
McCOURT, Rosemary   schoolgirl, Millicent, South Australia
McLAUCHLAN, Vi   housewife and mother, Melbourne
McMILLAN, Alan   dockworker, Sydney
MEERS, Athol   aircraft construction supervisor, Sydney
MENE, Charles   6th Division, 2nd AIF
MERENDA, Francesca   Australian-born Italian schoolgirl, Tully Queensland; internee
MILLER, Mary   union representative, munitions factory, Adelaide
MOWBRAY, Christina   war baby, Millicent, South Australia
MUGGLESTON, Ken   schoolboy, Katoomba, New South Wales
NOWLAN, Col   infantryman, Darwin
O'DONNELL, Lesley   shop assistant, Sydney
OLDHAM, Betty   Army nurse, 2/1 AGH, 6th Division
PARKER, Roy   pilot, US Air Force
PATERSON, Florence   department store clerk, Sydney
PELLEW, Anne   staff canteen worker, ARP warden, Sydney
PENROSE, Patricia   Isley's dress designer, Z Special Unit, Melbourne
PISATURO, Ric   Italian POW
POLLARD, Jack   cadet journalist, Sydney; soldier
PROCTOR, Phyl   technical college student, Sydney; AWAS
RAYWARD, Sandy   sergeant, Permanent Army, Sydney; 6th Division, 2nd AIF
RUSKIN, Alfred   German refugee, Melbourne; army medical corps
SAUER, Daisy   Army records clerk, Sydney; war bride
SAUER, Donald   sergeant, US Army
SCOTT, Jean   Land Army
SEIS, Harry   farmer, Gulgong, New South Wales

SHEPHERD, Kevin	schoolboy, Adelaide
SHEPHERD, Queenie	housewife and mother, woodyard proprietor, Adelaide
SLEE, John	Army engineer
SQUIRES, Robert	schoolboy, Warwick, Queensland; clerk, reserved occupation, Townsville, Queensland
STEWART, Harold	artilleryman, 2nd AIF
STONE, June	WAAAF
STRONACH, Nell	AWAS welfare worker
SYMONDS, Nora	textile worker, Sydney
TAYLOR, Bob	Post Office worker, Adelaide
TELFER, Betty	radio station typist and programmer, Adelaide
TELFER, George	bank clerk, Adelaide; infantryman, Darwin and New Guinea
THOMPSON, Ken	anti-aircraft gunner, Darwin
VANE, Amory	North Australia Observer Unit
WALLIS, Roma	store assistant, Gulgong, New South Wales
WILLIAMS, Peggy	Land Army
WINCKEL, Gus	Dutch pilot of evacuee plane, Broome

Index

Page numbers in italics refer to photographs